A Rational Approach to Animal Rights

A Rational Approach to Animal Rights
Extensions in Abolitionist Theory

Corey Lee Wrenn
Colorado State University, USA

© Corey Lee Wrenn 2016

Softcover reprint of the hardcover 1st edition 2016 978-1-137-43464-7

All rights reserved. No reproduction, copy or transmission of this publication may be made without written permission.

No portion of this publication may be reproduced, copied or transmitted save with written permission or in accordance with the provisions of the Copyright, Designs and Patents Act 1988, or under the terms of any licence permitting limited copying issued by the Copyright Licensing Agency, Saffron House, 6–10 Kirby Street, London EC1N 8TS.

Any person who does any unauthorized act in relation to this publication may be liable to criminal prosecution and civil claims for damages.

The author has asserted her right to be identified as the author of this work in accordance with the Copyright, Designs and Patents Act 1988.

First published 2016 by
PALGRAVE MACMILLAN

Palgrave Macmillan in the UK is an imprint of Macmillan Publishers Limited, registered in England, company number 785998, of Houndmills, Basingstoke, Hampshire RG21 6XS.

Palgrave Macmillan in the US is a division of St Martin's Press LLC, 175 Fifth Avenue, New York, NY 10010.

Palgrave Macmillan is the global academic imprint of the above companies and has companies and representatives throughout the world.

Palgrave® and Macmillan® are registered trademarks in the United States, the United Kingdom, Europe and other countries.

ISBN 978-1-349-55267-2   ISBN 978-1-137-43465-4 (eBook)
DOI 10.1057/9781137434654

This book is printed on paper suitable for recycling and made from fully managed and sustained forest sources. Logging, pulping and manufacturing processes are expected to conform to the environmental regulations of the country of origin.

A catalogue record for this book is available from the British Library.

Library of Congress Cataloging-in-Publication Data

Wrenn, Corey Lee, 1983–
    A rational approach to animal rights : extensions in abolitionist theory / Corey Lee Wrenn.
      pages cm
    Includes bibliographical references.

    1. Animal rights – Philosophy. I. Title.
HV4708.W74 2015
179'.3—dc23   2015023400

For Whitie and Petey,
Two very missed and dear friends

Contents

Preface	ix
Acknowledgments	xv
List of Abbreviations	xvii

1 Rationality and Nonhuman Animal Rights — 1
   The abolitionist departure — 1
   The reign of irrationality in Nonhuman Animal
      rights activism — 8
   An appeal to reason — 15
   Building a rational approach — 17

2 Irrationalities in Welfarist Organizational Pathways — 25
   A sociological perspective on Nonhuman Animal rights
      mobilization — 25
   Social movement rationalization — 29
   The irrationality of rational organization — 40
   A new age of rationalization — 49
   A working compromise in rationality — 59

3 Rational Advocacy and the Logic of Persuasion — 62
   Cognition and behavior change — 64
   Analogizing single-issue campaigning — 72
   Revisiting other popular tactics — 78

4 Reconciling Gender and Rationality — 94
   Individualism, feminism, and Nonhuman Animal
      rights advocacy — 95
   Patriarchy and the production of knowledge and reality — 105
   Power, politics, and science — 108
   A feminist-positive approach to rationality in Nonhuman
      Animal rights — 114

5 **Problematizing Post-Race Ideology** 120
  The invisibility of race in Nonhuman Animal advocacy 120
  Nonhuman Animal advocacy as a project of racism 133
  Authentic abolitionism 137

6 **The Case for Secular Activism** 141
  Religion and oppression 142
  Faith-based outreach 148
  Authority and resistance 157
  Atheism in the anthroparchy 163

7 **Conclusion** 172
  Minding the evidence 173
  An intersectional approach 178
  Capitalist complications 182
  Creating a community of accountability 189
  A new definition of abolitionism 192

Notes 195

Bibliography 204

Index 235

Preface

Are conventional approaches to Nonhuman Animal[1] rights advocacy rational? Are the theories and tactics based in evidence? Given the tremendous injustice currently imposed on vulnerable species, is the movement's decision-making process effectively moving society toward abolition? It might be presumed that movement organizations and leaders are prioritizing Nonhuman Animals' interests. Many times, however, the interests of other animals are relegated for human interests, compromised goals, or strategies that lack evidence to demonstrate their efficacy. The number of Nonhuman Animals exploited and killed per year continues to grow. Perhaps the movement is preventing this dire situation from worsening. More likely, movement efforts are actually facilitating and aggravating institutions of speciesism. If this is the case, they could be prolonging the systemic violence that the movement is supposed to be working to abolish. This book will argue the latter, insisting that it is past time that activists begin to think critically about the problematic ideologies that inform their goals and tactics.

Consider the following examples. In a comparative report intended for industry executives, People for the Ethical Treatment of Animals (PETA) suggests that Kentucky Fried Chicken (KFC) suppliers switch to "controlled-atmosphere killing" (suffocation by oxygen deprivation) to increase "meat"[2] yield, increase line speed, improve "meat" quality, extend shelf life, decrease contamination, reduce the cost to replace equipment, reduce worker turnover, reduce labor costs, reduce workers' compensation claims, and reduce energy and water costs. Acting as a sort of economic consultant, PETA gives detailed instructions on "reaching a return on investment":

> When other economic benefits are factored in, producers using CAK systems will begin to realize significant economic savings over electric immobilization in shorter time frames. [...] once the initial costs are recovered, this translates to an additional $1 million to $1.3 million in profit annually from improvements in meat yield alone. (2009, pp.27–8)

The Animal Liberation Front (ALF) and other direct action groups encourage activists to abandon peaceful tactics in favor of those that are often illegal, threatening, or violent. At an Italian conference titled "The Paralysis of Pacifism: In Defense of Militant Direct Action and 'Violence' for Animal Liberation," ALF leader Steve Best rationalizes that "Nobody knows what works, there's no formula for what works," thus necessitating approaches intended to terrorize:

> So, in some situations, a protest will be adequate. In other situations it's good to pick up the phone and make a threat: "Yeah, hi. I'm your friendly animal rights activist and if you don't stop breeding puppies in your backyard, I promise you I'll kick your ass." That may work. Or we have to break into a laboratory. [...] All tactics are on the table; nothing is taken off. And if that means that a guy who is killing cats in a neighborhood needs a lesson with the help of a baseball bat, then he's going to get the lesson with the help of a baseball bat. (2012)

In 2013, vegan lifestyle magazine *VegNews* launched an online series "Veganism Saved My Life!"[3] featuring interviews with individuals who claim to have been dangerously ill and subsequently saved by the "extraordinary health overhauls" that resulted from their plant-based diet. Participants report remarkably increased energy, dramatic weight loss, and, in the case of one woman who had abandoned her medication, a complete remission of stage IV cancer:

> My doctor did not support or encourage my vegan lifestyle. She never spoke about the power of food to heal and took no interest in what I was eating or doing to help myself out of her prescribed "therapy." [...] My immune system grew stronger and stronger – it's why I am here today. [...] I hardly ever get sick and I have more energy than ever. (Peraino, 2013)

Over the course of several American football seasons, PETA produced commercials in support of its "Veggie Love" campaign that depict young women performing sex acts on vegetables. They are filmed in a room made to resemble an amateur porn set, and the audience hears unseen men laughingly direct the women's actions. Women in string bikinis and high heels moan and writhe with tomatoes, give oral sex to cucumbers, and lustfully shove radishes into their mouths. The only woman of color[4] featured is animalized as she crawls across a pleather couch like a tigress and chomps broccoli with no hands. The accompanying internet advertisement reads: "Can't get enough veggies? JOIN NOW!!! All access starting at $16/year." It depicts a woman in a bikini poised to insert a long, curved cucumber into her open mouth. From PETA:

> "Veggie Love" was too hot for NBC, but the girls [sic] who didn't make the cut were too hot even for PETA! Still, these delicious hopeful models and their favorite crisp vegetables definitely piqued our interest and made us hungry for more.

Will Tuttle, author of *The World Peace Diet: Eating for Spiritual Health and Social Harmony* (2005), operates Circle of Compassion, a non-profit organization that promotes "kindness" to all living beings. The organization's approach is a spiritual one, advocating prayer and thought to hasten in a vegan world. Circle of Compassion maintains that veganism is optional, but it hopes to "elevate global consciousness to the awareness that all life is sacred and interconnected." Pointing to photographs that demonstrate that frozen water crystals receiving blessings form more "harmonious" structures than those receiving negative thoughts, it is thought that Nonhuman Animals might similarly benefit from such spiritual endeavors. In "less than a minute each day," advocates can "generate a universal energy field of compassion":

> What we focus our thoughts on expands. Therefore, it is essential that we take time to imagine compassion encircling the earth and that we have faith that we have the power to make it so. [...] What we are proposing is that we all increase the power of these actions exponentially by uniting our focused thoughts on this single phrase at least once a day: "Compassion encircles the earth for all beings everywhere." Imagine this phrase – this vision – being brought into the minds and hearts of millions of people each and every day and thus generating an energy field of compassion around the world. (Carman and Tuttle, 2008)

These excerpts were chosen to demonstrate the problematic nature of influential approaches in the field of Nonhuman Animal rights advocacy. When rights are promoted as economically beneficial to exploitative industries, speciesists are threatened with baseball bats, veganism is touted as a miracle cure, women are sexually and racially objectified, and prayers are believed to liberate other animals, there should be cause for concern.

The Nonhuman Animal rights movement is a social justice endeavor that is flooded with a number of irrational tactics that run counter to scientific evidence. The reasons for the adoption of irrational tactics like these are complex, generally relating to the influence of state, industry, and elite power and influence. This book seeks to unpack these complexities and encourages movement decision makers and participants to take a closer look at how and why the Nonhuman Animal rights movement has taken its current shape. Doing so can at times be uncomfortable and challenging, but it is a task worth tackling.

Major charitable organizations in the United States raise millions of dollars for their outreach efforts, but dishearteningly little of those holdings are invested into the evaluation of program effectiveness. Theorists publish dozens of books and postulate endlessly on podcasts and panels, but most of these efforts ignore the volumes of evidence that *already exist* from decades of research on social movements, social psychology, sociology, and other sciences. Scientists who research Nonhuman Animal rights activism remain relatively unknown, but philosophers who develop tactics through thought experiments rather than evidence-producing scientific experiments are commonly elevated to superstardom in activist communities.

The unfortunate result is a grave misuse of limited resources and ultimately the stagnation of Nonhuman Animal advancement. It is my ardent desire that readers will come away from this book with a galvanized commitment to critical vegan studies and activism. This book will not make a case for Nonhuman Animal rights. Those advocating for other animals tend to agree that Nonhuman Animals deserve equal consideration, but they generally are not aware of how to achieve it. There is a wealth of evidence-based social science research on the topic of social change, but ideological barriers, organizational pathway dependencies, and epistemologies of privilege have obscured them. While activists agree that Nonhuman Animals are worth fighting for, the movement has yet to agree on appropriate strategies for liberation. Constructing a coherent and effective path, then, will be the primary aim of this book.

This book also seeks to counterbalance the movement's religious-like disregard for evidence and reflexivity. Many solutions to the most pressing problems presented by the struggle to liberate Nonhuman Animals are already well documented. For reasons which will be explored in the following chapters, those who have the power to apply this knowledge may fail to do so for political reasons. Criticism is typically met with defensiveness rather than engagement. Bureaucratization, sexism, racism, and other structural barriers likely account for much of this reaction.

The movement hosts many celebrity icons who promote simplified and improvident solutions. It also reserves a platform for powerful professionalized organizations that posture for compromise. Most movement discourse is devoid of critical analysis. If evidence for effectiveness is valued at all, it is often construed to preserve the status quo. This book argues that a focus on fundraising, faith, and privilege too often biases advocacy approaches. Nonhuman Animal rights advocacy seems to be growing increasingly neoliberal and conservative, and, though the movement claims to respect diversity by adopting a wide variety of tactics, most simply replicate the tried themes of welfare reform, vegetarianism, sexism, and white-centrism. Much could be gained from exploring radical positions, but the hegemony of Nonhuman Animal rights advocacy has generally worked to protect dominant positions, even at the risk of abetting speciesism. A rational approach to Nonhuman Animal rights argues that advocates should reject that which does not work if abolition is to be achieved. Alternatively, I posit that the movement would benefit by applying a vegan, intersectional, anti-capitalist, secular, and *evidence-based* approach to dismantling oppression. To that end, participants must diligently evaluate their position and strategy. Either it works or it does not.

This theory is a critical one. It seeks to deconstruct norms and knowledges that shape attitudes, behaviors, and decision making. Importantly, this analysis will be limited by identity and place. As a white, heterosexual, relatively able-bodied cis-gender person living in the West, my approach will be restricted by these privileges. I value continued learning and self-reflection, but it is essential that these biases be acknowledged. Furthermore, the bulk of my analysis relies on my American perspective and is meant to apply primarily to the American Nonhuman Animal rights movement. Though much of my critique will apply to other Western experiences (and perhaps some that are non-Western), other cultures and governments have different policies and standards regarding social change work.

The radical nature of this work also warrants a disclaimer. Some topics and ideologies have historically been off limits to critical analysis or skepticism. Therefore, some discussions may create a feeling of discomfort or offense. The aim of this book is not to insult or antagonize but rather to provoke honest discourse and accountability in order to increase movement effectiveness. It is done so with the utmost respect for all those whose thoughts, opinions, and theories are analyzed in this book. Through open and civil discussion, appeals to evidence, and engagement with existing research and the scientific process, the movement can move closer to effective activism.

The writing of this book has not been easy. While I have received considerable support from many in the abolitionist community and I believe my ideas represent a growing attitude shift in that community, others have been less than enthusiastic about my deviation from the Francionian tradition. The professionalized movement, largely hostile to abolitionist voices, has also proved a formidable foe in my attempt to free abolitionism from the margins of movement claimsmaking. I have weathered considerable deliberations with my colleagues in the formulation of this critical approach to Nonhuman Animal rights. In hashing out what this approach might look like, I have drawn on the literature of a variety of disciplines. I expended great efforts to coherently assimilate this and have attempted to extend the abolitionist critique beyond the traditional philosophical realm to other disciplines, such as sociology, social psychology, and critical gender and race studies. I have also taken pains to ensure my approach holds up to scrutiny and offers a real plan of action for advocates. That being said, there are likely to be growing pains and considerable room for improvement, which will necessitate further dialogue. As with any critical approach, it is this invitation to contrary evidence and critique that underscores any truly useful theory. This is especially important in a movement that has, in fostering distaste for theory and rational reflexivity, exhibited significant stagnation. I hope this work initiates an approach to Nonhuman Animal rights that is ultimately practical, accountable, and successful. Let this be a starting point for many contributions to come.

Notes

1. The term "Nonhuman Animals" is capitalized to designate the status of Nonhuman Animals as a distinct social group. This is a liberty often taken by social scientists who recognize the power of language in enabling or disabling oppression. While Nonhuman Animals are hugely diverse and they do not necessarily share societies, they are part of one group, that is, a group of sentient beings that is *not* human and is subject to human violence. Similarly, as "white" would not be capitalized since whites already enjoy social privilege, humans would not need capitalization, as their status is already greatly elevated.
2. Euphemisms for Nonhuman Animal oppression are placed in quotation marks. Birke (1994, p.16), Nibert (2002, xiv), Stibbe (2001), and Dunayer (1995) theorize that language is often used to diminish, objectify, and otherize Nonhuman Animals.
3. See also their feature of the same name in their January/February 2012 issue, pp.32–7.
4. The phrase "of color" is American terminology most popularly used to respectfully refer to non-white persons

Acknowledgments

Thank you to Lucas Hayes, Dan Cudahy, Aph Kocięda, and Stevie Schafer for their invaluable insights and assistance in the formulation of this project. Stevie and Lucas graciously read the manuscript in its entirety, offering many valuable comments. Lucas was an important sounding board in my formulation of an anti-capitalist approach to vegan advocacy, and he also provided many helpful sources on the politics of population control. Aph and Lucas are not only amazing activists but also dear friends, confidants, and teachers whose support means the world to me. Dan Cudahy in particular offered a considerable amount of time and expertise. I am especially grateful for his single-issues campaign analogy, which I have discussed and expanded in Chapter 3. Thanks to Cheryl Abbate, a close friend and colleague I met while taking a Nonhuman Animal rights philosophy course at Colorado State University. She continues to be an important source of support as we navigate the very androcentric space of Nonhuman Animal ethics and academia. I also wish to acknowledge my colleague Sarah K. Woodcock of The Abolitionist Vegan Society for sharing her wisdom and friendship. To me, she is a beautiful beacon of hope in the movement. In addition to reading and commenting on part of the manuscript, Sarah literally fueled its writing with thoughtful vegan care packages. I would like to send a nod to the Animal Rights Coalition of Minnesota, Kathie Clarke of the Dabney S. Lancaster Community College, and No Kill Nation of Deerfield Beach, Florida, for their help in providing literature resources used in this book. I thank James, Tom, Casey Clague, Dr. Michele Spino Martindill, and Dr. Kate Stewart for their helpful feedback on part of the manuscript and also my mother, who spent considerable time printing out several drafts of this manuscript in the revision stages. Likewise, I sincerely appreciate the hard work of the anonymous reviewers who identified many areas for improvement and assisted me in sharpening my arguments.

    I would like to extend a friendly thanks to many of those authors and activists who unwittingly served as fodder for my criticisms regarding movement ideologies and tactics. I consider many of those mentioned in my analysis as respected colleagues, valuable resources, and selfless mentors. I also acknowledge an old friend and long lost colleague Stephen Laurent who set me on my radical abolitionist path many years ago in our student activist days. To that, I would like to recognize all of my activist colleagues and many readers for years of lively dialogue, criticism, feedback, and support since I began writing on Nonhuman Animal rights issues in 2009.

I also acknowledge my nonhuman family Petey and Keeley for their companionship throughout the writing of this work. Keeley kept my lap warm, while Petey sleepily supervised from his bed by my chair. They are both refugees in this anthroparchy, and they always guide my social change work.

List of Abbreviations

ACE	Animal Charity Evaluators
ALF	Animal Liberation Front
ARZone	Animal Rights Zone
CAK	Controlled-Atmosphere Killing
CSU	Colorado State University
EAA	Effective Animal Activism
FARM	Farm Animal Rights Movement
HSUS	Humane Society of the United States
KFC	Kentucky Fried Chicken
PETA	People for the Ethical Treatment of Animals
UPC	United Poultry Concerns

1
Rationality and Nonhuman Animal Rights

The abolitionist departure

During my graduate studies at Colorado State University, I enthusiastically enrolled in a Nonhuman Animal rights philosophy seminar in the hopes of broadening my sociological knowledge of Nonhuman Animal issues in preparation for my upcoming dissertation work. In this course, we explored ethical theories and the various weak justifications employed to defend the human exploitation of other animals. We debated the role of cognition, capacity for suffering, and death as harm. We deconstructed the immorality of vivisection, speciesist agricultural systems, and exploitative relationships with companion animals. In short, we were taught that Nonhuman Animals *matter*.

Sometimes we discussed vegetarianism, but veganism was never seriously considered. This omission would come into sharp relief later in the semester when our professor generously treated us to a pizza party. I was shocked when a stack of pepperoni pizzas arrived to the classroom. The very same students who had for months nodded along to our professor's lectures on the moral standing of Nonhuman Animals were diving into a dinner of pig's flesh and curdled breast milk from dairy cows long since slaughtered for hamburger. Was I in the right room?

Not long after, our professor led us on a field trip to the Colorado State University (CSU) research "farm," where a number of cows, sheeps,[1] and other animals were living under the "husbandry" of researchers and students. Along our tour, we met a fistulated cow. A gaping hole had been cut directly into her side straight through to one of her stomachs so that her digestion could be observed for research purposes. Despite having spent hours in the classroom studying the socially constructed and fundamentally arbitrary human/nonhuman divide, students could barely contain their excitement as they lined up for their chance to penetrate the restrained victim with their curious hands. The students laughed with each other, and many posed while their friends took pictures. In the classroom, students of Nonhuman Animal rights were learning to respect other animals as sentient persons. In the field, they were learning that it is acceptable to imprison, objectify, and violate other animals. More than acceptable, it can be *fun*.

At the end of the course, our professor offered the class some parting advice on where we might locally purchase "humanely raised" Nonhuman Animal flesh and other such products. This final lesson was understood as congruent with "rights" because Nonhuman Animals need not be protected from use and death, only especially egregious suffering. This protectionist conception of rights incorporates the suffering and death inevitably associated with the majority of Nonhuman Animal use. In other words, this perspective does not necessarily consider it problematic that cows, pigs, and other animals are killed for humans to consume. Killing becomes a problem only when Nonhuman Animals are not treated in a way that privileged humans – those who intend to kill and eat them – consider "humane." The meaning of humaneness is, both in theory and in practice, extremely variable. Some might envision that humaneness entails providing access to grass and sunshine, while others might reject these as luxuries and consider humaneness as relevant only to the reduction of stress in the slaughter line. In any case, the inescapable fact that Nonhuman Animals are being *used* and *killed* is often divorced from any conception of humaneness.

In this sense, the status quo of Nonhuman Animal rights philosophy and practice is quite suspect. I share these examples to demonstrate the troubling disconnect that often exists between intention and practice in the social justice space. It is difficult to accept that eating pepperoni pizza, violating fistulated cows, and shopping for Colorado home-on-the-range "happy meat" is congruent with humanity's moral obligation to other animals. But what accounts for this perplexity? How could students engage rational arguments at the seminar table, only to ignore or adulterate them when applied practically? According to ethicist Bernie Rollin (2006, p.166), it is relatively simple: human use of other animals is not going to end. Given this reality, ethicists should focus on improving the system to ease their suffering. The logic of welfare reform suggests that, given the magnitude of Nonhuman Animal suffering and the public's supposed unwillingness to go vegan and reject speciesism full stop, reforms are the sensible and responsible compromise (Phelps, 2013, no pagination). With so few options at hand, reforms work to alleviate the suffering endured by billions in the here and now. These reforms are also thought to interfere with industry profitability and are presumed to increase public awareness about Nonhuman Animal suffering. Some posit that welfare reforms will eventually lead to an abolition of Nonhuman Animal use.[2]

On the other hand, it is also argued that welfare reform is ineffectual and may actually be aggravating speciesism. American Nonhuman Animal charities, in pushing for reform, often emphasize to exploiters the many business incentives of cooperation. Compliance with welfare reform can actually become profitable for industries. Indeed, many speciesist industries actually take the initiative in such reforms (Salvage, 2012). One *Meat Science* report concludes that while most people claim that they care about the welfare of other animals and many are heavy purchasers of higher "welfare" products, their animal consumption does not actually decrease (Grimshaw et al., 2014, p.444). Likewise, "welfare" labeling is frequently quite meaningless, thus confusing a concerned public and subsequently protecting industry profits (Leitch, 2013; Parker et al., 2013; Swanson, 2013; Wrenn, 2013a).

This process is not unique to speciesist industry. Many others capitalize on the public desire for ethical production by creating their own definitions of social justice in order to control business and create growth. Dauvergne and Lister (2013, p.2) call this "eco-business," a form of corporate social responsibility that is

> proving to be a powerful strategy for corporations in a rapidly globalizing economy marked by financial turmoil and a need for continued strategic repositioning. It is also enhancing the credibility and influence of these companies in states, in civil society, in supply chains, and in retail markets. And it is shifting the power balance within the global political arena from states as the central rule makers and enforcers of environmental goals toward big-brand retailers and manufacturers acting to use "sustainability" to protect their private interests.

Like "greenwashing," "humane washing" can be good for business.[3] Dairies, piggeries, egg production facilities, and slaughterhouses are able to curtail government interference and assuage consumer guilt with proactive humane labeling. Alarmingly, Nonhuman Animal rights organizations often facilitate this process, as the compromise can be mutually beneficial. The promotion of "humane", "free range", "cage-free", and "pasture-raised" products creates an outward appearance of success and achievement for advocacy groups. This encourages public support for the cause, but there appears to be no consistent plan to abolish Nonhuman Animal use. In fact, some organizations, such as the Humane Society for the United States (HSUS), explicitly *reject* the need to pursue or achieve abolition (Pierleoni, 2011). Part of the reason for this resistance could be that achieving abolition would mean an effective end to many professionalized charity organizations. Nonhuman Animal suffering is a commodity that keeps both industries and nonprofits in business (Wrenn, 2013a). A vegan world means PETA, HSUS, Farm Sanctuary, Mercy For Animals, Compassion Over Killing, Vegan Outreach, and many other donation-driven Nonhuman Animal aid groups would have to downscale considerably or perhaps even close up shop. In other words, the non-profit structure itself may be responsible for facilitating a reformist approach that often contradicts the interests of other animals. The continual manufacture of grievances as is necessary to perpetuate organizational inertia is a phenomenon known to characterize many social movements (McCarthy and Zald, 1973, p.23).

The ideology of Nonhuman Animal rights activism has not gone without criticism. The perceived impotence of welfare-focused activism is the primary focus of Gary Francione, an influential participant in radical efforts to reform the modern Nonhuman Animal movement and a primary architect of the vegan abolitionist faction.[4] Francione's abolitionism prioritizes the advancement of Nonhuman Animal interests and firmly rejects any tactic that compromises those interests. This take on Nonhuman Animal rights theory and praxis insists that any meaningful action for other animals must include abolitionist tactics and an abolitionist goal. Indeed, the abolitionist position is highly critical of the professionalized approach that prioritizes reform and heavy moderation. The abolitionist critique is based on the belief that welfare advocacy not only falls short of liberationist goals but can actually impede them. Francione (1996, p.87) argues that welfare reforms have failed to create any significant improvement for Nonhuman Animals. They tend to be poorly enforced and minimally influential, and they ignore the systemic root of exploitation. Veritably, the system is often streamlined by welfare efforts. Animal exploitation becomes more profitable, more efficient, and more palatable to the uneasy consumer. Welfare reform, then, becomes a mechanism in the maintenance of Nonhuman Animal suffering and death. In reinforcing the notion that Nonhuman Animals are resources and property, regulation and protectionism become antithetical to achieving abolition.

Abolitionism is sometimes a vaguely understood position. Most advocates and organizations will identify as abolitionist; even the HSUS takes an abolitionist position on some issues. The reality of movement diversity, however, requires a more critical understanding of variation in position. Tactical preference is one means of disentangling abolitionism from professionalized reformist approaches. Abolitionism represents a small and marginalized radical faction within the larger Nonhuman Animal rights advocacy space. In addition to the goal of eventual abolition, this faction is identified by three factors: (1) a rejection of reformist tactics and a reliance on vegan education as the primary vehicle of social change, (2) its strict adherence to nonviolence, and (3) its recognition of oppression as an intersectional phenomenon. In other words, many large organizations that prioritize reform may self-label as abolitionist because they desire an end to speciesism, but this commonality in labeling is primarily a matter of semantics. While there is certainly overlap in goals and tactics among different entities in the movement, there is an identifiable difference in factional affiliation. In the larger context of social movement politics, abolitionism refers to a distinct radical faction identity. The division between hegemonic professionalized organizations that rely on reform and the anti-reformist radical offshoots that seek societal restructuring is a structural characteristic that is common to all social movements. As with any radical faction, the abolitionists tend to be overshadowed in the social movement space. Their voices are heavily suppressed, and their presence is often demonized. As will be explored in Chapter 2, much of this vilification results from the threat that radical groups pose to existing power relations. I argue that this exclusion may be rational for self-interested professionalized organizations, but it may be quite irrational in the grand scheme of liberation. With full acknowledgment that the abolitionist faction will not have all the answers and that it certainly acts irrationally in many ways itself, I will nonetheless argue that, with some modification, abolitionism can pack the greatest punch to speciesism.

The growing popularity of abolitionist activism in the Nonhuman Animal rights movement has manifested in an explosion of grassroots mobilization, internet groups, and websites. It is clear that these activists are having some sort of impact because professionalized welfare organizations and reform-minded advocates are beginning to countermobilize by reframing abolitionist messages as divisive or extreme, even labeling abolitionists as the enemies of Nonhuman Animal rights efforts (Best, 2012, p.301; Farm Sanctuary, 2012; HSUS, 2012; Joy, 2012; McWilliams, 2012; Pacelle, 2012). In one essay, Matt Ball (2012) of Vegan Outreach goes so far as to dismiss their critics as "loud, judgmental vegan-police types" who are "dogmatic," "arrogant," unrealistic, not "psychologically sound," "crazy," "misanthropic," "angry," and "obsessive." In Norm Phelps' (2013, no pagination) publication *Changing the Game*, he suggests that abolitionists are more concerned about feeling ideologically "pure, honest, and morally superior to the world" than they are with practicing "responsibility for results."[5] He further characterizes abolitionists as self-centered "hobgoblins" who "sit on their hands" while Nonhuman Animals suffer. Again, as a radical faction with a radical approach, abolitionists are rarely embraced by movement leaders.

Reformers and protectionists like Phelps have reason to take notice. Marginalized though it may be, the abolitionist movement has blossomed since the mid 2000s, during which many activists, organizations, and even sanctuaries have adopted the position. Its influence has encouraged some activists to reject ineffective or otherwise irrational tactics favored in traditional Nonhuman Animal rights approaches. Many abolitionists deny the utility in reforms, the effectiveness of political lobbying in a society that still legally binds other animals as property, and the clarity of promoting "humane" foods, vegetarianism, Meatless Mondays, or other reductionist diets. Abolitionists argue that to achieve liberation, advocates must challenge speciesism and work for complete cessation of *all* animal use. They aim to achieve this incrementally through the promotion of veganism and societal attitude change.

The primary emphases of abolitionism make it particularly congruent with a rational approach to Nonhuman Animal rights. Rationality is defined as *an adherence to reason, critical thinking, reflexivity, and skepticism*. Rationality requires a given idea to stand up to scrutiny, and that scrutiny must be ongoing to prevent ossification or stagnation. To withstand scrutiny, a rational idea must be based on evidence. It is not rational, therefore, to streamline speciesist industry if advocates want to achieve abolition. Nor is it rational to construct an alternate ideology that is as fixed and frozen as the problematic ideology it replaces – advocates must build a theory that values evidence and reflexivity with the goal of establishing the most effective approach to ending Nonhuman Animal use. To accomplish this, advocates would be wise to apply the tenets of the scientific method. A theory or tactic must be valid and reliable to some extent, and it must be open to critique. It cannot reliably resemble "truth" or "fact" until it can consistently hold up against attempts to discredit or disprove it.

The need for a strong methodology in advocacy efforts is a major point from which a new abolitionist theory might diverge from Francione's work. His version of abolitionist theory might seem more rationally consistent and evidence-based than competing theories of regulation and protection, but the rigidity of his approach is concerning. Changemakers should consider that regardless of how sound a given theory may appear to be, *no* theory ought to be exempt from evaluation. This includes abolitionist theory. Reason and critical thinking must be at the heart of outreach.

One example of this rigidity is seen in Francione's position on secular theory. Responding to grassroots calls for skepticism and flexibility from within the abolitionist faction, Francione posted a series of short essays on his website, *Animal Rights: The Abolitionist Approach*. In these essays, he asserts that secular abolitionists are "jumping on the New Atheist bandwagon" led by "political reactionaries" such as Richard Dawkins, Sam Harris, and Christopher Hitchens (2012a). He continues: "The idea that an abolitionist must be an atheist is as absurd as the position that an atheist cannot be an abolitionist." Francione's objections might not be surprising, given that even his relatively rational theory is greatly influenced by Jainism (specifically in his references to ahimsa and nonviolence) (Francione, 2009a).[6] One of his administrators, Linda McKenzie (2012), furthers this notion by suggesting that abolition should entail the "rejection of the institutions that maintain [...] inequality." She references secular abolition in specific ("reactionary New Atheism" as she calls it) as a guilty party. Secular abolitionism is framed as "discriminatory," "militant," "right-wing," misanthropic, and "completely at odds with the progressive values of abolitionism."

It is unlikely that secular abolitionists would insist that advocates adopt atheism; personal belief systems are not necessarily relevant to the advancement of other animals. What rational abolitionists *do* insist on is that advocates adopt an evidence-based approach to Nonhuman Animal rights, something that is fundamentally congruent with the progressive values of abolitionism. McKenzie is right to state that abolitionism must entail the rejection of institutions that maintain inequality, but she is wrong to overlook the institution of religion as one of the most powerful perpetuators of discrimination and exploitation. Rational abolitionism calls for a separation of personal beliefs, ideologies, spiritualties, superstitions, and any other ultimately irrelevant assumptions from Nonhuman Animal rights activism. Francione states that a concern for the plight of other animals "[...] can come from any source – it can come from theistic sources [...], spiritual sources [...], or wholly atheistic and non-spiritual sources." Again, rational abolitionism is not concerned with anyone's *personal* beliefs. Rather, it is concerned with how those personal beliefs encroach into what ought to be secular, evidence-based claimsmaking on behalf of other animals. In short, advocates should be mindful of ideological constraints in movement structures.

The reign of irrationality in Nonhuman Animal rights activism

Donald Watson, a founder of The Vegan Society, wrote in 1948 that activists "should use more care in sorting out facts that can be demonstrated, from personal beliefs and wishes." He was wary of false or exaggerated claimsmaking and the movement's refusal to advocate against the use of *all* Nonhuman Animal products. He determined that the vegan movement should adopt a secular, scientific, and logical approach to its advocacy. Doing so, he argued, would ensure that the argument for veganism would become "impregnable against nearly all the criticism it has ever received, or is ever, likely to receive." The vegan movement would "stand like a rock."

Many decades later, Watson's call for movement reform remains unanswered. It would seem that irrationality has usurped the Nonhuman Animal rights movement in both theory and tactic. Operating on celebrity, tradition, and unstructured emotional reactions, there is so little accountability that it loses credibility. Instead, whatever tactics seem to *feel* right and notions of "that's the way it has always been done" take precedence. Additionally, the domineering presence of welfare organizations becomes problematic in promoting limited tactics intended to rouse donations rather than liberation, as is the culture of unquestioning obedience that is facilitated by these traditions. In his critique of the Nonhuman Animal rights movement, abolitionist Bob Torres warns that, "leaving activism to the 'professionals' creates an environment where most people assume that the only way to be effective is by following the lead of the big organizations, the ideas and thinkers they promote, and the campaigns they head up" (2006, p.141). As to be explained in Chapter 2, the agendas promulgated by these large organizations are not always ideal. They often reflect path dependencies, whereby decision making is limited by previous decisions and historical circumstances which restrict the potential for innovation and reinforce a particular pattern of behavior. These agendas may also demonstrate what Torres calls a "cult of personality," a situation in which celebrities are wantonly revered: "a significant number of people within the animal rights movement seem to check their faculties of rationality at the door when it comes to certain movement 'celebrities'" (pp.149–50). He cites

the deity status of Peter Singer, who "can do no wrong, not because of his positions, but because of his history and standing" (p.150).[7]
Multitudes of scientific research exist in countless peer-reviewed academic papers, presentations, and studies that have explored the utility in various approaches, but rarely is any of it examined by activists. Of those few who *have* attempted to draw on scientific evidence, the evidence tends to be cherry-picked and misapplied to reinforce preexisting professionalized welfarist tactics. Nick Cooney (2011, 2014) and Melanie Joy (2008), for instance, pull on social psychology in an effort to present a meaningful evaluation of effective persuasion. The result, however, seems to be a reinterpretation of theory to support the status quo of welfare reform. If critical reflection is not consciously prioritized, authors and organizations may be tempted to misconstrue evidence to support that with which they already agree.[8] As to be explored in Chapter 3, social psychology actually has more potential to liberate advocacy from dead-end reformist pathways than non-profit researchers seem ready to recognize.

In a professionalized movement, the essence of "effectiveness" bows under the weight of non-profit growth. For instance, the newly formed organization Effective Animal Activism (2013) (later rebranded as Animal Charity Evaluators) purports to use objective research to determine which types of outreach work and which do not:

> We are pooling our resources to investigate which charities are really the most efficient at different tasks and to find out which activities most reduce the suffering of animals. The importance of this information on efficiency can't be overstated.

The quest for effective advocacy is a crucial goal, but the non-profit search process can be rather limited in scope. ACE is highly interconnected with professionalized advocacy organizations, which seems to influence perceptions of efficacy. Cooney, for instance, occasionally contributes to their social networking materials, while The Humane League – the organization he founded and directs – enjoys ACE recognition for being the most effective organization at the time of this writing. ACE executive director Jon Bockman founded a farm advocacy group as well. His organization, Justice for Animals, specializes in distributing Vegan Outreach literature (Bockman, no date; Bockman, 2013; Kurth, 2012). Non-profit understandings of "effectiveness" should therefore be scrutinized because they generally determine that farm animal advocacy is the best use of resources and because they reject that such advocacy must entail vegan outreach.[9] This type of advocacy entails primarily the promotion of welfare reforms (Animal Charity Evaluators, 2013).[10] The focus is on abuse, not use.

Efficacy evaluators often emphasize that success is measured in donations. Constituents of non-profit organizations are encouraged to donate as much as possible to help other animals. Cooney frames employment with a non-profit agency as "high impact activism" but also encourages constituents to enter a lucrative industry that could enable them to donate as much as possible to non-profits. With effective activism thus commoditized, other forms of nonmonetary advocacy, such as academic efforts, are discouraged. He explains: "Advocacy movements only respond to people who carry out a better approach, not describe one. Academics have virtually no impact whatsoever, regardless of how great (or groundless) their theories and suggested refinements are" (2013a). Professionalized claimsmaking of this sort that is critical of academic research and theory could be reserving political power for movement elites by restricting public participation to check writing. With its focus on fundraising and bureaucratic growth, however, the non-profit schema leaves little room for serious critical explorations. It is not uncommon for non-profits to dabble in efficacy research, but professionalized organizations are unlikely to challenge preexisting advocacy strategies and path dependencies, given their structural barriers. Efficacy will generally be conceptualized only in terms of funding appeal. As will be explained in Chapter 2, non-profits pursue growth to increase power, but that power comes with a heavy compromise. For one, it is expensive to create and maintain.

In *Uncaged: Top Activists Share Their Wisdom on Effective Farm Animal Advocacy* (Davidow, 2013), Cooney, Ball, and other organization leaders and movement elites also frame welfare reform and compromise as effective advocacy. Effectiveness is taken to mean requesting modest behavior changes from industries and the public, with priority given to particular Nonhuman Animal species exploited in the food system. In other words, representatives from the largest professionalized organizations suggest that effective advocacy entails prioritizing the suffering of some animals over that of others (as opposed to promoting comprehensive, all-inclusive vegan outreach as is favored by radical groups). It also appears to entail the engagement of reductionist measures such as Meatless Mondays, vegetarianism, and flexitarianism.[11] *Uncaged* sometimes engages data to support this "wisdom," but for the most part, it relies on tradition as evidence for effectiveness.[12] For instance, the extolment of financial growth again takes precedence as contributors communicate that effective, data-driven advocacy actually relates to effective, data-driven fundraising. Like so many publications dedicated to improving advocacy for other animals, *Uncaged* only reinforces commonly accepted welfarist pathways. Advocacy guidebooks of this kind read more appropriately as manuals for effective grant writing than they do for effective liberation strategies.

Sometimes, scientific rigor is ignored altogether when developing theory and tactic. Mark Hawthorne's (2008) *Striking at the Roots: A Practical Guide to Animal Activism* summarizes the traditional repertoire of Nonhuman Animal rights work (leafleting, letter writing, tabling, demonstrations, and so forth) with little to no reference to any research that might demonstrate its effectiveness. As with the contributors to *Uncaged*, Hawthorne relies on "voices of experience" – that is, anecdotes and interviews with leaders of professionalized non-profit organizations. Rather than "striking at the roots" of speciesism (which I argue would entail a radical, vegan-centric approach, as we shall see in Chapter 3), this publication merely reproduces tactics that have been adopted by professionalized organizations. These are sometimes tactics which are shown to benefit *organizations*, not liberation. When organizations become the authority on effectiveness in lieu of evidence, this is an indication that the Nonhuman Animal rights movement has become locked in path dependency and non-profitization. This position becomes a serious barrier to meaningful tactical development.

In another example, Kim Stallwood's (2014) *Growl* presents an approach to Nonhuman Animal rights advocacy that relies almost entirely on anecdotal reflections. Only two scientific studies are cited to support his policy-focused five-step plan for social movement success (p.196). This is not surprising, however, because the book intends to deliver advocacy recommendations based on personal experience, not scientific evidence:

> For almost four decades, I've worked at some of the world's foremost animal rights organisations in the United Kingdom and the United States. I've been intimately involved in the advance of the animal advocacy movement from the fringes of society to the mainstream. *Growl* is at once my first-hand account of that change, a reflection on the important lessons I've learnt, and an elucidation of the values I've come to believe must be at the centre of any effort towards implementing social justice." (pp.1–2)

Stallwood's career has been characterized by a strong commitment to direct action in combination with professionalized legal strategies

(Stallwood, 2004; 2013), but both of these approaches have been heavily criticized as inappropriate for advancing Nonhuman Animal rights given the current political climate (Cassuto, 2014, p.11; Francione, 1995; Hall, 2006).[13] Engagement with existing scientific research will be necessary to successfully navigate the path to social change. Stallwood himself admits his limitations in a 2011 presentation on anti-speciesist public policy: "I have no legal qualifications. In fact, I do not have any formal academic degrees of any kind. My qualification is my personal commitment and professional experience." Again, it seems that non-profit elites become the authority on effectiveness. The problem is that non-profit interests can easily conflict with approaches aimed at major structural change. This is not to say that Stallwood's activist experience is unimportant or irrelevant, only to insist that claimsmaking should be able to stand up to scrutiny.

Author James McWilliams (2013a) also seems to reject scientific rigor in advocacy efforts, relying instead on what he calls the "data of experience." In his approach, he suggests he knows what advocacy is effective based on how he feels afterwards. If he feels "good," if it "feeds into the machinery of common sense," then it works. Writing for Our Hen House, a popular non-profit advocacy group, Cassandra Greenwald (2013) is similarly wary of holding tactics up to scrutiny. Lamenting about "endlessly circular debates" and "in-fighting," she advises that the "secret to the best kind of activism" is "whatever kind you actually do." While diversity in strategy is important and activists are unique in the strengths and skills they possess (see Chapter 3), perhaps the best activism is really that which is *shown to work*. Without "debates" and "in-fighting," advocates may resort to an "anything goes" ethos that can hemorrhage precious resources.

Some leaders attract credibility and support for questionable tactics through violence and hypermasculinity. Consider Best's approach, which describes the liberation struggle for other animals as "war," or, as a "battle" against the "corporate-state complex." He explicitly rejects nonviolence as "a pro-violence stance that tolerates [Nonhuman Animal] blood-spilling without taking adequate measures to stop it" (Best, 2004, p.301). Like Stallwood, Best has many decades of personal experience that grant legitimacy to his position. The concern is that, in lieu of supporting evidence, ideas are taken to be fact simply based on the iconic status of movement leaders espousing them. Regarding Best's direct action approach, it is important to recognize that claims to the utility of violent tactics are not always supported by research. Indeed, social movement violence has had the unfortunate result of increasing state repression and eroding public support (Hall, 2006; Lovitz, 2010; Regan, 2004a, pp.234–6; Regan, 2004b, pp.188–92).

Indirect violence, too, is sometimes promoted as a means of improving the status of other animals despite a lack of evidence. Under the pretense that "sex sells," PETA celebrates the sexual exploitation of female volunteers (who it refers to as "Lady Godivas") as one of the most effective advocacy techniques. The organization has amassed a huge portfolio of erotic images as part of its "I'd rather go naked than..." campaign. The images predominantly feature celebrities, mostly women and girls (some as young as 16)[14] who are posed suggestively in various degrees of undress. Playboy "bunnies" are also featured in many PETA advertisements and demonstrations. One promotional video depicts a woman who was so violently penetrated by her recently veganized boyfriend, she has to wear a neck brace. According to PETA, he "knocked the bottom" out of this Lady Godiva (Huffington Post, 2012). PETA claims that its use of nudity has been highly successful because of the media attention that it solicits (PETA, no date b). However, this analysis does not acknowledge that media coverage of Nonhuman Animal rights activism is overwhelmingly negative (Cole and Morgan, 2011a; Freeman, 2009). Indeed, there is no evidence at this time to support the notion that sexually objectifying young women will arouse an anti-speciesist consciousness among audience members. Sex may sell food, cars, and movies, but research demonstrates that sex does *not* sell social justice, especially if the "sex" being sold involves the objectification and degradation of women (Bongiorno et al., 2013).

Moderate movement leaders and professionalized organizations are not the only harbingers of irrational tactics. Trends in irrationality develop within the abolitionist faction as well. Critical activists who seek to challenge traditional abolitionist theories and tactics experience further marginalization in a faction dominated by Francionian abolitionism.[15] The displacement of secular abolitionism discussed earlier in this chapter exemplifies this trend. Open discourse over tactical disagreements is difficult to come by. Instead, dissenting activists may be swiftly written off as discriminatory, ignorant, or selfish. The abolitionist faction's reluctance to engage in critical discussion and reflexivity may be evidence of some of the same path dependencies that plague the professionalized movement.

The politics of powerful non-profits are a primary concern, but radical factions have their share of problems as well. Therefore, welfarism, abolitionism, and direct action alike will be examined in the coming pages. That being said, I do argue that abolitionism is best positioned to adopt a critical approach to advocacy given its radical stance and its freedom from the pressures of professionalization. As outlined in Chapter 2, tactics and theories are sometimes promoted as a matter of tradition, but more often than not, they appear to be related to bureaucratization. Professionalized organizations must inherently prioritize their own sustainment. What this means is that a considerable portion of revenue must be allocated to salaries, further fundraising efforts, and other operational costs. Reformist tactics and single-issue campaigning are well suited to attracting donations. Rational tactics that are grounded in evidence have a greater potential for benefiting Nonhuman Animals, but they are significantly less useful in soliciting donations and thus may not be as attractive to professionalized groups. If this is the case, non-profit growth and Nonhuman Animal liberation are at odds with one another.

Welfare ideology and professionalized mobilization are deeply entangled. Large organizations have a vested interest in perpetuating compromised welfare reform and piecemeal single-issue campaigning. This is typical of any social movement. Many theorists and other leading activists, if not directly employed by these organizations, are subsumed by these popularized, prevailing, and professionalized approaches on which the movement has become dependent. Responsibility for challenging both ineffectiveness and movement stagnation is thus shifted onto radical activists in the grassroots sector who are not bound to or biased by organizational maintenance. Rather than assume blame for tactics that are self-interested and based on faith[16] or finances, movement players simply label those who demand accountability as "divisive" to the effect of stifling much-needed criticism.

Advocates have grounded their activism in faith with disastrous results. It is now that advocates must turn to reason. Age and experience, while helpful, do not necessarily equate to relevant or useful knowledge. Neither popularity nor celebrity should speak to the appropriateness of theory or tactic. To be relevant and useful, an approach must be grounded in reality and evidence. If reasonable attempts to procure evidence have failed, or if there is enough evidence to suggest that the theory in question is false or ungrounded, there should be an effort to revise or remove said approach. As it stands, there is scant evidence to support the effectiveness of welfare reform, single-issue campaigns, sexism, violence, and many other theories and tactics favored in the Nonhuman Animal liberation movement. If there is insufficient evidence, the theory or tactic must be rejected or adjusted and retested. In a rationalized advocacy system, there would be little room for personal beliefs or ideologies that might hinder objective analysis. Personal beliefs and suppositions are not reliable indicators of efficacy. Advocates should build a movement that works for other animals, not a movement that works for themselves.

My concern is that accountability and reflexivity in the Nonhuman Animal rights movement is largely absent and mostly discouraged. Reason often takes a back seat to faith. Participants in the movement spend considerable time postulating, recounting anecdotal evidence, and fervently defending ideology, but these efforts easily disregard the reality of tactical efficacy and existing scientific research. For a movement so desperately short of resources, this is an inefficient and irresponsible approach. To curb the exponentially growing number of Nonhuman Animals hurt and killed for human use, the movement must begin to deconstruct taken-for-granted tactics by adopting an ethos of healthy skepticism.

An appeal to reason

This book makes a case for applied critical thinking and accountability in outreach and mobilization efforts. For some time, the movement has rallied for membership and support according to the "by any means necessary" philosophy. This approach has been largely inappropriate, because few understand what research shows to be necessary. Resources tend to be funneled into inefficient and often counterproductive organizations, while activists may rely on baseless and fluid claims that speak to "compassion," "kindness," spirituality, sexual objectification, and subjective experience. Vague or flimsy claimsmaking is more commonly engaged over unequivocal demands for the recognition of nonhuman rights. For a movement that has seen limited success and has access to relatively few resources, it is essential that advocacy undergo critical evaluation. Simply having faith in an approach will not be enough. If it is not working, it must be amended or scrapped.

This process must begin in theory and tactics that are rationally bound. Does an approach hold up to scrutiny? Can it weather shifting public sentiments and cultural trends? Is it open to criticism, improvement, or invalidation? If not, it may likely represent little more than tradition and ideology – neither of which are reliably useful in advancing social justice. If advocates cannot apply these standards to their campaigning, it would be nonsensical to question those same characteristics that sustain a speciesist society. Advocates cannot fight tradition with tradition, ideology with ideology, or personal beliefs with personal beliefs. Advocates must be accountable in their claimsmaking. This is the heart of a rational approach: reason, critical thinking, and skepticism. The movement is asking a speciesist society to renounce its beliefs about the inferior status of other animals (which are strongly reinforced by cultural norms and state sanction) and assume the movement's beliefs instead. The problem is that the Nonhuman Animal rights movement tends to make this demand without any firm grounding in what makes its claims preferable. This approach creates an unnecessary vulnerability in anti-speciesist claimsmaking. Understandably, sometimes what counts as evidence is not easily separable from personal beliefs, and the difficulty in separating ideology from objectivity will be addressed in Chapter 4. What is important is that advocates and movement leaders move to implement new organizational values: reflexivity and accountability. True objectivity may be impossible, but the benefits to be gained from working toward that goal are certainly worth the effort.

From a sociological perspective, it is not clear that theoretical understandings of rationality have been sufficiently applied to the advancement of Nonhuman Animal rights, at least as a tactical matter. The abolitionist faction seeks to partially address this shortcoming by turning attention to the hegemonic presence of bureaucratization. Abolitionist theory, however, can be extended to also recognize the problematic nature of discrimination against vulnerable human groups by the movement and within the movement. This is a founding principle of the abolitionist faction that is theoretically acknowledged but unrealized in practice. An extended abolitionist theory might also engage criticisms of unchecked spirituality in movement processes. As will be explored in the coming chapters, bureaucratization, fundraising, discrimination, and spirituality are movement characteristics which prioritize the interests of advocates over those of Nonhuman Animals. As a result, the Nonhuman Animal rights movement becomes a space that caters heavily to careerists, raw foodists, New Age spiritual wanderers, dog and cat people, environmentalists, and pornographers. Variety is the spice of life, but these perspectives are sometimes only weakly connected to rights claims. Any person with an interest in sexual "empowerment," personal purification, detoxing, enlightenment, or "following their heart" can be counted as a representative of veganism. In no other social justice movement has the claim for equality been so thoroughly overrun by personal belief systems, mantras, and self-interest.[17] Desperate to expand a largely marginalized movement, advocates seriously weaken the movement's boundaries to be as inclusive as possible. The assumption seems to be that newcomers can be persuaded to adopt a rights-based approach at some point in the future. While this is most certainly a possibility, it does not necessarily follow in many cases. Without a clear anti-oppression identity, humanity's obligation to Nonhuman Animals is lost in a sea of unsubstantiated or indefensible claimsmaking and ineffectual outreach efforts. Veganism is all that Nonhuman Animals have,[18] and to dilute its meaning is an injustice. Unfortunately, abolitionists who criticize this deviation from the movement's original focus are more easily considered divisive than constructively critical.

Divisiveness has become a dirty word, but unnecessarily so. Social movements are not strangers to factionalism and the Nonhuman Animal rights movement should not think itself immune to this inevitable and even healthy process. Movements regularly undergo transformations in claimsmaking. This generally includes a reframing of outdated and erroneous beliefs and the installation of new, invigorated, and improved ideas (Snow et al., 1986, p.475). A top priority of abolitionist outreach is to challenge irrational, inappropriate, and counterproductive tactics and goals. Advocates of this position seek abolition and demand nothing short of that. This has ensured its position as a radical flank in Nonhuman Animal rights, but this radical position is essential to protecting liberationist goals long since obscured by the compromised claimsmaking of moderate groups. It is only with critical self-reflection that advocates can assess the utility of chosen actions and begin to move forward. Indeed, as the Nonhuman Animal welfare movement constipates with debilitating group think, it is the minority voice, unburdened by tradition, obedience, and organizational obligations that holds the greatest promise in securing innovative and effective solutions.

Building a rational approach

This book will add to the literature on social movement processes within a scientifically grounded, sociological perspective on identity, collective behavior, and social change in the context of anti-speciesism. Most contributions to Nonhuman Animal rights efforts take a philosophical approach, ignoring the role of powerful social institutions such as the economy, patriarchy, white supremacy, and religion. While philosophy has its place in shaping the activist imagination, it will ultimately be scientific evidence that determines how that imagination should materialize into meaningful action.

Rationality is a multipronged concept and can connote a number of things. This book will explore several of those interpretations. First, as this chapter has already discussed, rationality can refer to a basic exercise in reasoning. This could refer to whether or not a tactic or motivation is in sound judgment or good sense, for instance. Of course, what is rational to some will be irrational to others. To some extent, then, the meaning of rationality will always be subjective. It might be deemed rational for an advocacy organization to focus on fundraising and reform in order to maximize political presence, but it may be judged rational for a radical faction to take a different route and focus on creating a critical mass of vegans. Each entity could easily see the other's conception of rationality as irrational. The distinction will be found in the evidence. If the professionalized organization wants to end speciesism and is utilizing tactics that research shows can aggravate speciesism, then it cannot be said that this organization is behaving rationally. The same holds true of radical factions. Tactical outcomes must align with goals.

Rationality can also refer to organizational ideology. As will be examined in Chapter 2, foundational sociological theory identifies the rationalization process as a significant influence on institutional structure. Rational choice theory suggests that groups will make decisions based on a rational analysis of potential costs and benefits. Organizations can rationalize through a number of procedures with the intent of streamlining operations and maximizing effect. Again, the line between rational and irrational is a fine one. At some point, the degree of rationalization achieved can be so great that the organization actually becomes deadlocked. This state of impotent hyper-rationalization is difficult to describe as rational.

Rationality can also refer to spiritual or ideological beliefs. For instance, rationality is often used interchangeably with "free thought," agnosticism, or atheism. For many, all of life's questions can be answered with appeals to religion. For others, rational thinking is employed to determine attitude and behavior. Still others engage a combination of science and spirituality. Again, there is no hard-and-fast line between rational and irrational. It is a determinedly imprecise concept.

A rational approach will thus be a complicated one, but there are a number of steps that can be employed toward successful and reasoned advocacy. To achieve the strongest approach to abolition, this book proposes that the formulation and evaluation of theory and tactic should adhere to the principles of the scientific method. Many excellent reference books abound that might offer activists and movement leaders a more detailed understanding of the principles of scientific research, and a number of additional considerations will be offered in Chapters 3 and 4, but this chapter will offer some important fundamentals.

First, a useful theory must be *logical* and *coherent*. As to be explored in later chapters, welfare reform, violence, and single-issue campaigning quickly become impractical according to this principle. Streamlining the exploitation of other animals is not logical if advocates want to end that exploitation; engaging in violence is not logical if advocates want to end violence; single-issue campaigning is not coherent, in that it focuses on one form of exploitation or one species with the intention of addressing speciesism as a whole. All of these tactics are internally contradictory and are thus invalidated as appropriate approaches.

Second, knowledge must be based on *observation*. That which cannot be observed and subsequently measured will have difficulty garnering evidence. This has been a primary disadvantage for many theories. In failing to follow a path to knowledge built on reason and logic, advocates become unable to accurately judge what is useful and what is not. With little or no concern for evidence, it could follow that *any* claim could hold equal weight and equal potential. As previously discussed, the "anything goes" approach has been rather detrimental to the success of the movement. To be clear, however, difficulty in measurement should not outright disqualify any theory. For example, Chapter 4 discusses two very intangible concepts: patriarchy and power. Neither patriarchy nor power can exactly be *physically* observed, but their consequences certainly can be. For even the most difficult-to-observe phenomenon, the scientific method can generally be applied.

Third, advocates should adhere to the context of *discovery*. This would entail a serious consideration of various *possibilities*. A commitment to discovery and the allowance for other possible explanations, methods, and routes will prevent advocates from becoming locked in stagnated approaches; it stimulates creativity and innovation. Likewise, advocates could also adhere to the principle of falsification. Rather than simply assume that a given theory is true and search for evidence to support that assumption, advocates might assume their theory is *false* and look for evidence to *falsify* it (Popper, 2002, p.22). This keeps theory honest, and failing to find reasonable evidence to refute said theory, it can still demonstrate strength or accuracy. This principle of falsification also encourages eternal skepticism toward *any* theory, regardless of how robust it seems to be. Critique should be *"ubiquitous, systematic and relentless"* (van Peer et al., 2012, p.38). Advocates must constantly challenge that which becomes entrenched or taken for granted. In doing so, the tradition of welfare reform would be held accountable, but so would *any* approach, abolitionism included. After all, nothing can ever be fundamentally *proved* according to the scientific method, especially when making generalizations from particular findings.

Finally, activists should develop a *methodology*. Not only will a traceable system of operations coherently and logically guide investigation, but it will also provide a set of instructions for others who may likewise wish to test the theory. If others are able to follow the methodology and come up with a falsifying outcome, this would challenge the theory; if others come up with a similar result, this would lend weight to the theory. Fully disclosed procedures keep the process honest and invite others to test the theory as well. Another important consideration is the recognition of more than one appropriate method. No single form of analysis can provide a complete picture. For example, employing surveys, interviews, *and* statistical analysis would provide a more accurate result than using only one of those methods. This is known as triangulation: applying multiple, appropriate, and complementary methods to gain a more comprehensive understanding of the topic in question. A vigorous methodology should also include a review of the literature that acknowledges previous research. For instance, the Nonhuman Animal rights movement frequently develops repertoires with little or no reference to existing science on social change. This is undeniably irrational and disadvantageous. Existing research can assist movement actors in deciding which tactics will be most effective; it can also demonstrate which areas require further inquiry. Knowledge of what has already been researched preserves resources that would otherwise be wasted on repeated mistakes.

To summarize, first, applying rationality to Nonhuman Animal rights mobilization should entail coherency. Second, advocates must be able to observe the phenomenon in question directly or at least indirectly by way of its consequences. Third, advocates should be open-minded to the potential for many possibilities and remain dutifully critical of even the strongest of theories. Lastly, advocates must develop a strong evidence-based plan of action in testing the validity and reliability of theory. This should ideally be a multipronged approach that is replicable by other researchers, and it should build on existing knowledge. Again, this outline offers only a basic introduction to the tenants of the scientific method, and it is intended to be a working application of research methodology to shape mobilization processes. At the very least, the primary requirements have been highlighted along with the reasoning behind them and the expectations that they command. In the following chapters, the role of rationality will be further unpacked as it applies to organizational structure, individual attitude and behavior change, intersections between human and nonhuman oppression, religion and social change, and social behavior within the capitalist system. A rational approach to Nonhuman Animal rights must be cognizant of these large-scale processes in order to make appropriate tactical decisions.

In this first chapter, I have introduced a critical analysis of problematic ideologies that undergird theory and tactic in the Nonhuman Animal rights movement. Professionalized organizations and radical factions are known to structure collective action based on political pressures, celebrity, patriarchal norms, faith, and tradition. The abolitionist faction has been explored as a potential site for rational decision making based on its critical tendencies and freedom from the contagion of non-profit responsibility. However, all movement players stand to benefit from acknowledging the role of critical discourse and the benefits of scientific rigor in tactical development. To that end, core methodological requirements have been presented to inspire rational decision making.

Chapter 2 presents a sociological investigation into the rationalization processes of organizations. It will be argued that the modern Nonhuman Animal welfare movement has not been immune to societal trends in bureaucratization. In striving for efficiency and growth, Nonhuman Animal welfare organizations ultimately rationalize to the point of irrationality. This form of rationalization extends Francione's critique of professionalized Nonhuman Animal welfare charities, but it offers a more nuanced argument regarding the particular pitfalls of formal organization and incorporation into the non-profit industrial complex. I suggest that abolitionist mobilization should be wary of the many detriments inherent to professionalization. I also suggest that a continued commitment to more loosely coalesced and democratically structured grassroots organization types might prove the safest and most rational route.

Following this exploration of social movement structures, I will proceed with a scientific analysis of social change tactics. Chapter 3 examines the cognitive aspects of speciesism. How do humans rationalize relationships with other animals that are so frequently oppressive? In what ways can social change workers interrupt these processes and make a persuasive case for Nonhuman Animal liberation? This chapter investigates the complex relationship between emotion and reason in relation to attitude and behavior change. Analogy is explored as one reason-based strategy that invites audiences to consider evidence and apply logic to the dialogue of social justice. Single-issue campaigning is specifically examined via analogy to demonstrate the irrationalities of the prevailing social change imagination. As a favorite tactic of professionalized Nonhuman Animal welfare organizations, these campaigns target specific abuses or specific species. Drawing on an adaptation of Henry David Thoreau's "branches of evil" analogy first presented by Angel Flinn and Dan Cudahy for vegan non-profit Gentle World, it is argued that single-issue campaigns represent "branches" on a "tree" of Nonhuman Animal exploitation. In failing to promote veganism, single-issue campaigns do little to address the root causes of speciesism and the various branches of Nonhuman Animal exploitation eventually regenerate. Chapter 3 also assesses other popular anti-speciesism tactics, such as leafleting, video screenings, and food tastings. Social psychological concepts, in particular, are applied to underscore the peculiars of successful persuasion.

Chapter 4 extends this discussion of rationality by tackling the inevitable gender variable. The Nonhuman Animal rights movement is comprised mostly of women but is led mostly by men (Gaarder, 2011, p.12). A rational approach will necessarily aggravate this gender typing. The history of rationality is examined in this chapter as a means of disadvantaging women and other animals in general society but also within the Nonhuman Animal rights movement. First, masculinized rationality has been elevated in the movement to the effect of marginalizing female-identified advocates. Second, it seems to have been ill-applied to the improvement of tactics and theory, particularly in regard to campaigns that rely on sexism, sexual objectification, and sexualized violence against women. Yet, it is the *society* in which rationality is embedded that is the ultimate cause for said discrimination. This means that rationality itself retains a potential for usefulness, and its relationship with social inequality should not necessarily damn science. I will argue that rationality can be adequately rescued and may prove a powerful tool for all genders working in Nonhuman Animal rights advocacy.

Chapter 5 builds on the work of Breeze Harper to further explore the irrationality of unchecked oppression in Nonhuman Animal advocacy spaces. Specifically, there is a focus on the impact of white epistemologies on movement effectiveness. Not only are women objectified in anti-speciesism outreach, but people of color often are as well. Further, people of color tend to be tokenized in Nonhuman Animal rights claims-making, but they are largely excluded from outreach efforts (Harper, 2010a; Harper and Ornelas, 2013). The Nonhuman Animal rights movement problematically relies on a white worldview to frame strategy and depict veganism. White-centric advocacy is rational insofar as it has worked to attract other white persons of privilege. However, such an approach is illogical if advocates expect to widen their constituency in order to normalize anti-speciesism and achieve the numbers necessary to demand political and institutional change. As it now stands, the movement remains overwhelmingly white (Maurer, 2002, pp.9–11). People of color remain largely marginalized, and the oppression they endure is actually aggravated by a "post-racial" Nonhuman Animal rights project that ignores the needs of non-white communities and the continuing influence of institutionalized discrimination. White-identified vegans often bewail the tired thought experiment so often made by non-vegans which poses the possibility of having to kill and consume other animals if stranded on a deserted island. However, few seem to recognize that millions of Americans *do* live in food deserts. More than a thought experiment, this environmental racism represents a *real* and *ongoing* emergency situation that severely restricts the ability to make healthy or ethical purchasing decisions. A rational approach to Nonhuman Animal rights, then, must recognize the importance of race-conscious, intersectional advocacy and the irrationality of seeking justice for some vulnerable groups at the expense of others.

Chapter 6 continues the discussion of marginalized communities with an analysis of institutionalized religion as it pertains to oppression, social change, and secular politics. This chapter also explores religion's ongoing relationship with oppression and the unchecked discrimination against atheists in the modern Nonhuman Animal rights movement. Vegan atheists experience discrimination in ways that mirror anti-atheism in ordinary society: atheists are easily stigmatized, while religiosity remains relatively unexamined. Even the relatively liberal Nonhuman Animal rights community tends to privilege faith over reason. This allegiance to particular dogmas leaves little room for critical discourse. Based on studies that establish the relationship between secularism and support for Nonhuman Animal rights, this discrimination is also alienating one of the movement's largest demographics of potential participants.

Much of Francione's work engages rational discourse, but because it is heavily steeped in Jain tradition, this theory fails to consistently maintain rationality as a baseline in outreach efforts. Logic and rationality are necessary, he argues, but not *sufficient* (Francione, 2012b). I counter this position by arguing that social justice movements must be grounded in rationality as a means of centering the vulnerable group in question. Actor Alicia Silverstone's "Kind Diet," for instance, asks readers to go vegan to become a "superhero" for themselves, other humans, the planet, and *lastly* other animals. She suggests that going vegan allows humans to "see how amazing and joyous and peaceful life really is" (Silverstone, 2012, p.1). The organizational names of many large Nonhuman Animal charities also reflect this fixation on "kindness": *Mercy* For Animals, *Compassion* Over Killing, and the *Humane* Society of the United States, for example. Readers might imagine a "Mercy For Women" or "Compassion

Over Rape" to understand the problems that can manifest within this humane schema. This framework does little to challenge hierarchies of inequality and domination. Positioning social justice as a matter of "compassion" or "kindness" ultimately runs the risk of paternalism and removes the oppressed from the center of concern. Nonhuman Animals need equal consideration, not condescending sympathy that continues to otherize them.

While a secular theory of Nonhuman Animal rights is insistent that *personal* beliefs are not necessarily relevant to mobilization efforts and tactical repertoires, I suggest that faith-based claimsmaking at the movement's *institutional* level could be problematic. Importantly, a secular approach is not interested in individual level religiosity; it is concerned with the *structural* claims made at the group level. In this chapter, the movement's many appeals to religion are analyzed, and, ultimately, a case is made for secular activism.

The final chapter interweaves these topics in rationality to address the intersectional nature of social justice work for other animals. A new theory of abolitionism must recognize the importance of critical thinking, open discourse, and evidence-based improvements. This logic of accountability and reflexivity must also include a clear denunciation of nonhuman *and* human oppression. That is, there should be no tolerance for speciesist single-issue campaigning for Nonhuman Animals, but neither should there be any tolerance for single-issue campaigning that focuses on *only* Nonhuman Animals. The abolitionist Nonhuman Animal rights project should begin to ground itself in the larger framework of anti-oppression. It is only by recognizing the interconnectedness of various injustices that anti-speciesist work becomes logically coherent. For that matter, intersectionality is essential for political viability. These extensions in abolitionist theory will have significant implications for the way advocates treat marginalized activists and marginalized human communities affected or ignored by anti-speciesist activism. They will also require a reconfiguring of those tactics which remain embedded within the capitalist system. As the coming chapters will reveal, simply asking others to "go vegan" will no longer be sufficient. An anti-oppression perspective will necessitate innovations in traditional organizational structures and activist imaginations. A rational approach to Nonhuman Animal rights will need to be critical, secular, and evidence-based. To be successful, the movement will need to engage the bigger picture of social forces, and it will need to start holding itself accountable with honesty and rigor.

2
Irrationalities in Welfarist Organizational Pathways

A sociological perspective on Nonhuman Animal rights mobilization

Nonhuman Animals are beaten, raped, torn from their homes, separated from their families, enslaved, subjected to medical experimentation, killed, and even consumed by other members of society. For the most part, this is taken for granted as normal, acceptable, and even natural. This happens day in and day out in every human society to trillions of nonhuman persons. Nonhumans receive limited legal protection that tends only to respect the property rights of their "owners" (Francione, 1995, p.44). Without a doubt, Nonhuman Animals comprise the largest oppressed group in human society. They suffer the greatest number of injustices and receive the most limited attention and assistance. Because they, like human animals, are sentient and experience this inequality as a result of socially created hierarchies of power, they should not be excluded from moral concern and social responsibility.

Unfortunately, the field of sociology is not immune to socially normative prejudices and has largely ignored the plight of Nonhuman Animals (Arluke, 2002; Franklin et al., 2007; Peggs, 2012; Nibert, 2003, p.5; York and Mancus, 2013). Sociological research has focused primarily on the role that nonhuman companion animals play in the development of human identity (Carter and Charles, 2011; Irvine, 2013), food pathways and the impact of Nonhuman Animal agriculture (Beardsworth and Keil, 1997), and social movement mobilization (Gaarder, 2011; Jasper and Nelkin, 1992). Nonhuman Animals generally remain tributary characters and rarely the primary subject of study. This is not to say that sociology does not have much to offer to the anti-speciesism project. Indeed, the systems of oppression that have troubled other marginalized groups seem to apply quite readily to the experience of Nonhuman Animals. Many of the theories, methods, and subfield specializations applied to human inequality studies hold much potential in applications to other animals. Indeed, sociologist David Nibert suggests that it is impossible to seriously explore human inequalities without taking into account those inequalities experienced by other animals, as they are often mutually reinforcing and inextricably bound.

As it stands, the majority of work in the advancement of Nonhuman Animal rights is dominated by philosophy and political science. Looking specifically at the literature on abolitionism, it is primarily the work of Cole and Stewart (2014), Cudworth (2011), Nibert (2002; 2013), and Torres (2006) which speak to the sociological importance of Nonhuman Animal injustice. Nibert and Torres in particular offer a partial analysis of how anti-speciesism might be operationalized. Both authors point to the role of capitalism in exacerbating both human and nonhuman oppression and the subsequent shortcomings of a reformist approach.

While the contributions so far are relatively few, abolitionist vegan sociologists have offered pertinent explanations as to how nonhuman oppression occurs and how exploitative structures might be dismantled. Most prescribe the rejection of speciesist ideology, a commitment to vegan consumer-based resistance to the economic system that promotes that ideology, and an exploration into the possibility of alternative politico-economic systems. Nibert, for example, sees potential in a move toward socialism (2002, pp.243–54), while Torres advocates an anarchist approach (2006, pp.112–22). However, Nibert and Torres's focus on macro-scale oppressive structures, for the most part, do not extensively explore the relevance of social movement theory. This chapter will extend the sociological conversation by offering a critical analysis of movement structures as relevant to abolitionist Nonhuman Animal rights mobilization. The massive structural changes required to undermine inequality might be achieved through individual boycott, interest group lobbying, or even environmental or social health disasters exacerbated by nonhuman exploitation, but social movements act as important intermediaries that amplify individual actions and circumvent legitimated (but often limited) means of social change like legal reform. They are better able to organize and demand social change on their own terms. This is why abolitionist mobilization ardently encourages engaged participation beyond one's basic identification as a vegan. Personal abstention is an important political act in its own right (that is, veganism is inherently participatory), but *advocacy* collectively broadcasts abolitionist claims, counters hegemonic ideology, and puts pressure on industries, the public, and the state to reconsider the legitimacy of oppressive conventions.

Social movements circumvent, to some extent, the inevitable moderation of goals associated with political lobbying. They have the ability to cultivate marginalized attitudes and utilize extra-institutional means to create change. Legal changes are often expected to follow from these bottom-up social demands. This is not to say that social movements forgo legal mobilization efforts and political lobbying. Nor do I suggest that a social movement can fully succeed without some degree of negotiation with state agencies and political authorities. But, social movements are distinct from interest groups precisely because they champion the ability of collectives to protect their claimsmaking integrity by pressuring institutions and influencing change largely *independent* of legitimated means. That is, a group need not work within the system and risk significant compromise to enact change. This is especially relevant for groups who advocate minority positions and face significant ideological or institutionalized barriers.

True to this social movement typology, modern abolitionist Nonhuman Animal advocacy efforts have had a contentious relationship with the political system. Of course, many who hope to achieve abolition for other animals do utilize pre-existing legal channels. In his 2010 debate with Francione, for instance, Robert Garner suggests that a moral vegan crusade would be unlikely to create lasting large-scale change (pp.147–54). To supplement vegan outreach, he implores the need for strengthened legal protection for other animals. Francione counters that popular support is needed before any anti-speciesist law could be successful: "if the moral paradigm does not shift, the political and legal processes can do little" (p.254). A critical mass of vegans is required for sufficient execution of anti-speciesism legislation. Therefore, abolitionist mobilization has traditionally focused on creative vegan outreach (public speaking, tabling, art, food tasting, writing and research, social networking, et cetera). The intention is to foster a vegan-positive culture that encourages and facilitates the recruitment of new vegans and challenges the legitimacy of speciesism. In this approach, abolitionism stands in stark contrast with the larger, professionalized organizations which rely almost entirely on legislative tactics intended to reform welfare standards for Nonhuman Animals.

It could be argued that abolitionism and reformism actually represent separate movements. After all, abolitionists strive to *end* Nonhuman Animal use, but hegemonic welfarist organizations funnel their resources into *modifying* Nonhuman Animal use and may or may not seek abolition. However, the extreme division between abolitionists and regulationists is actually quite typical of social movement behavior. Welfare organizations and their proponents routinely call for movement unity and denounce abolitionist critics, hoping that abolitionists will stop disrupting established operations with their radical claimsmaking and instead adopt the dominant advocacy approach. Movement unity, though, is an unlikely goal simply because factionalism is familiar to any social movement environment. In order to amass power and resources, movements inevitably moderate their message, and this moderation spawns radical offshoots. Rather than bemoan this natural and unavoidable process, it may be wiser to recognize the value of radical mobilization in a social movement environment that is prone to moderation. Indeed, abolitionists have embraced this divide to some extent. Factionalism grants radical advocates the space to uphold goals without compromise and to challenge counterproductive or inefficient tactics.

Francione has championed this divide with a compelling case against the hegemonic dominance of welfare reform, but his legal focus overlooks a wealth of sociological theory on bureaucracy, organization, and social movements that have, for many decades, warned against the dangers of organizational professionalization in advocacy efforts. Abolitionists may be unaware of the hazards and snags befalling other movements without a working knowledge of this literature. It is the intention of this chapter, therefore, to explore the sociological perspectives on social movement hegemonies. I will also examine the underappreciated role of radical protest in challenging taken-for-granted advocacy repertoires, the irrationalities of concentrated power, and the ideologies that support them. Extending Francione's welfarist typology, professionalized welfarist organizations are defined as those which have achieved non-profit status, expend considerable portions of their resources on fundraising, and have compromised their tactics in a way that prioritizes welfare reform, single-issue campaigning, social services, and reductionism in consumption patterns (rather than veganism). These organizations mirror businesses with a paid staff, a hierarchical structure, financial and operational transparency, and regular cooperation with the state. Instead of working for radical structural change, they are also more likely to be fostering relationships with those industries and major donors that benefit from an exploitative and unequal social structure.

Social movement rationalization

The regulation of Nonhuman Animal use is an arguably irrational tactic. It has been suggested that instead of creating positive change for the Nonhuman Animals, welfare reforms are instead working to reduce consumer expectations about the meaning of welfare (Parker et al., 2013). As Regan (no date) explains:

> The hard truth is, it is wishful thinking to believe that the successful implementation of reforms will give birth to a vegan world. It is far more likely that great numbers of people will continue to eat animal flesh, even after supporting reforms, only now with a clear conscience, a gift, paradoxically, given to them by well-intentioned reformers.

Activists are unwittingly undertaking the public relations work of exploitative industries. Indeed, a *Washington Monthly* journalist reporting on the politics of "beef" production observes that the interests of activists and ranchers are "one and the same" (Mahanta, 2014). Nonhuman Animal rights organizations that engage this approach foster a post-speciesist ideology. Speciesism is no longer considered a serious social problem, due to a general understanding that major forms of animal discrimination have been adequately attended to. The rampant speciesism that continues in a species segregated world is made largely invisible by social movement alliances with industry. Because welfare reform tends not to work and can, in many cases, actually complicate society's potential for liberation by making industries more efficient and creating a culture of consumer complacency (Francione, 1995; 1996; 2008, p.16), it is curious why welfare reform continues as the dominant paradigm in Nonhuman Animal activism.

Sociological perspectives on groups and organizations lend well to this concern. First, Weber's classic work on bureaucracies predicts a potential for irrationality to develop in efforts to rationalize organizations. Secondly, the literature on social movements incorporates Weber's concerns in pointing to the tendency toward professionalization among social movement organizations. This professionalization, it is argued, inevitably results in a dilution of goals and moderated tactics. While increased bureaucratization and compromise may appear rational in securing social movement survival, it is decidedly *irrational* as a means of achieving desired social change. Finally, Ritzer's notion of "McDonaldization" extends Weber's thesis and offers an updated perspective on trends in organizational rationality. It speaks easily to modern social movement environments where organizations are increasingly moving toward irrationalized professionalization.

Francione's poignant criticisms of advocacy politics might lead to an assumption that the professionalized Nonhuman Animal rights movement is unique in its strange counterproductivity. The movement quite paradoxically promotes the consumption of "higher welfare" corpses; freely advertises and financially supports exploitative industries; "euthanizes" millions of healthy and otherwise adoptable Nonhuman Animals; singles out popular species for protection, and downplays, ignores, or criticizes veganism. These trends may seem incredible to some, but it is actually the case that *many* social organizations behave in ways that appear similarly irrational.

Sociologists look to the work of Max Weber (2001 [1905]) who theorizes extensively on the problems endemic to bureaucracy. Weber's work dates to the end of the 19th century and the early 20th century, a time when capitalism was blossoming under the Industrial Revolution and society was becoming highly specialized and alienating. His work casts a critical eye on the increasingly powerful role that bureaucracies play in Western society. Bureaucracies have been essential to the smooth and organized operation of an increasingly complex society, but they tend to centralize control and can be difficult to change. Responding to these trends, Weber observes an "ideal type" bureaucracy that is thought capable of accomplishing complicated and involved tasks in the most functional manner. To achieve this, a bureaucracy should display six characteristics: (1) a specialization of duties, (2) a hierarchy of offices, (3) an adherence to rules and regulations (4) technical competence, (5) impersonality, and (6) the utilization of formal, written communications. These idealized characteristics represent a move toward rationality, and this progression is thought to increasingly improve an organization's ability to manage important social functions.

Organizations are generally necessary to get things done, but successful operation can be complicated. Francione's criticisms of professionalized organizations highlight the restrictive influence of Weber's idealized bureaucracy in the Nonhuman Animal rights movement. Again, it is not alone in this regard. A number of social movement scholars have recognized the tendency toward bureaucratization in movement organizations (DiMaggio and Powell, 1983; McCarthy and Zald, 1973; Piven and Cloward, 1977, xx–xxi; Staggenborg, 1988; Zald and Ash, 1966). Social movement theory investigates the ways in which people come to participate in collective action and how that participation is structured. Organizations play a critical role in shaping these behaviors. Social movements seek to address social problems that are ignored or otherwise unsatisfactorily addressed by existing social institutions. They also tend to advocate for relatively powerless or otherwise marginalized groups. Organization within movements is essential for mobilizing resources and efficiently utilizing those resources. Organization helps to stabilize and secure a collective group in an often harsh social movement environment that routinely faces fluctuating public support and droughts in resource availability. Social movements that advocate for particularly powerless groups face greater burdens of limited resources and scant support.

Social movement participation poses heavy costs and risks to individuals. It would therefore seem irrational for an individual to participate in social movement activity if that movement proved to be draining on personal finances, time, or mental health. Participation is all the more puzzling if that involvement is somehow stigmatized (as documented in the gay rights movement) (Taylor and Raeburn, 1995). Thus, social movement theorists are interested in how and why an organization originates in response to a social need, how it structures itself to meet that need, and how an organization overcomes the potential risks and costs to recruit participants. Considering these challenges, rationalized bureaucratization, with its potential to efficiently tackle complex social problems, might appear to be a fundamental necessity to bring about successful social movement mobilization.

Social movement organizations, acting bureaucratically, emerge within the intention of effectively addressing a social problem. The limited and inconsistent nature of resource pools, in tandem with the enormity and complexity of many social problems, often forces a movement to professionalize in order to stabilize, efficiently utilize resources, and manageably tackle social problems. Because building a constituency is essential for stabilizing public support and ensuring a durable resource pool, movements expend a great effort in overcoming the costs of participation and the tendency to free-ride.[1] Rationalization becomes a means of achieving profit and power, both of which are considered essential to social movement success. Movements often rationally adopt similar tried-and-true strategies and thus become strikingly isomorphic (DiMaggio and Powell, 1983). Indeed, it can be difficult to detect the difference between major Nonhuman Animal organizations, as most exhibit a similar formula for advocacy and financial solicitations.

The Nonhuman Animal rights industrial complex

These very rational reasons for professionalization often lead to some unfortunate side effects. As professionalized groups become increasingly focused on self-preservation, they necessarily moderate their claims-making to attract the largest possible amount of resources (Choudry and Kapoor, 2013, p.5). Because tactics and claims that are considered "radical" are likely to find limited support and tend to have long incubation periods before noticeable progress can be realized, organizations have little to gain in promoting them. Immediate successes are required to solicit support, maintain media presence, and motivate participants. Continued support and a regular intake of resources are necessary for maintaining a movement organization. Organizations cannot afford to back goals and tactics that do not garner immediate returns. While this may be to the organization's benefit, the social problems that initially spurred the organization's emergence go largely unaddressed. This is because moderated goals tend to work within the system as it is. They do not always seek the system's elimination, nor do they call for the radical restructuring required for measurable change.

Calling for relatively conservative modifications to social problems means that organizations can expend a minimal number of resources. They can also win easy victories when the institutions being challenged have little to lose from cooperation. Indeed, cooperation can be beneficial. Movement organizations earn victories that are important for fundraising activities and motivating participants, while the speciesist institutions that undergo these minor changes can reap the benefit of an improved public image per the social movement's endorsement and the facilitation of a post-speciesist ideology.[2] However, the underlying social problem remains largely unchallenged and will continue unabated, with the public left to assume that the problem has been adequately addressed. The social movement organization, after all, is thought to have expertise in regard to its chosen social problem. If the professionalized movement organization routinely strives for minor reforms, there is little reason for the public to question its tactics. These circumscribed efforts obscure the likelihood that the professionalized organization has become bogged down in its unremitting need for income, a need that demands bureaucratization and compromise.

In *Making A Killing: The Political Economy of Animal Rights*, Torres (2006) describes the modern movement as an "animal rights industry" to highlight the tendency for Nonhuman Animal charities to prioritize resource mobilization over tactical efficacy. Torres's concept can be extended to more accurately describe this industry as an industrial *complex*. This latter description indicates an overlap between Nonhuman Animal rights advocacy groups and the industries that exploit Nonhuman Animals. Nonhuman Animal rights mobilization is inextricably embedded in capitalism, and empathy for other animals has become commoditized. As Torres argues, the close relationship between advocacy groups and exploiters is primarily a result of social movement professionalization. As an organization bureaucratizes, emphasis shifts from social change to organizational maintenance and survival. This phenomenon has entailed significant compromise for liberation efforts.

Barbara Noske (1989) first coined the phrase "the animal industrial complex" to describe the capitalistic nature of humanity's relationship with other animals: "The animal industries are built around principles of greed and profit, not just around human needs. This human-animal relationship is embedded in a web of exploitative practices, in which one type of exploitation is carried over onto another level" (p.38). Torres frames the Nonhuman Animal rights movement as an "industry" that is similarly distracted by capitalist gain, one that has resulted in a bizarre alliance with exploitative industries. Such a partnership tends to be mutually beneficial, and the reforms they promote tend to be only minimally effective in reducing animal suffering. More often than not, they are promoted as a means to increase efficiency and profitability. Nonhuman Animal exploiters can cultivate a public image of concern for Nonhuman Animal welfare, and Nonhuman Animal rights organizations can declare victories with which to mobilize donations. The Nonhuman Animal rights industrial complex is evidenced, for example, in the HSUS decisions to hire a piggery owner as Vice President of Outreach and Engagement, to assign Whole Foods president John Mackey to its Board of Directors, and to place HSUS executives on the board of Tyson Foods (both Whole Foods and Tyson Foods are leading American industries in the slaughter and sale of Nonhuman Animals) (Erickson, 2013; LaVeck and Stein, 2012; Lynch, 2012). Advocacy and industry can be quite heavily intertwined.

The Nonhuman Animal rights movement is not alone in this direction. Professionalization, bureaucratization, and non-profitization have been manifesting in most social movements for several decades. Scholars refer to this phenomenon as the *non-profit industrial complex* (Smith, 2007, p.8). As evidenced in the above discussion of Nonhuman Animal advocacy, organizations are under incredible pressure to professionalize. This is for several reasons. First, professionalizing makes an organization officially recognizable to the state, foundations, and the public, which qualifies it for funding. Second, professionalizing protects the organization to some degree from state harassment because it must adhere to state rules and state observation. Third, by moderating tactics, the organization becomes increasingly attractive to state and foundation funding, which tend to be extremely conservative. Most foundations are created and maintained by wealthy elites who use them to protect and grow their assets and to avoid state taxation. Elites are required by law to redirect those monies to the public, but they tend to do so in ways that reflect their interests. Elite foundations are not likely to fund radical social change efforts that could undermine the structures that benefit them (McCarthy and Zald, 1973, p.26).

Take, for instance, the larger Nonhuman Animal welfare non-profits that also fund the various vegan education ventures of other groups. As they rely on grants to sustain themselves, they refrain from advocating or sponsoring radical tactics that might be favored by less powerful collectives. Most events that the larger groups sponsor involve food tastings, film viewings, and leafleting that use materials provided by professionalized organizations. As the beneficiaries of grant money, the larger groups get to decide which causes are appropriate for funding. Not surprisingly, they tend to work with groups that promote a moderated message.

As another example, organizational language is often compromised to appeal to funders, meaning that "veg" language is often substituted for vegan terminology. "Veg" could imply vegetarianism, pescetarianism, or any number of diets that compromise Nonhuman Animal interests. This has an intentionally deradicalizing effect. Vegan Outreach cofounder Matt Ball (2011) explains: "Foundations and rich non-vegans give to groups with similar philosophies/approaches, but won't give to 'Vegan' Outreach." Veganism is presented as an option by moderated organizations, but that option is often buried under reductionist choices that receive more active support. Instead of asking their constituency to go vegan, groups usually ask only that they cut back or go vegetarian. For example, recall from Chapter 1 that Animal Charity Evaluators explicitly avoids veganism in favor of welfare reform in its mission statement. Veganism is presented as only one of many ways to alleviate suffering. This could suggest that the continued consumption of Nonhuman Animal corpses and other products of exploitation can be consistent with effective advocacy. This is far from a radical position. Reductionism does not require structural change, and similar arguments are already supported and promoted by other social institutions and medical professionals. It is a diluted version of liberatory goals, but one that is far more appealing to conservative donors.

The capitalist system is one of exploitation and inequality. Usually those few who own the means of production will accrue great wealth at the expense of the many workers who have nothing but their labor to sell for survival. The state requires that a certain percentage of this extracted wealth be redistributed to society, but loopholes exist. Elites are able to protect the profit gained from exploiting vulnerable groups by storing them in tax-exempt foundations. At this point, they can carefully select where to reinvest those funds. Rarely are they redistributed in a manner that would relieve those who are hurt by the capitalist system in the first place (Ahn, 2007).

For example, Nonhuman Animals suffer and die by the trillions each year to the extreme benefit of elites who profit from their flesh, labor, and other products. Rather than redistribute that wealth in a way that would improve the well-being of Nonhuman Animals, elites funnel the funds into professionalized non-profits that are reluctant to advocate for any radical structural change that could upset the exploitative structures that elites depend upon. Importantly, conservative foundations are far less likely to issue grants to leftist causes to begin with. Those few liberal organizations that do receive help realize that their message will need to be modified significantly to suit these conservative interests. Grassroots coalitions – the groups which are most likely to harbor radical goals – are largely excluded altogether, lacking the non-profit organizational requirements, networking connections, and administrative training necessary to apply for and receive funding (King and Osayande, 2007).

As with elites, the state also has much to gain in pushing organizations toward professionalization. Radical collectives are a threat to the state, meaning that the state has an interest in suppressing them. Researchers have noted that violent suppression can work to the disadvantage of the state by inadvertently garnering public sympathy and support for crushed protesters (Rodríguez, 2007, p.29). For example, images of nonviolent civil rights protesters accosted by malevolent police officers sparked outrage across the nation in the 1960s. In lieu of this backfire, the state has come to see the value in less visible soft control. Since the Civil Rights Era, the state's approach to social unrest now involves offering certain incentives to collectives with the intention of regulating and moderating them. Social movements are channeled through non-profit institutions, effectively quelling them (McCarthy et al., 1991, p.70). Not only is organizational efficacy stunted by this process, but also the public is made to believe that the social problems in question are being seen to, thus reducing public awareness and propensity for protest. The process of institutionalization is essentially a means of facilitating hierarchy and control, one that suppresses critical thought to the benefit of the state (Ward, 1996, p.119).

State incentives not only compromise those organizations caught within the complex, but also the power differential created in the social movement arena puts considerable pressure on non-professionalized radical groups that must scramble for the few remaining resources. As funding and membership swell for the professionalized groups, their clout also grows. Marginalized radical factions must contend not only with dwindling resources but also with the power of the professionalized organizations that have usurped the social movement space. These organizations often do the work of the state in attacking the legitimacy of marginalized radicals, defaming them and denying them access to resources.

Another disempowering effect of the non-profit industrial complex, then, is the atmosphere of competition that it creates. For professionalized organizations, there is little to be gained in cooperating with radical factions that not only compete for the same funding, but can sully their reputation as an attractive grantee. It would be unlikely for a large non-profit to partner with abolitionists who *unequivocally* demand Nonhuman Animal liberation and veganism. Professionalized organizations rely on large, conservative, elite-driven foundations that would likely balk at this radical claimsmaking. Although abolitionists and many professionalized rights organizations theoretically seek the same goal (a vegan world) – and this commonality should encourage cooperation – the two groups essentially become adversaries. This partially explains the tendency for professionalized groups to vilify abolitionism, ignore it, or manipulate abolitionist language to suit their message of reform. Furthermore, large organizations often accuse abolitionists of being "divisive," insisting that activists of all persuasions ought to work toward the same end. This insinuates that abolitionists should abandon radical claimsmaking and either join ranks or withdraw to allow professionalized organizations unrestricted access to resources and agenda-setting. There is a lot at stake for those groups that have prioritized fundraising. They must appeal to funders at all costs, and sometimes this entails marginalizing radical groups and appropriating their rhetoric. A contentious, uncooperative social movement field is good news for the state. If every group is out for itself, the movement becomes fractured in a way that poses much less of a threat to the established social order.

The state also benefits from a network of weakened social movement organizations by unloading its responsibility to citizens onto non-profits

(Gilmore, 2007, p.45). Unable to engage radical tactics, professionalized organizations are often reduced to social service work. This work is not entirely altruistic. In providing immediate relief to their constituents, non-profits are able to keep up appearances by working to help those whom they claim to be in service of. They are also able to fundraise behind these efforts. Trap-neuter-release programs, abuse prosecutions, open rescues of sick and dying farmed animals, and free or low-cost services to companion animal owners in impoverished areas are all important social services that do provide immediate and important relief to those fortunate enough to experience them. They also make for especially heartwarming stories and photo opportunities that will headline websites and accompany mailed brochures with donation requests.

As will be explained in the next chapter, drawing on emotion is useful for motivating viewers, and most activists, regardless of non-profit affiliation, heavily utilize this tactic. However, they may be obscuring important social justice claims in doing so. For organizations, intensive emotion-based persuasion tactics are also low-cost, minimal investment practices that can garner considerable financial reward. Given the limited nature of funding for leftist movements, these types of sellable social service projects probably seem like an efficient use of what little is available. The concern, however, is that a focus on funding can be extremely counterproductive. Organizations adhere to compromised practices in order to appeal to the limited available funding, and then they apply those limited funds to affordable social service work that can be advertised for additional funding. This cycle leaves little room for social change because it prioritizes sustainment and survival. Non-profits become preoccupied with providing immediate relief to constituents, but they spend little to no effort in attempting to solve the structural problems that create the suffering of their constituents in the first place.

Sanctuary non-profits, for example, regularly take in Nonhuman Animals rescued from the agricultural industry, though these efforts represent little more than a drop in the bucket of rampant globalized speciesism. Importantly, these refugees represent more than a few saved lives: they become fundraising mascots. Many sanctuaries encourage members to "adopt" or sponsor rescued animals living on the premises, but for larger non-profits, these funds are likely directed toward reform campaigns. By way of an example, Farm Sanctuary's (2013) net assets of 12.4 million dollars are presumably more than enough to care for the animals on their California and New York sites. Again, social service work is important, but funding raised on its behalf is not necessarily congruent with radical structural change.

Local "humane" societies fall into a similar trap. Instead of working to dismantle the speciesist social structures that create the problem of companion animal suffering and homelessness, these organizations prioritize fundraising in order to keep their doors open and to continue providing services to local communities and their Nonhuman Animals. Like sanctuaries, these organizations tokenize dogs and cats in need, in order to bring in more funding. This funding pays the salaries of a few and provides temporary relief to some Nonhuman Animals, but kill rates are high, adoption rates are low, and the stream of animals in need is unrelenting. Indeed, dismantling oppressive structures would mean the eventual demise of these organizations (and the countless salaried positions they support). While some might welcome this eventuality, it may not be an attractive prospect for corporatized organizations that have prioritized survival and growth.

Non-profitization also undermines grassroots work by standardizing social change advocacy. Activists are drawn into salaried careers, and community organizers are transformed into managers. They are funneled into leadership training programs that effectively deradicalize them and indoctrinate them with the established professionalized advocacy approach. Large non-profits often train advocates and grassroots groups according to their brand of effective advocacy. The presumption is that large, professionalized, and heavily funded organizations are the epitome of successful mobilization and activism knowledge. Advocates are directed to replicate the tactics and rationale of professionalized organizations, most of which center on welfare reform and reductionism. Rather than encourage and support grassroots mobilization where radical ideas blossom, these groups infiltrate with their own moderated approach, providing their branded literature for distribution and dictating what topics and targets warrant attention. Grassroots activists are transformed into street teams that will promote their sponsoring professionalized organization free of charge. Becoming a part of the non-profit "team" usually means forgoing a radical agenda, but the allure of networking, recognition, support from major movement players, and other perks can overshadow this compromise.

For those who *are* paid to advocate, working for a non-profit can be quite lucrative in the US. Many salaries are well above the national average, and some reach well into the six figures.[3] Job announcements usually call for expertise in fundraising and marketing with little or no mention of social change skills or any personal commitment to anti-speciesist values. In other words, non-profit leaders and employees need not be vegan or trained in creating change for other animals. Presidents, directors, managers, and other executives need only be an expert in raising money. Furthermore, qualifying for these career positions requires substantial privilege by way of social, economic, and political capital. Non-profit employees often brandish advanced degrees in public administration, non-profit management, economics, mathematics and statistics, and computer science. It is not uncommon for professionalized non-profits to enjoy access to elite workforces. Unfortunately, the educational, occupational, and networking privileges available to non-profit careerists are largely out of reach to poor persons, people of color, and many women. It is thus argued that professionalization can undermine efforts to dismantle species inequality, but it can also work to maintain social inequality among humans. As will be shown in Chapter 5, this hierarchy of social movement advocacy also has implications for at-risk human populations who could benefit greatly from the resources and outreach efforts of large non-profits. For now, it is important to recognize that advocating for a paycheck is a privilege often reserved for white, middle-class Westerners who are usually male (King and Osayande, 2006). Certainly, the homogeneity of leadership will impact decision making in ways that could bias tactics, limit resonance, and restrict movement growth.

Largely excluded from the non-profit model, marginalized people have been pushing for change with creative, low-cost campaigns in their communities. This legacy of unpaid activist labor may be devalued in the non-profit model, but it is certainly not ignored. While professionalized organizations have paid staff, some of whom are making very handsome salaries, they continue to rely on the free labor of interns and volunteers. Although these organizations draw in millions of dollars in funding, professionalization is expensive and the funding leftist movements receive is significantly less than conservative ventures.[4] Salaries cost money, as do the basic social services they offer. For instance, Farm Sanctuary claims they require $26,270 to operate *each day* (Baur, 2013). Recall that the state hands over many social service responsibilities to non-profits. This translates to significant savings for the state and a comparatively tight budget for non-profits. The actual labor associated with providing social services is managed through thousands of unpaid positions. Most of the larger organizations offer unpaid internships to accomplish much of their work. Many of these volunteers work to distribute outreach literature that doubles as fundraising material. Sometimes female volunteers are, for lack of a better word, prostituted on public streets, encouraged to wear lingerie or go naked to raise public awareness to the organization and raise funds (Wrenn, 2015, p.13).

Again, the compromises associated with professionalization fuel the emergence of radical factions that emerge in the social movement environment (Fitzgerald and Rodgers, 2000, pp.580–3). Radical factions, dissatisfied with movement moderation, play an important role in filling the gaps left by professionalized organizations. They also pull the movement back toward the core social change goals that first inspired mobilization. Free from the restrictions felt by larger organizations that have business expenses to satisfy, radical movements have the space to challenge prevailing ideologies and to demand meaningful and substantial social restructuring. Importantly, radical factions also tend to favor a democratic or grassroots structure as a precaution against the many bureaucratic pitfalls associated with professionalization. Of course, this comes at the cost of much-needed stability in a hostile social movement environment. Resources are more difficult to collect. The inability to affect any immediate social change can also be demoralizing and thus might fail to solicit significant public support. With such handicaps, many radical factions find it difficult to weather the tide. Radical factions may struggle to realize any significant power within the movement, but their presence is absolutely critical in maintaining goal ideals nonetheless.

The irrationality of rational organization

Having introduced the role of organization in social movements and the complications imposed by the state and industry elites, I will return to Weber's theory of bureaucratization for a closer analysis of organizational irrationality. Thus far, I have argued that the movement's tensioned relationship with rationalization has influenced considerable conflict between the professionalized organizations and radical factions. Major Nonhuman Animal rights groups focus on welfare reform, an approach that is especially conservative and easily promoted. Consequently, the abolitionist faction has emerged as a radical challenge to that moderation. Professionalized groups are bogged down with requirements for fundraising and small, easily won campaigns, but they have a large presence and a greater resource pool. Abolitionists are limited in their influence and resource access, but they possess a genuine commitment and a strong, unadulterated, and consistent message.

Undoubtedly, in the fight for legitimacy and power, abolitionists will face important decisions about how to structure their faction for optimum efficiency and how to rationalize without compromise. In the meantime, abolitionists have not been shy in their critique of professionalization in the Nonhuman Animal rights movement. Recall that the benefits to professionalization come with significant risks. Weber's six characteristics of bureaucratization demonstrate that a well-intentioned move toward rationality can quickly slide toward irrationality. While bureaucratization values a specialization of duties, hierarchies, rules, regulations, competence, impersonality, and formality, those same ideals can also create alienation, inefficiency, ritualism, inertia, declines in privacy, and a fixation on time. The following sections will explore these strained relationships in further detail.

Specialization and alienation

Specialization can improve efficiency, but it corrodes communality. Henry Ford's automotive production line, which assigned each worker a particular task, is an example of this. This specialization allows for mass production at affordable costs, but the process takes a heavy toll on employees. Individuals and groups within the organization are distanced from one another, as are groups inhabiting the larger social movement space. Indeed, organizational specialization can even distance various social justice efforts, making alliances across issues difficult. Social change workers will need to decide how far to engage specialization before it begins to impede individual innovation. While important for efficiently and objectively managing specific tasks, the specialization of duties and impersonality typical of large organizations can distance both participants and potential participants from genuine movement activity. That is, a divide can materialize between the organization and its support base. Alienation in a movement organization can be especially problematic as social movement mobilization relies very heavily on creating an identity for activists and providing networks to nurture their participation.

Professionalized organizations can depersonalize to the point at which activism is restricted to petition signing, letter writing, financial donations, and disengaged memberships that operate only to encourage more petition signing, letter writing, and financial donations. Torres (2006) argues that this alienated activism is ultimately tempered and impoverished:

> As long as PETA (or any other large organization) encourages them to donate money, rather than doing their own activism, they are producing a centralized economy of activism that further

disempowers people; if people are just handing over money, they're libel to continue to feeling isolated, angry, and frustrated. (p.141)

Gone are the days of local chapters and grassroots activism. Today's participants are more likely to be urged into signing a petition or a check; they are rarely encouraged to seriously engage the issues or to participate in any significant way. This is unfortunate as Nonhuman Animal rights activism is an inherently personal endeavor. Supporting antispeciesism in a way that seriously considers the interests of other animals entails a complete overhaul in what one puts in their shopping carts, on their bodies, and *in* their bodies. These are explicitly personal actions. A serious accommodation of vegan politics also entails a substantial challenge to a prevailing speciesist ideology. Taking a few moments to sign a petition or to donate keeps the power of social change in the hands of the professionalized organizations and almost completely removes the participant from the process. As it stands, advancing the cause for Nonhuman Animals is an uphill battle, and the movement could be compounding this difficulty by ignoring the immense potential in its constituency. To fully enjoy the diverse resources that the Nonhuman Animal rights constituency can furnish, it would be wise to encourage them to participate beyond signatures and donations.

Long accustomed to limited financial resources, the marginalized abolitionist faction appears more cognizant of the potential in people power. Abolitionists ask those interested in advancing Nonhuman Animal rights to make the very important commitment to veganism but to also *promote* veganism in ways that utilize their own unique skills and talents (Torres, 2006, pp.145–7). In becoming vegan, a participant immediately reduces demand for Nonhuman Animal products, but that participant also makes an important political statement that can influence others with little added effort. As veganism becomes normal and legitimate, a positive vegan culture is created. Vegan networks can sustain a commitment to veganism and also welcome newcomers (Jabs et al., 1998). By encouraging participants to go beyond their own personal commitment and to advocate as well, that impact can be multiplied substantially.

Advocates should also recognize that supporting Nonhuman Animal liberation and becoming vegan in a speciesist society entails significant social costs. An organization that has become so large and bureaucratic that it is effectively removed from its constituency makes for a poor welcoming committee. Interestingly, internet communities have exploded online to fill this critical void. While participants might have an extremely limited relationship with major organizations, they can at least network with one another online. The internet has also acted as an important vehicle for the similarly alienated voices of radical factions. Low startup and maintenance costs allow for considerable entrepreneurialism. In online spaces, activists need not defer to social movement organizations for leadership and structural regulations (Earl and Schussman, 2003, pp.177–80). Abolitionists, for example, are largely ignored by professionalized organizations, but they have been able to create a plethora of online gathering points, including blogs, Facebook groups, and websites. As a radical faction with limited collective resources, the internet gives presence to a group that would be otherwise overshadowed or outright silenced.

It could be argued that professionalized organizations enjoy a public presence that acts as a sort of beacon to those interested in Nonhuman Animal rights who lack access to local networks. Professionalized organizations also possess the resources necessary to reach out to those isolated individuals. For instance, even as a young person growing up in a rural, low-income Appalachian "hunting" community in an era before widespread internet access, I knew about PETA and was able to write to them and receive information. Likewise, groups like PETA also have the financial ability to proactively mail out literature and information to the uninitiated. The problem begins when those isolated folks are given the message that "anything helps" and that they can realize their concern for Nonhuman Animals simply by becoming a paid member. The problem is further exacerbated when that membership entails a postal onslaught of donation requests thinly disguised in shocking anti-cruelty campaigns that exploit their emotional vulnerability to Nonhuman Animal issues. Some may see through these fundraising tactics, but these organizations wield incredible power in shaping the "common sense" of advocacy paths.

Therefore, a constituency alienated from the professionalized organizations that shape the movement is potentially very dangerous. Most people will freely admit to caring about Nonhuman Animals in some way or another and thus exist as an immense pool of potential revenue. Unfortunately, large organizations in the Nonhuman Animal rights movement, bound by bureaucratic requirements, find it too risky to encourage interested parties to realize their moral concern in meaningful action. Kept at a distance, these participants exist in a mass of anonymity and lack access to those fulfilling relationships within the movement that are so essential to motivating continued interest and participation.

Hierarchy and inefficiency

As a theoretical matter, the application of a hierarchical structure to a social movement seems counter to the goal of anti-speciesism. Activists paradoxically erect new hierarchies with the intention of dismantling others. While bureaucratic organizations exist to perform social functions or address societal needs, remember that Weber notes their frustrating tendency toward ineffectiveness. They can be made impotent by self-interest, ideology, or overly rigid hierarchy, rules, and structure. Perhaps the most glaring consequence of excessive bureaucratization in the professionalized Nonhuman Animal rights movement, then, is this ironic downward spiral into inefficiency. As an organization becomes overly hierarchical and compartmentalized, it can become less flexible in its ability to tackle the social problems that it was originally designed to address. Thus, the more efficient a bureaucracy becomes, the more it risks becoming inefficient.

Large organizations can be limited in their ability to respond effectively when complex steps must be undertaken before they act. Local groups which are more in tune with the characteristics of their region enjoy close ties with their community and abbreviated levels of command. Therefore, they are often in a position to act more quickly and appropriately. Unfortunately, local groups tend to be replaced or absorbed by larger organizations to increase resource access and public presence. This was the case with PETA, which, at one time, was comprised of several local divisions until consolidating as a national organization in Norfolk, Virginia.

As previously emphasized, the focus on financial stability and increasing public support tends to moderate a movement's goals. Certainly, if a group must divert a large portion of its efforts and funds into further fundraising, and those funds are being expended on organizational overhead rather than social change goals, then that group could be said to be inefficient. If a group has amassed millions of dollars, saves much of it, and spends most of the remainder on further advertising with only a small fraction going toward Nonhuman Animal relief efforts, then this group is prioritizing its own needs above those of the nonhumans it represents and is thus behaving inefficiently. This is not to ignore the financial requirements of a large organization and the important influences these professional groups can have at the national level, but rather to suggest that they have significant inefficiencies *inherent to their size and responsibilities*. This, in turn, highlights the importance of abolitionist activism as a site of decentralized, democratic, and grassroots mobilization, with no definitive leadership and activists who are dispersed across the globe. The structure of abolitionism lends to the flexibility necessary for quick, personalized action suited to local needs, and it does so within the context of large-scale goals of structural change.

Rules and ritualism

These types of inefficiency may endure because of another symptom of bureaucratic over-rationalization that encourages repetitive, inflexible behavior: ritualism. Ritualism speaks to a professionalized organization's tendency to adhere to rules and regulations in a manner that prioritizes the organization's internal interests over originally stated goals. Sometimes manifested in "red tape" and tedious paperwork, efficient problem solving is impeded by a complicated bureaucratic process.

For the Nonhuman Animal rights movement, ritualism often develops in restrictive procedures that hinder goal attainment. Many practices are carried out according to the status quo with little to no critical assessment in regard to their effectiveness. For example, Francione (1996, p.78) and others (Nibert, 2013, p.259; Torres, 2006, p.91) have argued that welfare reform has not been shown to significantly improve the status of Nonhuman Animals. In fact, both US and global consumption of Nonhuman Animals has increased considerably despite the movement's notable expansion over the past century (Simon, 2013, p.5; Wrenn, 2011, p.12). It is also questionable if single-issue campaigns, another favorite tactic of professionalized Nonhuman Animal organizations, are effective in achieving the liberation of other animals. As will be explored in the next chapter, single-issue campaigns squander resources on tactics that single out one species or issue as more important instead of expending those resources on more comprehensive vegan outreach (Wrenn and Johnson, 2013). Increased vegan numbers would improve the status of *all* nonhumans, not just that of a few popular species. Many groups also continue with campaigns that sexually objectify female activists despite research that finds them to be counterproductive (Bongiorno et al., 2013). Professionalized organizations are also likely to favor the killing of healthy Nonhuman Animals, although research indicates much higher potentials for adoption than commonly acknowledged (Winograd, 2009, xi–xvii). Considerable evidence suggests that welfare reform, single-issue campaigning, sexism, and the killing of healthy companion animals is detrimental to the goal of Nonhuman Animal liberation, but the movement continues to utilize them as a matter of course.

These professionalized organizations also engage in a considerable amount of counter-framing to protect their inefficient and often irrational procedures. Vegan Outreach and PETA, for example, often portray veganism as unachievable or overly restrictive (Norris, 2009; Friedrich, ~2010). Declaring the No Kill movement the "biggest threat to homeless animals today" (Matthies, 2013), PETA routinely publishes material that vilifies No Kill shelters as either torturous prisons or elitist facilities that turn away countless needy animals. Sometimes No Kill rescue is even conflated with hoarding (PETA, 2010), a serious and debilitating mental disorder. Alternatively, PETA reframes their support of companion animal killing as "dignified," "compassionate," and "animal rights uncompromised." Thus, the credibility of No Kill advocacy is called into question, while the mass killing of millions of Nonhuman Animals is considered "animal rights." It is telling that professionalized groups deem these deadly approaches as necessary given their access to millions of dollars in organizational funds fed by foundations, elites, and membership donations. These are lifesaving funds that No Kill shelters and their refugees could desperately use.

These organizations often argue that vegan or No Kill alternatives are impractical or impossible and will not resonate with the public. It could be, however, that professionalized organizations are themselves creating these ideological barriers and unfavorable attitudes. The public is rarely exposed to an unequivocal vegan message, meaning that its potential for resonance is still unknown. Counter-framing can effectively obscure alternatives from their constituency as preferable options. By withholding resources and challenging the legitimacy of radical alternatives, they make the work of life-affirming, liberatory advocacy that much more difficult. Thus, professionalized organizations become bound to their long established and often antiquated procedures. Unfortunately, this ritualism has become a significant hindrance to engaging in the critical self-reflection that is so necessary for healthy movement growth, adaptation, and improvement. Instead of exploring alternatives that might prove more rational and efficient, professionalized organizations remain stubbornly committed to rules of advocacy that may work in the disservice of Nonhuman Animals. While rules are needed for efficient operation, they can come to dictate an organization to the point of discouraging innovation.

Competence and inertia

Another strength associated with bureaucratic organization is its ability to competently address social problems. That is, organizations develop in sufficient quantity and complexity to ensure adequate attention and proper functioning. An ideal rational organization will exhibit competence in technology, leadership, and other characteristics useful to adequately performing its function. Sometimes, however, organizations may find it difficult to self-regulate this process. How do organizations know when competence is achieved? Is there a cap on organizational growth?

Bureaucratic inertia refers to the tendency for organizations to perpetuate themselves. On the surface, this might seem important to a social movement that hopes to entrench its influence and extend its reach, but organizations can expand in areas or regions where they are of little use. When this is the case, resources may be unnecessarily squandered. Such squandering is seen in the steady diffusion of Walmart stores in every nook and cranny of the US, for example, or in the spread of government agriculture regulation departments in areas that are non-agricultural.

The Nonhuman Animal rights industrial complex, too, experiences wasteful inertia. It is certainly not accurate to suggest that Nonhuman Animal rights representation could exist in areas that are not in need of it. Speciesism is far too widespread. However, professionalized organizations *do* tend toward increased infrastructure, which is not necessarily a precursor for successful social change (it is also very expensive). These groups also demonstrate inefficiency of growth by failing to consistently assess the efficacy of tactics. Millions of dollars raised by Nonhuman Animal organizations are routinely funneled into programs that have been shown to be ineffective.

Furthermore, single-issue campaigns are infinite. Protests against individual Nonhuman Animal injustices dominate the anti-speciesist repertoire, while a more encompassing vegan campaign is neglected. Inertia of this kind is most certainly related to fundraising concerns. The itemization of activism ensures that organizations can fundraise behind each issue individually in order to maximize return. Professionalized groups appear to expand indefinitely and develop hundreds of single-issue campaigns, though vegan outreach might offer a more succinct approach to liberation. Therefore, while the Nonhuman Animal industrial complex is restrained by ritualized procedures, it becomes even more encumbered by an inertia that encourages unrestrained bureaucratic growth and sustains the inefficient use of resources. Organizations become fixated on the task of maintaining their inertia as a matter of survival and growth. As a result, they will be less focused on eliminating the structural problems that necessitate and support the existence of these organizations.

Impersonality and declines in privacy

Another important consequence of bureaucratization identified by Weber is the attack on privacy. Affiliation with large organizations often entails disclosing personal information. Perhaps to compensate for the tendency for rational organizations to depersonalize procedures, personal data is required for many tasks and operations. To become a "member" of a large non-profit, individuals are generally asked to supply credit card information, a mailing address, an email address, and a phone number. Inevitably, this information is shared among other organizations and is used to solicit further donations.[5] Some organizations provide member information to other activists who need assistance for local projects. As activist networks expand in online spaces, additional risks to identity security could arise.

Within the abolitionist faction, too, it is not uncommon for individuals to find their activity monitored, recorded, and shared. That information can later be used to police activist behavior and may stand as evidence to ostracize and exclude them. Scholars have identified the gay rights movement as "high risk" for this reason. Like advocates working to liberate Nonhuman Animals, lesbian and gay activists face "substantial legal, financial, social, or physical costs" (Taylor and Raeburn, 1995, p.254). In an age of identity theft, activist surveillance and stigmatization, as well as heavy legal sanctions against Nonhuman Animal rights activism, the decline in privacy could become a significant problem in the future. Loss of privacy might also be linked to increasing the costs of participation to the point of diminishing motivation and discouraging participation. This possibility is outlined in Will Potter's (2011) *Green is the New Red*, an exposé of government monitoring and harassment in radical environmental and anti-speciesism activist spaces.

Formality and time orientation

Excessive formality in organizational procedure can become detrimental to a social movement that could otherwise benefit from some degree of spontaneity. Formality can become a liability when it comes to dictate the pace, place, and duration of advocacy. Parkinson's Law identifies the tendency for work to expand to fill the time available. What this means is that an organization will fill that time regardless of the time actually needed to complete the task. This relates to inefficiency in that it sometimes squanders human power and other resources to meet the typical eight-hour workday required of a paid advocate. Volunteer advocates, too, may seek to complete a set amount of volunteer time, even if those efforts are unneeded.

Consider, for instance, the problem of recruiting several activists to staff an information table for several hours when only one or two individuals would be required. I am reminded of a colleague who commuted over an hour in response to a call for volunteers needed to staff a vegan information booth in downtown Boulder, Colorado. The event was poorly coordinated. With six people volunteering in the booth, my colleague's presence was superfluous. She returned home frustrated, as her participation was unnecessary and it took her away from her antispeciesism research for the entire day. In this example, it is inefficient for multiple activists to participate for several hours when the event's traffic is very low or non-existent. Wasting time and activist energy in this way is irrational, but Parkinson's Law encourages that available time be filled with more work.

Furthermore, organizations concerned about long-term survival may need to find work to justify their continued existence (and continued funding), even if that work constitutes an inefficient use of limited resources. The fixation on time among professionalized organizations also leads to a devaluing of strategies that do not bring quick or immediate results and those goals that require substantial time investments. Organizations need to kill time to demonstrate that they are useful, but they also need a regular supply of evidence of their effectiveness. Because the push for Nonhuman Animal rights involves a challenge to deeply ingrained systems of oppression and a widespread speciesist ideology, radical approaches that involve incrementally achieved structural changes tend to be rejected by the mainstream movement. Most radical and meaningful changes to social structure will require time. Unfortunately, this is a luxury that large Nonhuman Animal rights organizations, oriented toward time (and inextricably toward fundraising), cannot afford. Time is money, and money is the priority for a professionalized organization that must fundraise to survive.

A new age of rationalization

An analysis of bureaucratic rationalization has illustrated many setbacks related to professionalization in the Nonhuman Animal rights movement, but contemporary sociological theory warns of additional problems that could negatively impact advocacy organizations. George Ritzer's theory of McDonaldization expands and modernizes Weber's theory to include these recent organizational trends. Used to explain the increasing rationalization of social structures in the age of technology and homogenization, Ritzer (2010) recognizes a move toward efficiency, predictability, uniformity, and automation in everything from the food industry to the educational system. This model can be extended to social movements as well. The McDonaldized system emphasizes efficiency on a scale previously unknown by prioritizing calculability, predictability, and control. As with Weber's ideal type bureaucracy, this modernized rationalization is also known to aggravate the tendency toward organizational irrationality.

Hyper-efficiency

Recall that it is a common tendency for rationalized organizations to adopt technologies and practices that optimize efficiency. While Weber understood that efforts to improve efficiency could have serious consequences, he could not have predicted the level to which "McDonaldized" organizations have reached. In a modern capitalist society, Ritzer observes that organizations may push for efficiency to the point of *hyper-efficiency*. In fast food corporations, for instance, every variable is meticulously structured. Employees are separated into individual stations and are made to memorize particular sales pitches designed to maximize customer purchasing. Food products may arrive to the store premixed or precooked, order processing is timed, and inventory is closely counted. Even the number of condiment packets allotted to each customer is regulated. When I worked for Hardee's (an American fast food chain) as a college student, we were instructed to give each customer precisely three packets of ketchup and only then if ketchup was specifically requested. Such an intense focus on efficiency leaves little wiggle room for behavioral variations and adaptations that may sometimes be necessary to manage unexpected problems as they arise.

Like fast food chains, social movement organizations work to develop an optimum method for mobilizing resources that reifies their preferred pathways for activism through a predesigned process and organizational rules and regulations (Oliver and Marwell, 1992). But hyper-efficiency makes switching tactics extremely difficult. Advocates stick to what they know to avoid risk and protect fundraising. Vegan Outreach (no date), for example, often reiterates their utilitarian approach: "we make our choices based on which option will lead to the least amount of suffering." This organization argues that, in specifically targeting more open-minded college students, a handful of paid activists and volunteers can distribute thousands of pamphlets in a short amount of time with relatively little cost. Other organizations rely on mail-delivered donation requests and viral internet petitions. These professionalized groups can reach large numbers of people, expending the fewest resources as is possible. As previously explained, this resource expenditure tends to be efficient in maintaining the organization in advertising and fundraising, but not as much in achieving social change. The rhetoric of reducing suffering presupposes that achieving a vegan world is a utopian fantasy best compromised with welfare reform and reduced flesh consumption. A model of hyper-efficiency thus begs the question: what are the hidden costs that may go undetected? Some tactics might be rejected because they are less efficient, but some goals cannot be achieved without substantial investment.

Calculability

Calculability lends well to this utilitarian objective of achieving greater good for the least cost. According to this variable, more is preferable and bigger is better. For example, a fast food restaurant will emphasize how much food one can get for a minimal price. As one of many potential examples, Hardee's launched a "Big Box Lunch" deal in 2011 that offers two double cheeseburgers, fries, an apple turnover, *and* a 20 ounce drink for only five dollars. In emphasizing calculability, movement organizations also push out massive quantities of "cheaply produced" goods that are of low cost or risk to consumers. Welfarist organizations engage calculability by churning out hundreds of single-issue campaigns, petitions, legislative actions, donation requests, and the like. As of this writing, PETA's "Action Alerts" website contains five categories of issues that span 12 pages. Though there is something to be said for the power of numbers and presence, Ritzer warns that quantity can quickly surpass quality. Indeed, the belief that economic growth can solve any number of social problems is a popular one, but this approach has its limits (Higgs, 2014).[6]

Organizations presume that issuing large numbers of advocacy products will ensure the "best deal" for other animals, but in doing so, many negative consequences are overlooked. Fast food restaurants, for example, inflict untold suffering on the Nonhuman Animals killed for their products. They are also responsible for significant environmental and public health damage. While elites who own the restaurants profit considerably from these "deals," it will be vulnerable populations who shoulder the real cost of production (Carolan, 2011). Most impacted are the Nonhuman Animals who constitute the product and poor communities and communities of color who are most likely to live in areas polluted by production. These are the same communities that experience the highest rates of life-threatening diet-related diseases (see Chapter 5). None of these costs are included in the low prices offered. Elites create a cheap product by transferring the cost to the public, but the profits are not likewise redistributed.

Neither can professionalized social movements escape this tradeoff. As will be explored in Chapter 3, single-issue campaigning tends to fall short of comprehensive anti-speciesist claimsmaking. It ignores root causes and fails to impact many less popular species. Single-issue campaigns tend to avoid veganism altogether, thus missing an important opportunity to create meaningful change. This is because a comprehensive and in-depth challenge to speciesism cannot be "mass produced" cheaply and quickly. To adopt such a strategy would require significantly more resources for a professionalized organization by way of a time commitment.

By way of example, the film project *Vegucated* immersed three individuals in a vegan education program that carefully explores the ethical, environmental, and personal benefits to adopting a vegan lifestyle (Wolfson, 2011). Participants were introduced to vegans in their local community, whereby mentors shared recipes and demystified vegan grocery shopping. The process relied on the strengths of a supportive vegan network and required a commitment of several weeks (with continuing support after the program's completion). This intensive community-based approach is typical of many grassroots vegan groups not distracted by fundraising requirements.[7] Achieving full public comprehension of humanity's moral obligations to Nonhuman Animals requires more than a fleeting emotional appeal; it takes a significant reconstruction of one's attitudes and behaviors. This necessitates a much more complex approach than simply flashing images of suffering Nonhuman Animals in leaflets and television commercials in the hopes of soliciting donations. This approach would interfere with the profits more easily gleaned from cheaper products, but cheap production obscures root problems. Welfare reform is sold to the public in hundreds of campaigns and petitions, while speciesism itself is largely overlooked.

Another consideration is that the mass production of campaigning is largely incapable of tailoring to specific demographic requirements. As will be elaborated in Chapter 5, Nonhuman Animal rights groups stand accused of adhering to a post-racial logic. Most organizations abide by white-centric claimsmaking that can either alienate or fail to resonate with people of color (Harper, 2010a; 2010b, xiii). Treating all individuals with rigid similarity – a hallmark of McDonaldized rationality – could be especially unrealistic and ultimately detrimental. McDonald's attempts to overcome cultural barriers by adapting their menus to local regions. There are sandwiches made of lobster flesh in the Northeastern US and there are restaurants in India that do not serve hamburgers made of cow flesh. However, the goal remains to assimilate all cultures into the

Irrationalities in Welfarist Organizational Pathways 53

homogenous McDonald's culture (Watson, 2005). When a corporation can process all customers equivalently, it allows for increased efficiency. New demographics are exposed to new foods that are more or less consistent across the globe (the burger with fries and soda combination), and they learn to adhere to the same procedures of food service. People learn to stand in line, to bus their own tables, and to expect a consistent product (Yan, 2005). In this way, a culture of consumptive behavior is learned, a particular way of knowing is adopted, and expectations of certain standards are created.

PETA India may tailor its advocacy package to suit Indian custom, but, ultimately, the tactical formula is the same. Nonhuman Animal advocacy is sold as something that is appropriate for the larger organizations to manage. Those concerned with Nonhuman Animal suffering are taught that advocacy is best conducted by reporting to these large organizations and following their script. PETA's advocacy Happy Meal often involves donating, employing PETA's tactics, and promoting vegetarianism, "euthanasia," and welfare reform. There is no real space for diversity. For those who cannot or will not ascribe to this brand of advocacy, they are simply marginalized and ignored. Many cannot compete. Like McDonald's, hegemonic Nonhuman Animal rights groups with an international presence create an advocacy culture that dominates the social movement landscape, making alternatives seem infeasible, if they can be imagined at all.

Predictability

Another key characteristic of a McDonaldized organization is the value placed on predictability. Predictability ensures that the organization's behavior and products are reliable across time and space. For example, one can expect to get the same hamburger product at a McDonald's in Denver, Colorado as one would find in London, Paris, or Beijing. Predictability creates a feeling of security and comfort for consumers. Initially, advocates should be suspect of such an approach applied to a social movement organization, as any degree of predictability is at once a point of vulnerability. If exploitative industries know what to expect from Nonhuman Animal organizations, they can effectively prepare their countermobilization (Jasper and Poulsen, 1993, p.643).

Unfortunately, predictability has further-reaching consequences. Foundations and paying members who support an organization with grants and donations come to expect regular victories. This relationship of expectation restricts movements to relegating their efforts toward minor changes that may have little to no effect on the well-being of

Nonhuman Animals. Movement organizations become locked into familiar approaches to advocacy with little room for deviation. They formulate single-issue campaigns, plea for donations, achieve minimal successes, declare victory, and then request more donations. This pattern is repeated across many, if not most, Nonhuman Animal organizations. Radical abolitionists, on the other hand, are reproached for challenging the organizational status quo and for shirking their "responsibility to real animals who are experiencing real suffering and real death (Phelps, 2013, no pagination). Following the protocol of professionalization is equated with "real" help for other animals. The "common sense" of professionalized advocacy effectively squeezes out alternatives.

Predictable advocacy efforts create scripted approaches that routinize interactions. Welfarist scripts that ask the public to "end animal cruelty," "stop animal abuse," or "halt factory farms" create predictable approaches to Nonhuman Animal rights. Abolitionist claims are generally omitted, as they exist outside the dominant knowledge of Nonhuman Animal advocacy. Larger groups understand that packaging outreach into attractive grant proposals and glossy leaflets which promote reform and prioritize donations will predictably result in the funding needed to keep the organization afloat. Radical tactics lack this important predictability. In a competitive social movement environment, large organizations cannot afford to take such risks.

Control

Finally, the McDonald's system values control. This control ideally encompasses production, consumption, employees, and customers, as these are variables that may create considerable uncertainty and efficiency if not sufficiently managed by the organization. In the social movement space, this control regards participants and mobilization pathways. What this means is that professionalized organizations dominate and shape the ways in which advocacy is conducted. For the average participant in the controlled social movement space, getting active for other animals almost instinctively entails particular behaviors predetermined by non-profits. If an individual wants to help other animals, they will have to become a paying PETA member or "walk for the animals" in a Farm Sanctuary fundraiser. Certainly, there are other options, but those options are rendered invisible in this highly controlled movement environment.

Control also entails the tendency toward automation, whereby the unpredictable human factor becomes increasingly obsolete in outreach efforts. A McDonald's restaurant, for example, features timers on the deep fryers, automatic soda dispensers, cash registers that calculate change and accept credit cards, and even pre-recorded greetings in the drive-thru. A similar trend is observable in the Nonhuman Animal rights industry. Participants are increasingly recruited by brochures and social media, while activism is relegated to impersonal signatures and check-writing. To become an advocate for Nonhuman Animals, a person need not ever interact with another human being. They can simply click the donate button and supply credit card information. This degree of control is considered rational and efficient, but for a movement that relies so heavily on identity and networking, this trend in depersonalization in tandem with a fear of innovation and creativity could be especially detrimental. Some amount of control should be reserved for grassroots activists and other participants not affiliated with large nonprofits. What works for McDonald's might not work for Nonhuman Animal liberation. A corporate agenda may be incongruent with social justice goals.

Disneyization

Related to the process of McDonaldization is the move toward "Disneyization" (Bryman, 1999). Here, four additional organizational trends are thought to manifest in Western societies: theming, dedifferentiation of consumption, merchandising, and emotional labor. The Disneyization process is intended to manipulate the consumer experience to maximize profit to the organization. This is an extension of rationalization because the ultimate intent is to improve efficiency in order to increase profits and reduce costs. Epitomized by Disney amusement parks, the theming process works first to attract the public, and then to differentiate the organization from competitors.

This process also seeks to divert customer attention from the organization's less-than-glamorous capitalist interests through the use of a *theme*. Visitors know why Disney parks are unique from other parks. They know what special theme to expect: magic, fantasy, storytelling, cartoons, nostalgia, and family fun. It is this theme that attracts visitors from all over the world. Visitors will bring family and friends and pay exorbitant admission fees, food costs, and souvenir prices because the theme *attracts* them and the theme *distracts* them. In the Nonhuman Animal rights movement, professionalized organizations create a "theme" of empathy for other animals. This theme encourages participants to buy into particular advocacy recommendations by triggering strong empathetic emotions meant to distract participants from thinking critically about the utility of their actions. This helps to explain the popularity in counterproductive welfare reforms that are promoted within this theme of compassion. The public will view shocking leaflets or commercials, experience strong emotional reactions, and then presumably donate at the organization's behest to demonstrate their empathy. Swept up in the theme, consumers can be persuaded to buy without thinking.

Themes also help to differentiate particular organizations. This differentiation is especially important in a highly competitive and largely homogenous social movement environment. If an organization could successfully recruit donations through an attractive theme, it would certainly gain an advantage. The HSUS, for example, with its focus on dogs, cats, and free-living animals, can attract a large demographic interested in the protection of popular species, while PETA and Farm Sanctuary cultivate a theme inclusive of farmed animals and vivisection victims. PETA attempts to be culturally relevant, edgy, young, and sexy; Farm Sanctuary takes a mature approach that is more likely to appeal to middle-class audiences. What is important here is that recruited individuals are not encouraged to think critically about their involvement or their "purchases" (or, more specifically, their donations). Audiences are invited to be part of the experience or the image and atmosphere cultivated by a particular non-profit brand. While technically in operation to challenge Nonhuman Animal use, themes of compassion deride the organization's original purpose, allowing welfare reforms to proliferate. Theming gives organizations a competitive advantage and distracts from the group's originally intended purpose.

Dedifferentiation, another characteristic of Disneyization intended to improve profit in a competitive environment, speaks to the *interlocked* nature of organizational behavior. Dedifferentiation occurs when different institutional spheres overlap to the point where they can no longer be distinguished from one another. For example, casinos in Las Vegas also serve as hotels, restaurants, shopping centers, *and* spas. It is a great advantage to the organization if it is able to serve multiple functions to the customer. Becoming a "one-stop shop" means that the organization can attract more business. Nonhuman Animal rights organizations demonstrate this tendency in several ways. First, they compartmentalize their campaigns to appeal to a variety of public interests. Those who care about seal clubbing can look to the HSUS, those who care about dogs and cats can look to the HSUS, and those who care about the environment can also look to the HSUS. As Nonhuman Animal liberation is an inherently intersectional issue, dedifferentiation should not be a problem. Social movement researchers refer to this professionalized phenomenon as "product diversification" (McCarthy and Zald, 1973, p.24). Unfortunately, many organizations fail to synthesize these concerns into a comprehensive vegan logic. Interested parties are encouraged to turn to professionalized organizations to satisfy their varied empathetic curiosities, but rarely do these organizations explicitly explain the interconnectedness of these various social problems. Compartmentalizing speciesism is more conducive to fundraising.

Merchandising is another important source of profit for an organization. It is so important, in fact, that an organization's intended purpose can gradually become superseded. Disney theme parks may earn certain profit from admission tickets, but they can pull in substantially more capital through the sale of clothing, toys, gifts, and a multitude of other souvenirs. Licensing with other organizations increases the effect. For instance, McDonald's offers Disney toys with their kids' meals and Walmart sells shirts with Disney characters. Importantly, one need not even visit the park to purchase these items. Similarly, the Nonhuman Animal rights industry peddles hundreds of T-shirts, books, stickers, and the like. PETA has its own brand of chapstick, nail tattoos, shoes, socks, and ties. Likewise, one need not even be a member of the organization to shop in the PETA "Mall." Licensing extends organizational reach as well. Farm Sanctuary has partnered with fashion designers to create their "The Ambassador Collection," a farmed animal theme clothing line. For several years, PETA has been tagging along with the Vans Warped Tour (a highly successful and long running youth-oriented music festival), scoring countless promotional advertisements from popular performers.

A favorite tool of American advocacy organizations, merchandising discourages individuals from seriously engaging the Nonhuman Animal rights discourse. Instead, they can buy a T-shirt or attach a sticker on their car. Advocacy is thus commodified through consumable items. The political message becomes lost behind brand names and images. The fact that most of this merchandise will inevitably brandish the group's name or logo alongside (or often superseding) the anti-speciesist message is further testament to the weight given to branding over the cause. Merchandising could potentially be useful in spreading awareness and networking, but more often than not, these items act only as an important source of revenue and free advertising for the organization.

Finally, dedifferentiation demands that organizations increasingly expect employees to engage in emotional labor. Workers must demonstrate to customers a particular demeanor of excitement, happiness, and enjoyment manipulated through carefully crafted scripts and training. Like many aspects of McDonaldization and Disneyization, this is intended to improve the customer's experience (at the expense of the employee) to improve sales. Disney employees are rigorously trained to master a particular demeanor that both placates and pleases the customer in even the most stressful of situations. A satisfied customer is a customer that will buy more and buy often. The cost imposed on the employee, however, can be significant. Emotion work is known to be alienating and dehumanizing (Hochschild, 2012, p.7).

Advocacy for other animals, too, requires a substantial amount of emotion work. Indeed, Nonhuman Animal rights activism can be very emotionally draining or even traumatic (Adams and Messina, 2004, p.110). Like Disney employees, advocates are expected to abide by particular standards for attitude and behavior. Advocates who engage the public are expected to uphold professionalism, acting as a positive representation of the organization and the cause. They must keep their cool and combat natural impulses to feel angry, sad, or distraught. Vegan Outreach even encourages activists to keep a "sense of humor" about them (Ball, no date). This is a remarkable request given the gravity of Nonhuman Animal suffering:

> It is not enough to be vegan, or even a dedicated vegan advocate. We must remember the bottom line—reducing suffering—and actively be the opposite of the vegan stereotype. Just as we need everyone to look beyond the short-term satisfaction of following habits and traditions, we need to move past our sorrow and anger to optimal advocacy. We must learn 'how to win friends and influence people,' so that we leave everyone we meet with the impression of a joyful individual leading a fulfilling and meaningful life. (Ball, 2008)

In the rationalized organization, the "bottom line" must be adhered to at any cost, even at the expense of one's humanity. Recall that a rationalized organization sees the human factor as a potential liability to efficiency. Expectations regarding emotional labor seek to exert control over the uncertainty of human emotion. Indeed, emotionality has been so heavily stigmatized (particularly because the Nonhuman Animal rights movement is a largely feminized endeavor), masculine approaches to discourse and activism are often encouraged and celebrated (Groves, 2001, p.212–13). Not surprisingly, many leadership positions in the largest American organizations are delegated to men as well (Gaarder, 2011, p.87).

These emotional requirements are typical of moderated activism, but they also manifest within radical factions, including abolitionism.

While hostile emotions might indeed be detrimental to effective advocacy, to *completely* stifle reactive emotion in a feminized and inherently emotional movement could be unrealistic and would certainly disadvantage and discriminate against women. Managing unpleasant and off-putting emotions and delivering a more welcoming message tends to be favored by professionalized organizations that are primarily concerned with protecting their brand image and donor base, but abolitionists might enjoy considerably more leeway in applying this tactic sensitively.

A working compromise in rationality

Surfacing in tendencies toward bureaucracy and professionalization, McDonaldization, and Disneyization, rationality has significantly impacted the structure of the Nonhuman Animal rights movement. Efficiency is valued, but the process of rationalization that is needed to achieve that efficiency often entails a considerable degree of irrationality. This has the potential to significantly stunt advocacy efforts, and has provoked the formation of radical abolitionist approaches. Certainly, some degree of organization is necessary to address massive and complex social problems. Unfortunately, rationality can expand to the point of counterproductivity as organizations become increasingly burdened by procedure and self-perpetuation.

Critics of non-profitization in the social movement arena have cited the role of professionalization in perpetuating and aggravating social problems. In the Nonhuman Animal rights movement, Francione's work repeats this finding by underscoring the tendency for organizational behaviors to worsen the prospects for other animals. Those individuals with a genuine concern for other animals unknowingly donate their time and money to professionalized organizations that have prioritized survival over social change, organizations that have been incapacitated by the inefficient trappings of bureaucracy.

The relentless pursuit of organizational rationality has culminated in an ideological adherence that neglects accountability and critical self-reflection. Weber identifies this phenomenon as an "iron cage." Here, organizations trap individuals within a safe and strong but extremely limiting rationalized system. A particular pathway is cultivated that prevents flexibility and stifles creativity. Nonhuman Animal activists have become trapped in the iron cage of Nonhuman Animal welfare hegemony. Squandering resources with the continued implementation of tactics that do not work or that even *worsen* the condition of other animals is irrational. Refusing to hold veganism as the bottom line in the promotion of Nonhuman Animal equality is also irrational. The movement's precious few resources – time, money, and volunteers – are frequently wasted or underutilized. Participants have become alienated from the meaning of activism, and alternatives for more appropriate activism lie just out of reach from their confinement behind the cage bars. The cage of professionalized welfarism may offer many reliabilities and securities, but it ultimately instills subordination and rigidity. It stifles freedom and an ability to make truly rational decisions. Activists can become disenchanted, and participation can become limited and routine.

Abolitionists hoping to increase their presence face a very real conundrum: to what extent should they embrace organization? What are the limits to rational behavior? Thus far, abolitionism has been relegated to grassroots mobilization. Theoretically, central leadership is denounced.[8] Most abolitionist work is focused in localized, unaffiliated groups and individuals spread across the globe. Torres (2006) calls for an eschewing of large non-profits in favor of smaller affinity groups. There is also value in individual activism. Recall that this democratic structure and lack of central organization means a sacrifice in presence and efficient resource mobilization. The internet has acted as a powerful compensation, allowing abolitionists (at least those with access to English-speaking spaces) to form dense networks, share resources, and cultivate an identity that will motivate and sustain them.

This is not to say that abolitionism as a movement faction is immune from the detriments of rationalization. In particular, declines in privacy and the policing of activist lifestyles have emerged as significant problems. Socialized subordination, common with larger organizations, exists in abolitionist circles as well. Many activists who support novel tactics or theory are shamed, silenced, or exit the movement entirely for fear of retribution. Furthermore, the act of being vegan itself requires a significant imposition to one's private life. Activists are told what not to wear, what not to eat, what not to support, and so on. This is unavoidable in what is essentially a very personal movement. Yet, when activists are policed in how they date, if they should procreate, how they should parent, what they feed their companion animals, who they interact with, and even what they post on social networking sites (as is common within some abolitionist communities), the movement risks undermining itself.

That being said, a review of rationalization processes in organization makes a powerful case for the importance of radical abolitionist mobilization. In avoiding the detrimental limitations of professionalized organization, abolitionists wield a unique ability to advocate for other animals in a *manageably* rational manner, a manner that does not compromise goals for the sake of bureaucracy and fundraising. The democratic nature of abolitionism also lends itself well to the reasoned allocation of movement resources. It remains to be seen, however, if abolitionists can overcome the significant handicaps of decentralized mobilization and the hegemonic control of institutionalized advocacy. Success will inevitably entail a careful and cautious application of rationality.

3
Rational Advocacy and the Logic of Persuasion

Professionalization brings with it many complications and compromises. It also works to normalize and naturalize particular tactics and goals which come to dictate the "common sense" of Nonhuman Animal advocacy. As explored in the previous chapter, the rationalization processes of large non-profits may lead to problematic *irrationalities* that can actually work to hinder or worsen progress toward Nonhuman Animal liberation. Organizations prioritize tactics and goals that are best suited to fundraising and organizational longevity, not necessarily those which would be better adapted to dismantling speciesism. It is therefore problematic to take for granted the efficacy and appropriateness of popular tactics promoted by these groups. Attention should be paid to whether or not tactics work for liberation and, to a much lesser extent, their economic potential. Advocates should be accountable to other animals, not to funding agents.

This chapter will explore some of the popular tactics in Nonhuman Animal advocacy and will discuss them as they are relevant to scientific research. As of now, there is very little work done to ascertain the effectiveness of many tactics. What little research is being done tends to be conducted by professionalized organizations. This can be a problem for two reasons. First, this represents a direct conflict of interest. The nature of the non-profit industrial complex is such that organizations are under intense pressure to achieve victories and hide failures. These groups need to regularly prove to their funders that what they are doing is working and that it is worth funding in the future. Second, the standards of efficacy used by these organizations are based on welfarist ideologies of compromise and the capacity for the tactics in question to raise more funds (raising money is sometimes conflated with creating social change). In other words, many professionalized organizations are setting their standards rather low, and success means something very different to a non-profit that focuses on funding. Subsequently, this chapter explores the movement's favored tactics with the acknowledgment that most have not been implemented in an unadulterated state. This chapter will also attempt to refine these tactics in a manner that is more conducive to the change sought: a vegan world.

Vegan advocacy has one major advantage that makes social change work somewhat easier than it does in other movements: *humans like other animals*. Many people care about the plight of other animals, but a key problem is that they are not aware of how Nonhuman Animals are exploited or how they can help them (Jamieson et al., 2013). Furthermore, Public Policy Polling (2013, p.4) finds that about one third of Americans are unsure of what to think of veganism, leading the Humane Research Council to suggest that outreach efforts could improve public perception and acceptance (Gutbrod, 2013). This would suggest that educational outreach that seeks to inform and empower the public could be a worthwhile focus. This chapter will explore tactical approaches that could address this area of concern.

Writing on current challenges in Nonhuman Animal advocacy, abolitionist Tom Regan (no date) also emphasizes the importance of veganism and education:

> We take an important step down this path [Nonhuman Animal liberation] when we voice the ideal that even now many of us dare not speak: veganism. And though there are many ways to awaken the conscience of the general public, the three most important are now, always have been, and always will be: Educate. Educate. Educate.

Vegan education is likely the most efficient use of movement resources because legislative and other institutional changes tend to *follow* public sentiment, not precede it. Achieving a critical mass is a necessary first step before anti-speciesism can be codified into law. Major social institutions are, at this point in human history, extremely oppressive. They represent the interests of the privileged and work to normalize, naturalize, and legalize the exploitation of the vulnerable. In a speciesist society, speciesists control social institutions, and those social institutions will reflect and reinforce speciesism. It is counterintuitive to expect that institutions created to protect privilege will willingly reform without considerable public support to reinforce the desired shifts. Given these circumstances, education is an important factor in achieving social change. Research suggests that educational campaigning (particularly that which recognizes socioeconomic contexts) is useful for transforming public attitudes and behaviors regarding the consumption of other animals (Deckers, 2013, p.32).

The following discussion will relate the research on social change to rational abolitionist advocacy. Rather than throw the baby out with the bathwater, many favorite welfare tactics are salvaged and reconfigured for abolitionist goals. What is most important is that social change workers pay attention to the science. Many savvy researchers have spent entire careers decoding human behavior and conducting experiments to test the various theories of social change. While very little efficacy research has been accomplished in the name of Nonhuman Animal rights, and what little that exists has been applied to welfare reform,[1] this wealth of social psychological research can offer a strong starting point in guiding informed activism. Does shocking imagery of suffering Nonhuman Animals hurt or help? Do vegan cupcakes engage or distract? Are vegan leaflets efficient or just a waste of time? All of these questions are vital to constructing a useful and effective advocacy plan. Many of the answers contradict common sense and evade a simple yes or no. Doing the research is a crucial first step in work to liberate other animals.

Cognition and behavior change

Change in the brain

Attitude and behavior change are extremely complex phenomena. What works for some audiences will not work for others. Some respond primarily to logical approaches, while others are more apt to follow emotional reactions (though emotions generally have the greatest influence overall). Never are the two disassociated or necessarily incompatible. Engaging reason involves some degree of emotional work, while experiencing emotion involves some sort of reasoned interpretation. Careful thinking and mental elaboration can lead to enduring change (Petty et al., 1995; Petty et al., 2009), but emotion is also essential for effective persuasion. In the case of Nonhuman Animal advocacy, Elizabeth DeCoux (2009) argues that logic-based persuasion techniques are not as effectual, because they dilute depictions of suffering and stifle the potential for emotional reactions. In most cases, successful change will require the combined efforts of emotion *and* reason (Heath and Heath, 2010, p.8). They are coexisting, complementary, and overlapping.

While both emotion and reason are integral to social change, some activists may reject emotional appeals out of respect to rationalist values or for fear of repelling the public with sentimentality. This position could be a mistake. Social psychological research demonstrates that humans are primarily motivated by emotions (Heath and Heath, 2010, p.8). They provide the "oomph" necessary to push individuals out of their comfortable, habitual behaviors and jumpstart them into adopting new and unfamiliar behavior change. Responding to gender norms that encourage empathetic and relational responses, many women (who comprise the Nonhuman Animal rights movement's largest demographic) are especially motivated by emotion to advocate for animals (Gaarder, 2011, p.43). Reason and logic serve their purpose, but they are never fully separated from emotion in the business of attitude and behavior change. Cognitive and affective systems are integrated in the process of moral judgment.

However, unharnessed emotion can be problematic. In relying too heavily on emotional responses and too lightly on rational thinking, many actors in the Nonhuman Animal rights movement follow an unstructured desire to end large-scale violence against other animals without laying the necessary groundwork for establishing an approach that works. In some cases, there is an outright hostility toward theory by those exacerbated by the urgent situation of Nonhuman Animals who need help "*right now.*" Emotionally charged activists and organizations may rush into the fray without first developing a much-needed rational plan of action. With the little organizational accountability and limited direction that those organizations provide, participants are apt to act without fully understanding the implications of anti-speciesism and the need for critical thinking in strategy. While increasing participation is fundamentally a positive gain, without careful guidance, social change could be slow coming and recidivism may be high. As one example, an ill-conceived dietary switch to plant-based eating may backfire without careful consideration of associated social justice principles and lifestyle changes. There are many reasons that vegans and vegetarians revert to omnivorism, including time, cost, and conflicting or dissolved relationships with friends and family. Those who come to veganism with a concern for Nonhuman Animal ethics, however, are far less likely to revert (Menzies and Sheeshka, 2012, p.167). A critical mass of vegans can only do Nonhuman Animals so much good if that mass is wavering or unstable and directs its efforts toward irrational, unsuccessful tactics.

Everyone is guided by both reason and emotion, but individuals do vary in how these two cognitive components interact. Effective use of reason and emotion in outreach first depends on the audience. If the audience is well educated or analytically minded, they will be more responsive to a rational approach (Cacioppo et al., 1983, p.815; Cacioppo et al., 1996). Neuroscience research suggests that it is the rational part of the human brain that is activated by social injustice triggers, and individuals with higher levels of justice sensitivity demonstrate a stronger response (Yoder and Decety, 2014). People uninterested in the message, on the other hand, tend to be swayed by peripheral information or a simple liking of the messenger (Chaiken, 1980; Petty et al., 1981, p.853). Additionally, how people's attitudes were *initially* formed matters. If they were initially persuaded by information, it will take more information to persuade them in the future; if emotion first persuaded them, further emotional appeals are most effective (Edwards, 1990; Fabrigar and Petty, 1999).

Tactics intended to trigger emotions should not to overwhelm the cognitive responses of their audience. Those who are distracted when presented with new information are more likely to accept a message and are less likely to counter-argue (Keating and Brock, 1974; Osterhouse and Brock, 1970). For vegan activists, this means that particularly distracting commercials, websites, or information stalls might be more effective in persuading people. However, activists should recognize that, as with any peripheral attitude change, earnest change based on cognitive processing is not likely to happen under such conditions. Indeed, Regan and Cheng (1973) find that complex messages are actually lost on people who are distracted. Distraction only increases persuasion for *simple* messages. The multifarious message of anti-speciesism, then, is likely not appropriate for such a technique. Likewise, advertisements steeped in violence and/or sex run the risk of being *too* distracting. Marketing research demonstrates that those who view commercials that feature either of these elements are less likely to remember what the advertised brand was (Bushman, 2007). This information is especially relevant to vegan campaigning that favors gory or nude imagery. Advertisements that rely on exploited and objectified naked female bodies might be entertaining for some viewers, but they are not likely to persuade.

Analogy

Before attitude or behavior change can be embraced, some degree of deliberation is needed. That is, rather than making an instant change, most will take time to think over the arguments and issues. Analogy, in particular, pulls on this cognitive process in an attempt to trigger a reasoned response. This tactic has a long history in Nonhuman Animal rights advocacy. Antebellum abolitionists drew parallels between the ownership and exploitation of African Americans and Nonhuman

Animals (Beers, 2006, p.12). Victorian-era feminists like Frances Power Cobbe likened the brutality experienced by women to that of other animals. Cobbe was especially critical of the powerful scientific community that objectified and otherized both women and Nonhuman Animals (Obenchain, 2012, p.72). Today, feminist intersectionality politics continue to create analogies hoping to inspire critical thought. The work of Carol Adams (2000a) demonstrates that women are effectively treated as consumable "meat," while Nonhuman Animals are often sexualized and feminized to facilitate their consumption as well. Margorie Spiegel (1996) published *The Dreaded Comparison* which aligns the treatment of human slaves with that of Nonhuman Animals. Jewish Holocaust comparisons are readily made as well (Davis, 2005; Patterson, 2002). Finally, Nibert's *Animal Rights/Human Rights* (2002) ambitiously explores how Nonhuman Animal exploitation is functionally similar to that of *all* vulnerable human groups.

Analogy can be a powerful way to provoke thought and emotion. It can convey unfamiliar, complex, or difficult concepts and disrupt taken-for-granted assumptions. It can also demonstrate the verity of contested claims based on claims already established or accepted. In short, analogy is a powerful tool for education. Because much of the public is largely unfamiliar with thinking about Nonhuman Animals within a social justice schema, drawing comparisons with human groups who are familiar within this paradigm might be imperative. However, these analogies often provoke anger and backlash against the messenger. Indeed, some have criticized this tactic as hopelessly offensive (Bailey, 2007; Kim, 2011). When applied as what Socha (2013a, p.237) calls "fast food activism," trans-species analogies can easily backfire because they are usually presented by privileged persons who insensitively and superficially draw on the experiences of oppressed groups for the sake of argument (see Chapter 5 for further discussion). Trans-species analogies should be used carefully and appropriately, if used at all.

The appropriateness of their use depends largely upon the messenger and the intended audience. Perhaps due to a long history of feminist Nonhuman Animal rights activism and a centuries-old and sometimes positive association between women and other animals, analogies between the two have met with better reception. When crafted by women and intended for largely female-identified audiences, there is usually a *conscious* and *engaged* application that respects both the history of misogyny and the ongoing problems with women's oppression. Alternatively, white-led organizations that, more often than not, reflect white experiences and target mostly white communities can run into problems. By way of example, PETA erected a panel outside the Museum of Natural History in Washington D.C. and used Martin Luther King Jr. quotes and images of enslaved Africans to demonstrate that Nonhuman Animals are the *new* slaves (insinuating that human slavery is a thing of the past). The stunt created considerable controversy (Wright, 2011). Under these circumstances, analogy appears exploitative and cruel. Importantly, this is not to relieve analogies between human and nonhuman females, as advocacy materials sometimes crudely compare the rape and abuse of women to that of Nonhuman Animals. Given that so many girls and women are victims of rape and violence (see the following chapter), these analogies are likely to be both triggering and unwelcoming.

Mental blocks
It is worth considering that much of the discomfort elicited by analogies stems from an unquestioned sense of human superiority and the subsequent inability to recognize the unfortunate similarities. This possibility would most accurately apply to those groups less burdened by systemic discriminatory oppression themselves. Anger or humor may be used to deflect the importance of the message, and this is a common symptom of denial (Hobden and Olson, 1994). These reactions work to deflect persuasion efforts and reject responsibility. Denial is often related to cognitive dissonance, which is an uncomfortable recognition of disconnect between one's behaviors and one's attitudes (Festinger, 1957). Denial (Cole and Morgan, 2011b, p.152) and other forms of moral disengagement (Graça et al., 2014) are likely major barriers to adopting anti-speciesist attitudes and behaviors. Few people see themselves as corrupt, unfair, or otherwise bad. Most like to think they are decent individuals who contribute positively to their community. Many purport to be "animal lovers," but only a tiny fraction are vegan. When confronted with vegan outreach that challenges this animal-friendly self-perception, some may react negatively in an attempt to deflect the validity of the claim.

Evolutionary psychology suggests that the human brain is a compartmentalized organ designed for efficient multitasking and problem solving (Kurzban, 2010). However, theories of compartmentalization also suggest that, while brain modules can sometimes cooperate, they can also come into conflict. Compartmentalization is frequently evidenced in human relationships with other animals. For instance, vivisectors psychologically distance themselves from the vulnerable Nonhuman Animals used in their research (Fox, 2000, p.467). Most Americans also compartmentalize Nonhuman Animals into categories of "pets," "food," and "wild animals," which entail varying levels of moral concern (if any at all) (Joy, 2010). Unfortunately, most Nonhuman Animals find themselves in compartments outside of moral concern for the sake of cognitive convenience. Conceptualizing how human relationships with other animals may be altered is not easy work: it requires a major reconfiguring of world views and behavioral processes. In many ways, it is simpler for the human brain to go with the flow and to relegate otherized groups to a separate compartment that will not require attention.

Humans also have a tendency to selectively expose themselves to information that supports what they already believe and to avoid contradictory information (Fischer and Greitemeyer, 2010). Humans prefer validation over correctness, especially when they are personally involved with the practice in question (Hart et al., 2009). For instance, folks are more likely to be tuned in to popular media publications that espouse the dietary need for animal protein or report that Nonhuman Animals killed for food are treated humanely. Those same people are less likely to go out of their way to explore the scientific literature that contradicts these popularly held beliefs. Just as the devout are more likely to expose themselves to religious media and religious social networks and are not likely to delve into atheist spaces for contradicting information, those who regularly engage in the exploitation of other animals (by eating and wearing their flesh, for instance) are not likely to seek out vegan information to contradict their social reality. It takes considerable cognitive energy to constantly challenge one's understanding of the social world. It is much easier to stick with what is familiar and reinforce that way of knowing.

Furthermore, the brain takes longer to process information that is contradictory to pre-existing beliefs, and it is accomplished with less accuracy (Shtulman and Valcarcel, 2012). Factually inaccurate beliefs can be suppressed by scientific inquiry, but researchers find that pre-existing false knowledge is not eradicated altogether. This means that some people may be exposed to irrefutable evidence that speciesism causes Nonhuman Animal suffering, human suffering through diet-related disease, and environmental suffering from heavy pollution and resource extraction, yet they may still latch on to the naïve theories that they began with. In this way, the human brain is quite resilient to change.

Selective exposure can also lead to a phenomenon known as "motivated blindness." This entails intentional problem avoidance which derives from personal or institutional loyalty (Bazerman and Tenbrunsel,

2011). For example, to explain why Nonhuman Animal "rights" organizations and companion animal "shelters" maintain astoundingly high kill rates, No Kill advocate Nathan Winograd suggests that those responsible are actively ignoring uncomfortable ethical dilemmas:

> Were leadership at groups like HSUS or PETA to actually acknowledge No Kill success to the public, it would immediately create an expectation that they would champion it. And because championing No Kill would require sincerity, dedication, hard work and, most threatening of all, acknowledging that their friends and colleagues who are currently running shelters are not meeting these standards or that they themselves failed to do so when they ran shelters and needlessly killed animals, they don't acknowledge it or the effort required to make it happen elsewhere. In fact, they fight it. (2012, p.60)

Humans reduce dissonance by reaffirming their beliefs. Put simply, they assure themselves that they really *believe* in what they are doing and that makes them feel better. They might also maintain faith in the system that produces the practice in question: if it is not an acceptable or necessary practice, why would it otherwise exist legitimated and unfettered? By simply existing in the first place, many assume that the practice is good or functional. Vegan activists come across this logic often masked in the language of "tradition": humans eat "meat" because it has always been that way. Why would zoos exist if they were not a good thing? Experimenting on other animals is necessary; why else would science rely on vivisection?

In a similar vein, many exhibit the "just world" phenomenon (Lerner, 1980). That is, humans usually believe that bad things happen only to bad people. This is because it is easier to ignore how unfair and downright horrid the world can be. This process happens routinely with rape victims. Rather than come to terms with the normalcy of toxic masculinity in society, many blame women for wearing certain clothes, going to certain places, behaving like a "slut," being "stupid," or being careless. The influence of this psychological phenomenon convinces many that women are raped because they deserve it. The myth of meritocracy is another example: in a highly stratified social system, people of privilege mistakenly believe that they are well off because they have worked hard for it. The other side of that coin is that poor persons must be lazy, intentionally ignorant, and undeserving. The belief that people are rewarded for persevering or stricken because they did not try hard enough makes for a happier picture. It is much easier to believe in personal culpability than to acknowledge an inherently exploitative, patriarchal, white supremacist capitalist system.[2]

Likewise, rationalizing a just world results in victim-blaming other animals to the effect of naturalizing human supremacy. Consider the following examples. Humans eat cows because cows are presumed to be "stupid." Humans shoot free-living animals because they would otherwise overpopulate. Nonhuman Animals are killed on roadways because they were too ignorant to stay out of the way. Humans are at the "top of the food chain" because they are smart, clever, and resourceful. Bad things happen to Nonhuman Animals because they deserve it; good things happen to humans because they have earned it and they are simply better. Structural oppression becomes invisible according to this logic. The socially constructed prejudices and discrimination created to support oppression also become invisible. In reality, cows are actually quite intelligent. They are killed because they are intentionally brought into existence for the sole purpose of exploitation. Likewise, "hunting" is a multi-million-dollar industry that encourages state and federal "wildlife" and forestry agencies to intentionally create populations of "game" for humans to kill (Anderson, 2012, pp.237–42). Death on roadways occurs because roads are constructed in the homes of free-living animals with the unrealistic expectation that they will adapt to automobiles speeding through at all hours of the day and night. Humans "got to the top" by manipulating social structures to benefit them, creating untold amounts of suffering for others in the process.

The constant burden of grappling with inequality and oppression wears on the psyche. Presuming order to the chaos allows humans to push injustice out of mind in order to get on with living. While these notions can be comforting, the just world phenomenon generally has the effect of both blaming the victim and relieving bystanders of their responsibility to intervene or assist.[3] This cognitive division that manifests between victim and bystander is not incidental. There is a tendency for humans to create in-groups that work to privilege and protect themselves and those closest to them (Emswiller et al., 1971; Miller et al., 2001, pp.56–7). Inevitably, however, an in-group necessitates an out-group for comparison. Because humans are biased in favor of themselves, there is a tendency to ascribe positive attributions to the human in-group. This happens at the expense of the nonhuman out-group which is often vilified or ostracized (Nibert, 2002, p.5).

Hence, persuasion is difficult; it oftentimes requires considerable persistence and a nuanced approach. As uncomfortable as they sometimes are, analogies can generate discussions that illuminate speciesism in relation to other forms of oppression. A number of psychological defense mechanisms seek to protect an individual's self-image as a good, loving, caring person. Most like to think that they would never be complacent in state, elite, or corporate endeavors that hurt the vulnerable. Likewise, most individuals would not like to think themselves responsible for the suffering of other animals. If most people do not see themselves as engaged in systemic violence, it would follow that violence must be the work of deviants, but those capable of extraordinary injustice are not abnormal. In truth, rather ordinary people can adhere to social norms that facilitate great suffering. This is what political theorist and Jewish refugee Hannah Arendt (2006) refers to as the "banality of evil." Social psychological research attests that most humans experience a self-serving bias and believe themselves to be more virtuous than others (Hoorens, 1993). If there is any suffering taking place, it is suspected to be caused by *others*. Very few, if any, participants in Stanley Milgrim's (1974) famous obedience study would have thought themselves capable of inflicting terrible harm or even death on their "victims" in the experiment – but most of them did.[4] In this study, ordinary people were placed in a laboratory setting and instructed to electrocute a test subject out of view in another room to the point of death (the subject was not real, but the participants did not know this). Researchers did not expect that many of the participants would follow through with the fatal instructions, but that would not be the case.

It should be considered how, collectively and individually, the "banality of evil" applies to human/nonhuman relationships. Most humans unthinkingly perform very ordinary and routine roles in Nonhuman Animal exploitation, humans who are otherwise ordinary loving and caring people. Like so many other social atrocities, speciesism is maintained by Nonhuman Animal users who perform individual roles that may appear insignificant, mundane, and isolated. Collectively, however, what happens is unimaginably horrific and destructive. Most would like to believe that they would opt out of or resist malevolent social pressures, but Milgram's research (and the high rate of Nonhuman Animal consumption) is a warning to reconsider this presumption. Social norms, especially those aggravated by obedience to authority, can be a powerful influence over human attitudes and behavior.

Analogizing single-issue campaigning

> There are a thousand hacking at the branches of evil to one who is striking at the root, and it may be that he [sic] who bestows the largest

amount of time and money on the needy is doing the most by his [sic] mode of life to produce that misery which he [sic] strives in vain to relieve. – Henry David Thoreau[5]

Analogy and other reason-based approaches to persuasion have many social psychological barriers to overcome in order to be successful. Recall that trans-species analogies have been favored tactics in the Nonhuman Animal rights movement for some. As will be discussed in Chapter 5, glaring insensitivities to ongoing human suffering have made these analogies considerably unsuccessful and largely inappropriate. Analogies, however, might be useful on a more nuanced level *within* the Nonhuman Animal rights community. The majority of Nonhuman Animal advocates continue to participate in mass violence against other animals in their support of highly problematic welfare reforms and inefficient single-issue campaigning. Analogy offers a means to break through those irrationalities that have become normalized and unexamined in advocacy spaces.

Many advocates are beginning to question the utility in welfare reform, but far too few have given pause to the shortcomings of single-issue campaigning. The movement accepts that single-issue campaigns aimed at welfare reforms create steps in the right direction. It is thought that single-issue campaigns could eventually lead to the abolition of property status and, ultimately, to the elimination of Nonhuman Animal exploitation (Regan, 2004b, p.179). To illustrate this argument, an analogy developed by Angel Flinn and Dan Cudahy (2011) is helpful in likening speciesism to a tree. According to Flinn and Cudahy, the "tree" of Nonhuman Animal exploitation is divided into several sections. Their analogy is presented here with some modification:[6]

- The soil that facilitates the growth of the tree represents the prevailing economic mode of production. The economic mode of production influences and legitimizes social structure. In this case, Western nations operate under a capitalist economy, which necessitates extreme levels of exploitation and oppression. Oppression is "embedded in and largely protected by the state and by the laws and practices it produces" (Nibert, 2002, p.5).
- The tree is sustained by rain and sunshine, or in this example, by the state and its social institutions and ideologies. Without these ideological and institutional supports, the tree cannot access the "energy" needed to support the growth of oppression.
- The root of the tree – or, the root of the problem – represents oppression. Nibert explains: "Sociologists have come to believe that racism,

sexism, classism, and the like have historical and social structural causes that are rooted largely in unjust social arrangements – arrangements that significantly shape human consciousness and that are reflected in individual behaviors" (2002, p.4). The roots of this tree grow within the economic "soil" of capitalism and these roots also facilitate the tree.

- The base of the tree trunk serves as the foundation for the tree's growth and represents oppression as it affects Nonhuman Animals. As Nibert explains, speciesism "results from and supports oppressive social arrangements" (2002, p.10). That is, the "trunk" of speciesism is a product of its oppressive "roots" in unjust social arrangements (the capitalist "soil"). The trunk of speciesism also supports the many acts of prejudice and discrimination that afflict Nonhuman Animals.
- The lower trunk of the tree that hosts the largest branches represents the human use of Nonhuman Animals for food, as the food industry accounts for the bulk of all Nonhuman Animal exploitation. The larger limbs that grow from the trunk represent the production of dairy products, birds' eggs, and "meat" (including fish flesh). Each of these leads to many smaller branches that represent the specific exploitations associated with these industries. This might include intensive confinement and physical mutilations. Other smaller branches that originate in the food section of the speciesism tree might represent less common practices such as foie gras production.
- Farther up the tree, past the most sizable branches of the food industry, the medium-sized branches represent other speciesist industries, including experimentation, clothing production, and entertainment. Like the food branches, these branches will also host many smaller ones. For instance, the limb that represents animal-based clothing branches off into "fur" production (which branches off again into issues such as trapping free-living animals or seal clubbing).
- A number of dead and dying branches linger at the edges of this tree, which represent specific practices that are no longer economically optimal. Killing chickens by electrocution is one example (a practice that is distinguished by industry and advocates alike as less economically efficient) (Hoen and Lankhaar, 1999; PETA, 2009).

Examining speciesism as an interconnected system demonstrates that the core problem with single-issue campaigning is that it focuses on the peripheries of oppression. Single-issue campaigns not only ignore the trunk and main branches, but the roots themselves, which are continually working to deliver vital nutrients to every part of the tree.

Pruning makes a tree grow stronger

Single-issue campaigns generally seek to "clip" small or dead branches, ultimately making the tree healthier. Even when welfare groups attempt to cut off a medium-sized branch, such as seal clubbing or animal-hair production, it is generally the case that the tree is robust enough to continue thriving despite the loss of a live (in other words, profitable) branch. If a part of the branch is cut or prevented from growing (as was the case with Nonhuman Animal hair production in the 1990s) (Barnett, 2010), the tree is still powerful enough to regrow those branches. This was certainly the case with "fur" production since the early 2000s (Dasgupta, 2006; Hix, 2013; We Are Fur, 2012). Attempting to prune the tree not only fails to harm the tree in the long run, but it can actually encourage it to thrive. Furthermore, branches grow back. For those single-issue campaigns that succeed in cutting off small or middle-sized branches, new growth can occur in other areas to replace cut branches in a global economy. For example, when the United States banned horse slaughter, the industry simply shipped doomed horses to Mexico (Sandberg, 2007). In another example, Ringling Brothers and Barnum & Bailey took the initiative with an announcement that it would remove elephants from its circuses in 2018, only to relocate them to a breeding facility (Pérez-Peña, 2015) and introduce a new camel act to the show (Collins, 2015). Both supply and demand will shift to other jurisdictions as required so long as speciesism, rooted in oppression, persists.

Nonhuman Animals are both property and economic commodities, thus creating a wide divergence in norms regarding their treatment. On one hand, the law permits extreme cruelty for the most trivial of economic benefits, so long as the use is considered socially acceptable (Francione, 1995, pp.4–7). Single-issue campaigns reinforce these irrational dichotomies by singling out specific uses of other animals as though they are worse than others. When campaigns seek to eliminate one branch of the tree, while ignoring other branches, they insinuate that certain forms of exploitation are worse than others. The movement thus presents a hierarchy of concern to the public. Francione exemplifies this in his analysis of the tremendously popular anti-"fur" campaign. This particular campaign sends the confusing and false message that Nonhuman Animal hair production is somehow worse than that of other animal-based fabrics such as "leather," which are produced just as brutally but are much more widely used (Francione, 2008, p.93). Single-issue campaigns could avoid this shortcoming by calling for veganism and an end to *all* Nonhuman Animal use, but a clear vegan message is, more often than not, absent from single-issue claimsmaking.

For that matter, it is not clear that single-issue campaigns are at all an efficient use of resources. Granted, using a particular issue or event to draw attention to a vegan argument can be useful. However, funneling resources into a single-issue *campaign* will necessarily dilute the vegan message and promote one species or type of exploitation as more deserving of public attention. Instead of pooling resources into a consistent vegan message, single-issue campaigns divide resources among those issues that *advocates* care most about, what they suspect *others* care most about, or what they suspect will solicit the most *donations*. For instance, the Peace Advocacy Network operates a campaign to ban the horse carriage industry in their vegan abolitionist agenda. However, the campaign largely obscures their abolitionist message. Indeed, the campaign literature makes no mention of veganism, though it does request donations (Peace Advocacy Network, no date). The sheer number of campaigns is another area of concern. Social psychological research warns that inundating the public with countless single-issue campaigns is likely to result in decision paralysis. With so many pressing concerns vying for attention, many will shut down and make no decision at all (Schwartz, 2004).

The vegan solution: Uprooting and eliminating the tree

The tree of Nonhuman Animal exploitation flourishes and continues to exist because of oppressive social structures and, to a lesser extent, consumer demand. In this case, it is capitalist exploitation that nourishes every aspect of the tree and fuels consumer demand. An anti-capitalist vegan collective works to the detriment of the tree's health. Educating and mobilizing others aids the process of uprooting oppression. As the movement's political strength grows and the support systems of the tree diminish, the outer branches that single-issue campaigns target will naturally die off until the tree can no longer survive. Rather than wastefully expending energy "hacking" at the branches of this tree, it might be wiser to "strike at the root" with a comprehensive, politically focused vegan approach. Dismantling oppression will mean the countless offshoots will fall, too. Therefore, veganism is a far more efficient line of attack. With the destruction of speciesism, there is room for egalitarian, liberatory regrowth.

Single-issue campaigns and welfare reforms ultimately help sustain the tree and cannot lead to abolition, because they do not challenge the underlying oppressive social structures. Because this understanding may seem counterintuitive, analogy works to disrupt taken-for-granted assumptions. Specifically, this analogy illustrates that welfarism is a paradigm of *exploitation*, rather than *protection*. Welfare reform does more to ease the psychological distress of human exploiters and consumers and far less to ease the actual suffering of Nonhuman Animals. Aiding industries of exploitation with improvements to their efficiency and public image only worsens the Nonhuman Animal condition. The post-speciesist imaginary is insidious because it obscures the ongoing brutality experienced by vulnerable animals with a veneer of mutually beneficial human–nonhuman relationships in a "just world." This analogy illustrates how welfare measures are healthy for the institutions of Nonhuman Animal exploitation in much the same way as watering, pruning, and fertilizing help a tree to thrive.

Of course, there are bad analogies, too. For example, one popular, but bad, analogy involves "picking the low hanging fruit" from the metaphorical tree. This analogy refers to the movement's tendency to prioritize easy welfare reform victories.[7] The fruit is "low hanging," however, because the public *already agrees* that these reforms should be made. There is little or no challenge to the notion that Nonhuman Animals are resources and things. Note also that "fruit is sweet" in the sense that welfare reforms reward professionalized organizations with fundraising opportunities. They also reward industries by bolstering consumer confidence and increasing production efficiency. Most important, *a healthy tree will continue to produce fruit indefinitely*. Welfare reforms come and go and laws are often appealed or unenforced, providing non-profits with an indefinite source of campaigning material.

The immunity of an analogy to counter-analogy also matters. The ease with which an argument can be countered speaks to its weakness, creating a resistance to attitude change (Cialdini et al., 2003). For example, the low-hanging fruit analogy is a bad analogy for welfare proponents because it ignores the root causes of Nonhuman Animal exploitation. However, it lends itself well to counter-analogy and thus functions as a good analogy for abolitionists who point to the regenerative nature of "fruit" production.

Assessing the age and educational level of the intended audience is also helpful. Is the intended audience incapable of understanding the nuances of a given analogy? Or, will they understandably misinterpret out of ignorance or inexperience? An audience might also deliberately misunderstand the argument in reaction to cognitive dissonance or as a result of some ulterior motive (such as an economic reliance on speciesism). Recall also that rational arguments tend to be more effective with those who are more analytically minded. On the other hand, those who are more affectively minded respond to more emotional appeals. A complex analogy, then, may not reach everyone equally; nor are they universally appealing.

The audience's involvement with the message is also important. If the message is relevant to them, individuals will be more likely to centrally process (and thus retain) the information. Otherwise, individuals will likely rely on peripheral cues, which would be difficult to convey in an analytic analogy. Those persons might be best reached through photographs, videos, or repeating slogans. In the following section, these concepts will be explored in greater detail. Analogy is heavily utilized in Nonhuman Animal advocacy, but it is best placed within the confines of particular spaces and approaches. Effective use of analogy relies on a nuanced approach that acknowledges the identity of the audience. Analogy may seem tricky to operationalize, but most tools of persuasion are highly dependent upon context in this way. Social psychological research demonstrates that other tactics require carefully considered application as well.

Revisiting other popular tactics

Screenings

Documentaries and films with a message have been shown to improve public awareness about important social issues (Chung et al., 2006; Levine, 2003). Social issue documentaries can also influence civic engagement, especially when combined with a discussion after the screening (Cocciolo, 2013). Indeed, documentary screenings have been central to many social movement efforts, including the women's movement (Rich, 1998) and the Nonhuman Animal rights movement (Freeman, 2012). Freeman (2012) has suggested that film screenings can be strategic for those advocating on behalf of other animals because they engage public interest and build a framework for anti-speciesist imagination. It would be difficult to conceive of anyone surviving a screening of PETA's *Meet your Meat* and feeling nothing.

Images are powerful. The Nonhuman Animal rights movement primarily recruits new members through networking, but also through morally shocking visuals (Jasper and Poulsen, 1995). Eliciting intense emotional reactions through imagery has been associated with increased support of a given charity (Burt and Strongman, 2004). Braunsberger (2014) and Nabi (2009) find that participants who watch a disturbing video on Nonhuman Animal experimentation or "hunting" are more likely to experience attitude change.[8] Several professionalized organizations utilize pay-per-view stalls in a manner that extends the premise of these studies. The assumption is that exposure to morally shocking video can influence the consumption patterns of viewers. The Farm Animal Rights Movement (FARM) launched a campaign that offered $1 to participants who watch a four-minute film that documents Nonhuman Animal exploitation. Following one event in the San Francisco Bay area, FARM (2011) reports that 75 per cent of the 725 viewers pledged to reduce their consumption of Nonhuman Animal products, and, one month later, 50 per cent of their survey respondents reported having done so. After two years, FARM (2013) claims that the campaign has reached 160,000 people, stating that "80 per cent of viewers make a pledge to work toward a vegan diet."[9] Importantly, FARM does not always explicitly advocate for veganism in their campaigning efforts. Instead, it tends to accommodate non-vegan, reduction-based approaches. Questionnaire wording that describes the desired behavior change as "work[ing] toward a vegan diet" is intentionally vague. Reducing one's consumption of Nonhuman Animal products could mean any number of things. It may mean abstaining from cow's flesh, or it could mean ordering cheese pizza instead of pepperoni. Vague question wording means researchers are able to accommodate a larger, more positive response.

Two complications might also arise from this approach. First, respondents are likely to fudge their responses to make them more appealing to the researcher. This is known as the social desirability bias. Most agree that hurting Nonhuman Animals is a bad thing, and, if asked, most would likely downplay involvement in that suffering. Subsequently, respondents tend to over-report their "good" behavior. Researchers have warned that this bias is especially problematic when measuring dietary intake (Herbert et al., 1995). Second, the Hawthorne effect often arises among research participants who know they are being studied (Cook, 1962). Similar to the social desirability bias, participants will work harder to meet researcher expectations simply because they know they are under surveillance. Those who participated in the FARM pay-per-view study were made to fill out a questionnaire on site and provide their contact information. This could lead respondents to believe they would be contacted in the future to measure their behavior change. While the Hawthorne effect does actually create behavior change, there is no assurance that the change will be lasting once the research is complete. Another problem is that the professionalized version of the pay-per-view framework presents veganism as only one of many legitimate responses to Nonhuman Animal oppression. This may have the effect of diluting the importance of veganism. If advocating for veganism *in specific*, it is possible that pay-per-view methods could be more effective in increasing vegan numbers. Also, further research is needed to addresse the potential for response bias.

The Humane Research Council (2012) conducted a comparative study on the effectiveness of screenings that relied on feedback from over 500 teenagers and young adults. Participants viewed four different videos that were approximately four minutes long and were related to Nonhuman Animal rights, vegetarianism, and veganism. Videos varied in their tone and message, but all were at least somewhat effective. About 29 per cent reported that they were considering a reduction of their Nonhuman Animal consumption, and 8 per cent reported that they were considering complete elimination. Thirty percent stated that they would like more information about vegetarian or vegan food. Interestingly, the film depicting the production of animal-based foods[10] had the most people drop out and stop viewing, but it also inspired the most attitude change. This is important evidence for the utility in using morally shocking imagery. This same video is cited as an important motivator by respondents in a study of Facebook outreach conducted by The Humane League (2011). While it is expected that most respondents who "liked" the video's webpage were already interested in changing their Nonhuman Animal consumption patterns, results do indicate that about 26 per cent of respondents went vegan or vegetarian and 38 per cent reduced their intake of Nonhuman Animal products. A survey also conducted by The Humane League (2014) found that leaflets with depictions of suffering Nonhuman Animals on the cover were least preferred by respondents, though narratives of cruelty resonated more than health arguments.

There is evidence that offering participants a little something for their time can improve results. FARM may be onto something with their pay-per-view strategy. Research has shown that compensating individuals with small gifts or other incentives increases their compliance (Strohmetz et al., 2002; Whiteman et al., 2003). A small incentive such as a free food sample or a small monetary reward is an effective and cost-efficient means of achieving attitude change. VegFund often provides vegan food samples along with video screenings, and FARM offers $1 to those who watch their four-minute video clip. The pay-per-view strategy could be useful in attracting a wider array of participants who are not already considering going vegan, and it may also increase the number of participants who watch the entire video clip.

While increasing vegan numbers is a victory, one serious consideration is that graphic imagery may shock viewers into welfarist pathways (Wrenn, 2013b, pp.8–12). Gory depictions of suffering and death might turn some away, as was indicated in the Human Research Council's study, but for those who stick it through, advocates should be worried about the message garnered from their emotionally charged viewing experience. First, Hall (2010, p.229) worries that using "victims in pictures" actually works to reinforce their victimization and to aggravate their objectification. Second, she suggests that these pictures maintain human supremacy because they so often draw attention to *abuse* rather than to *use* (p.222). For that matter, images and videos that depict horrific scenes of Nonhuman Animal suffering are most often paired with welfarist messages requesting donations, promoting reform, and suggesting only a reduction in consumption. The concern is that viewers may learn to associate graphic images with a desire to help other animals "right now" through welfare-focused actions. That is, they may be swayed by the hegemonic presence of welfarist organizations that equate reform with immediate relief, portray veganism as extreme, and deride abolitionism as a utopian pipe dream. It is clear that these images trigger an emotional reaction, but it is possible that the professionalized Nonhuman Animal rights movement has manipulated the "common sense" reaction to this suffering as one of moderation and compromise.

For that matter, visual channels are generally effective for only certain types of messages. Chaiken and Eagly (1983) find that while television messages were able to persuade using peripheral cues (fast talking, music, sounds, and flashing lights, for example), more complex messages are lost and viewers become distracted by other things present in the video. Visual persuasion, the researchers suggest, is best reserved for simple, easily comprehended messages. More complex messages would fare better if written, but screenings may work well if they cut to the chase and encourage viewers to go vegan. Complex Nonhuman Animal rights and anti-oppression theory would be best offered as a supplement in leaflets, blogs, books, and face-to-face interaction. Visual media that simply repeats simplistic messages (such as the beloved "Go Vegan" mantra) over and over might be effective, but meaningful attitude changes are not necessarily going to follow.

In spite of these challenges, screenings appear to be a useful avenue for promoting Nonhuman Animal liberation. They engage audiences and trigger strong emotions. They are also very cost effective and can reach a large audience. Attitude change can be facilitated by embedding videos within a dialogue of anti-speciesism. Food samples, financial compensation, or other incentives can also improve behavior change. Advocates should be wary of morally shocking imagery that may push viewers to adopt welfare reform instead of abolition. Films should also be clear in the importance of veganism and the shortcomings of vegetarianism and other reductionist approaches.

Tastings

One of the major obstacles to adopting the vegan diet seems to be unfamiliarity with vegan foods and their perceived cost and distastefulness (Hoek et al., 2011; Schösler et al., 2012; Tucker, 2014). Food tastings offer the public an opportunity to try vegan food options at no cost or inconvenience to them. Food tastings also allow advocates to educate non-vegans on the accessibility of vegan food options. This activity is a relatively low-cost effort, as food samples may be donated by vegan businesses and can usually be presented in small servings that will accommodate more people. Not only are food samples useful for overcoming stereotypes about vegan food, but also they act as icebreakers. Tastings allow advocates to introduce veganism and distribute literature.

Research has also shown that individuals who are given food or drink to snack on when exposed to new information are more likely to be persuaded (Janis et al., 1965). Offering food may also encourage behavior change by evoking the recipient's desire to return the favor. The reciprocity norm suggests that individuals are likely to help those who have helped them in the past (Gouldner, 1960). Social scientists sometimes include a dollar in mailed questionnaires as this can increase the response rate. Welfare organizations rely on the norm of reciprocity when they include stationary gifts in mailed solicitations for donations. Vegan educators, however, could tap into this norm by offering food samples. Some advocates advertise free vegan cupcakes in exchange for conversation. Most people will act according to social norms and be willing to listen if they accept the gift.

Face-to-face contact is generally the best channel for persuasive efforts (Eldersveld and Dodge, 1954), but the reciprocity norm works anonymously as well. By way of an example, I once left a plate of vegan food samples in the kitchen of my workplace along with vegan leaflets. By the end of the day, both the food samples *and* the leaflets had all been taken. On another day, I left vegan bake sale leftovers in the kitchen with a cup for donations for my student group and this was also successful. Reciprocity has its limits, however. If people are not able to reciprocate as expected by social norms, they may react negatively. In some cases, receiving help can threaten one's self-esteem (this has been documented in interactions between elderly persons and their caregivers) (Newsom, 1999). Advocates should be careful to utilize this technique only in ways that will not threaten the self-esteem of the recipients. For instance, the Food Not Bombs program that provides free vegan food to homeless persons might run into this problem. Offers and subsequent expectations should be relatively modest. Exchanging a cupcake for conversation is likely to be more successful than offering cupcakes in the expectation of a complete, on-the-spot vegan conversion.

The primary shortcoming of food tastings in vegan advocacy is that they are often accompanied with problematic messages. First, many tastings rely on volunteers and literature that actually recommend vegetarianism and other forms of reductionism instead of veganism. In these cases, a chance for a clear vegan message is lost in the welfarist rhetoric of compromise. Second, many organizations use naked or nearly naked young women to hand out food samples. PETA is most notorious for this tactic, recruiting young white women to dress up as "Lettuce Ladies" and hand out veggie hot dogs and the like. This approach combines two popular means of grabbing attention: free food and naked women. Unfortunately, the two are not compatible in the context of anti-oppression work. Free vegan food works in the context of social justice, but titillating displays of naked women work in the context of patriarchy and violence. It is illogical to serve up women's bodies to the public as a means of promoting Nonhuman Animal liberation. This tactic only reinforces the notion that vulnerable populations are freely available to the privileged to consume for their pleasure. This is decidedly antithetical to a liberation movement.

Third, quite a lot of vegan tastings offer up expensive specialty items that are financially or geographically inaccessible to the majority of the American population. Handing out samples of vegan ice cream sandwiches and vegan pizza will demonstrate that veganism does not mean losing favorite and familiar foods, but it may also demonstrate that veganism is simply out of the budget for many. Finally, focusing on specialty treats and junk food may distract from the stereotypes about bland and boring vegan food, but it could potentially represent veganism as unhealthy, which would be a misrepresentation. Because concerns over healthfulness is another reason why people may continue to eat or resume eating Nonhuman Animal products (Childers and Herzog, 2009; Lea, 2001, p.102; Toronto Vegetarian Association, 2015, pp.4–6), cookies, pizza, and ice cream may not always be the ideal samples.

Food is an important incentive to behavior change, but advocates should take care to choose appropriate foods and appropriate distribution techniques. Samples should be offered with a clear vegan message. Many people will choose to reduce rather than eliminate their intake of Nonhuman Animal products with or without the encouragement of vegan advocates. It is better to clarify that veganism is the ideal response to concerns with Nonhuman Animal suffering and personal health. It is on advocates to honestly explain what social change they hope to achieve.

Furthermore, advocates should carry themselves professionally and expect the same of others. Stationing half-dressed young women on the street corner to hand out veggie dogs is objectifying and counterintuitive to an anti-oppression message. An Australian study demonstrates that men exposed to PETA's naked campaigns found its dehumanization of women off-putting, and these men are not likely to support the antispeciesist cause (Bongiorno et al., 2013). Finally, advocates should be mindful of their audience. It may sometimes be wiser to promote easy to obtain, easy to prepare, healthy, and affordable vegan foods. Distributing nutritional literature with food samples may also be important to countering any misconceptions about the unhealthiness of veganism.

Leafleting

Leafleting is favored by many activists for its low cost and the ease of distribution. Vegan Outreach relies almost entirely upon this method, insisting that leafleting on college campuses is the most efficient use of resources. It argues that leafleting allows advocates to distribute the information necessary to adequately explain a vegan argument, more than is typically granted in the media coverage sought by other non-profits, which tends to be both limited and biased. It explains, "Even though we reach fewer people, we reach them with the information required to allow them to change" (Norris, 1997). While face-to-face interaction and networking is the strongest form of advocacy, leafleting is an adequate supplement, allowing activists to reach beyond their personal networks and make contact with community members. Providing information to passersby to take with them and revisit at their leisure is also useful for those individuals who are not likely to consider an immediate change in behavior. After all, research has shown that many become vegan only after a substantial incubation period involving further learning and consideration (Beardsworth and Keil, 1992, pp.266–76; McDonald, 2000, pp.6–7).

Research outside the vegan community has confirmed the utility in leafleting. For instance, leaflet distribution has been linked to improving the comprehension of healthcare programs (Azoulay et al., 2002) and public confidence in a given organization (Hohl et al., 2010), especially when used in combination with verbal engagement (Regner et al., 1987). That is, handing out leaflets is helpful, but handing out leaflets with a debriefing increases the leaflet's effectiveness. Importantly, one study measured the effectiveness of mass leafleting on public knowledge about nutrition and found that without the verbal engagement, no significant changes in attitude were detectable (Nichols et al., 1988). Other nutrition research has shown that those who are personally contacted by heart disease campaigners are more likely to change their health habits and thus reduce their risk for illness (Farquhar et al., 1977). Therefore, advocates should ensure that volunteers personally hand out literature or are at least present to discuss the literature picked up from information tables.

Advocates can establish credibility with leaflet recipients by creating a perception of expertise and trustworthiness. That is, they should appear knowledgeable on their topic of concern. Speaking confidently can also increase the perception of expertise. However, an audience can often reject the expertise of someone who is delivering messages that are contrary to the audience's pre-existing beliefs. Researchers have suggested that this is one reason why climate change experts have been unpersuasive for half the American population (Kahan et al., 2010). Trustworthiness, however, can be achieved if recipients do not think that the messenger is attempting to persuade them (Walster & Festinger, 1962). For example, if the audience believes the messenger has nothing to gain and has no vested interests in persuading people, they will be trusted more. Looking people straight in the eyes (Hemsley and Doob, 1978) and speaking quickly can also increase trustworthiness (Miller et al., 1976). Advocates should become comfortable enough with the material to speak confidently and without hesitation. To improve these factors in vegan outreach, advocates would do well to increase their knowledge by reading, researching, and keeping up to date on the issues. Advocates will also have to be mindful of the audience's beliefs and perhaps target those more receptive to a vegan message (this is why many organizations target college students who tend to be left-leaning). Utilizing persuasion techniques that invite conversation and are not overbearing should also be more useful.

Sometimes more superficial methods work. Some research has shown that the messenger can be more effective by simply being attractive and liked. Physical attractiveness increases persuasiveness (Chaiken, 1979). Of course, applying this concept to vegan advocacy risks marginalizing activists who are not considered conventionally attractive. Likewise, the movement's use of "sexy" models to promote veganism can backfire in normalizing objectification. However, demonstrating *similarity to the audience* can increase attractiveness, as individuals tend to like those who are like them. So perhaps hired models may not always be the best approach, but a sensitivity to gender, class, and other identity markers would be useful. Similarity matters even in the details. Mimicking the body posture of those who receive the message can increase persuasiveness (Bailenson and Yee, 2005).

Advocates can benefit from this research by improving personal appearance: messengers should appear professional and kempt, *or not*, depending on the context. Wearing a button down shirt with slacks while leafleting at Burning Man Festival is probably not advantageous, but those looking to attract conservative funders might benefit from adopting the corporate look.[11] Likewise, choosing advocates that an audience can relate to is important. For example, if one is leafleting on a college campus, college-age advocates might be best suited to the task. Existing power dynamics between privileged and underprivileged groups will also be relevant. A female-identified advocate might be most appropriate for an engagement at a women's conference. Recruiting male-identified volunteers for the purpose of persuading feminists on how they should think and act might be taken as an offense or even as a threat. In some cases, conversations among equals are more effective.

Face-to-face interaction tends to increase the success of leafleting, but it is not always required. Making print information available for people to take at their leisure without volunteers present to clarify the message is not ideal, but as leaflets are relatively inexpensive to produce, it certainly cannot hurt. Furthermore, providing this option may be helpful for introverted persons who are not keen on interacting with volunteers and for those who are in a hurry and cannot spare the time to speak with an advocate. Research has shown that simply being in a hurry will reduce people's likelihood of engaging in pro-social behavior (Darley and Batson, 1973). Haste interferes with pro-sociality even when people have been primed prior to the opportunity, though priming does usually help (Beaman et al., 1978). This may be one detriment to Vegan Outreach's favored approach of soliciting college students who are rushing between classes. Even if students are primed prior to their contact with advocates – say, if they are just leaving an Animals & Society lecture as they run into a Vegan Outreach volunteer – they may *still* be unreceptive if they have little time before their next class starts. This is because people in a hurry are preoccupied and less responsive to the priming. For advocates, this means that having a volunteer available to prime recipients is helpful, but not absolutely essential. Furthermore, having information available for busy people to grab at their convenience may be the difference between their receiving some information and their receiving none at all. Alternatively, targeting areas where people are milling about or otherwise have the free time to spare would be useful. This might include parks, community buildings, or bus stops.

Limited research into the effectiveness of leafleting on vegan conversion demonstrates modest success rates. In 2012, Farm Sanctuary and The Humane League conducted a follow-up study on students who had received Farm Sanctuary leaflets two months prior to ascertain their levels of behavior change. Between two and 12 per cent of students reported reducing some of their Nonhuman Animal product consumption (Cooney, 2013c). No significant number of students went vegan. However the Farm Sanctuary literature does not specifically advocate for veganism but primarily encourages vegetarianism and other reduction strategies. This runs into the same shortcoming of FARM's pay-per-view campaign. The content of leaflets should coincide with abolitionist goals. Another consideration is that leaflets are often not tailored to their audience. Many vegan outreach leaflets have reading levels that far exceed the literacy rates of the average American (Humane Research Council, 2011). Furthermore, many leaflets appeal to a limited demographic, that of middle-class whites. Underprivileged groups may be better reached with an appeal to their unique social circumstances. Legacies of colonialism, slavery, environmental racism, and institutional discrimination are important considerations in the construction of outreach messages. In other words, leaflet resonance may be improved if speciesism is integrated into the larger framework of oppression.

Whether or not non-white demographics can be reached by a message that specifically emphasizes speciesism is not the issue. The presumption that people of color do not or cannot care about Nonhuman Animal suffering is a lingering racist stereotype that was developed following the abolition of slavery to maintain white supremacy and legitimate ongoing discrimination (Lundblad, 2012, p.78). The problem is that vegan advocacy is often portrayed as (and interpreted as) a "white people thing." It is maintained as a lifestyle of privilege that is out of reach to many vulnerable human groups. The motivational discrepancies that may exist between white vegans and vegans of color is not one of apathy to Nonhuman Animal suffering but rather one of cultural and racialized differences maintained by a white-centric Nonhuman Animal rights movement that is generally insensitive to structural oppression as it pertains to humans (see Chapter 5). Campaigns that focus on Nonhuman Animal suffering and feature pricey vegan substitutes may appeal to college students who are disproportionately white and middle-class, but this same presentation is not generalizable to other populations. Many organizations focus on campus outreach with the presumption that college-aged young adults are more receptive to attitude change. This relationship is supported by research (Krosnick and Alwin, 1989), but advocates might also be concerned that prioritizing a privileged population ignores the suffering of disadvantaged populations. Lower income families are more likely to be impacted by the negative health consequences of eating Nonhuman Animal products (Wiig and Smith, 2008). These families are sometimes restricted by inflexible work schedules, limited income, limited transportation, food deserts and food inaccessibility, and inadequate or obfuscated nutritional knowledge, all of which make healthful eating difficult. Accordingly, advocates might emphasize that a vegan diet can reduce food costs by as much as 50 per cent (Flynn et al., 2013, p.74; Wigg and Smith, 2008, p.1728). Indeed, omitting Nonhuman Animal products from the shopping list could save a low-income family enough money to feed a child.[12]

Newsletters, blogging, and creating communities

Newsletter and blog activity is another low-cost opportunity to engage the public and volunteers. Social movement media intends to keep interested parties up to date on activities while offering information on effective outreach practices, theory, and current events. Most often available by mail or the internet, this type of information would also appeal to busy individuals who can peruse the information when it is convenient, meaning that the message would not be completely lost to people in a hurry (recall that haste acts as a distraction and is negatively correlated with pro-social behavior). Newsletters and blogs are convenient to advocates as well as constituents. They are available to anyone with the means to create and distribute them, offering a relatively diverse array of voices and specializations for the interested public and activists to relate to.

Blogging has exploded as a means of accessible, do-it-yourself outreach as computer and internet access has increased. While many blogs do associate with formal organizations, this is obviously not a requirement, and many individuals can find considerable agency and empowerment in blogging (Somolu, 2007). Instead of relying on professionalized interpretations of appropriate activism, bloggers can themselves create and distribute knowledge (Fine, 2006). The feminist movement in particular has credited blogging with being an important factor in improving women's rights and with expanding public knowledge about women's issues. In addition to the ease and affordability of newsletters and blogging, they may also serve a vital function in maintaining vegan interconnectedness for the Nonhuman Animal rights movement. Research has shown that fostering vegan communities, identities, and networks is one of the most important factors, if not *the* most factor, in both encouraging and maintaining veganism (Cherry, 2006; Haverstock and Forgays, 2012, p.1034; Jasper and Poulsen, 1995; Lea, 2001, pp.105–10). Nurturing community is essential because humans are social animals that learn what behaviors and attitudes are considered normal, favorable, and legitimate through processes of socialization.

Group identity can be a powerful motivator. The gay rights movement, as one example, has very successfully mobilized identity (Armstrong, 2002; Bernstein, 1997). Identity creates a sense of belonging and a sense of responsibility to the group. A positive vegan culture has the potential to resocialize individuals toward adopting a sense of moral responsibility for other animals, the environment, and at-risk human populations. This has certainly been the case with efforts to raise environmental consciousness as well. Today, many individuals and communities recycle, responsibly dispose of garbage, and utilize alternative modes of transportation because of structural changes that have increased the convenience of doing so and the political culture that has popularized concern for the earth (Diekmann and Preisendorfer, 1998). Creating social norms conducive to a desired social change can encourage positive behavior. That behavior change can, in turn, change attitudes as well (Cross, 2013).

Activist projects that seek to increase familiarity with veganism and support networks have the potential to create a vegan-positive culture that is conducive to both increasing and sustaining vegan ranks. For instance, psychologists studied the impact of Michael Pollan's (2006) *The Omnivore's Dilemma* on college students and found that while the book initially sparked substantial attitude changes, a year later, those attitudes had largely reverted (Hormes et al., 2013). It is likely that the absence of a supportive network (students in the study were first- and second-year psychology students) may be largely responsible for this recidivism.[13] In building a vegan culture and a safer vegan community, the stigmatization from the outside non-vegan world loses its sting. In bolstering a communal feeling and a sense of belonging, identity can preserve motivation.

Creating a vegan culture is also important for combating the bystander effect. Common sense suggests that in a situation that behooves pro-social behavior, the more people present means the more likely that assistance will be given. This is not the case. Nonhuman Animal suffering is "witnessed" by millions of humans, so it might be expected that more people would want to help. In reality, the more people present, the *less* likely anyone is to help. This happens not only because people are less likely to notice their surroundings when in a group (Latané and Darley, 1968; 1970) but also because people read the reactions of others to determine the appropriate response, which can cause delay or inaction. Many humans witness the suffering of other animals, but fail to act simply because others around them have also failed to do so. If exposed to slaughterhouse footage, an individual may feel compelled to act, but as everyone else continues to eat animal flesh, they are likely to do nothing. As a society, this response is cemented through socialization processes and social institutions that are created and protected by elites who stand to profit from speciesism. The bystander effect has been documented in small groups and public settings, but when *entire populations* fail to act in the face of oppression, the compulsion to conform is nearly inescapable. Paradoxically, willingness to help declines as the number of people aware of the situation increases. This creates a diffusion of responsibility whereby no one person feels obligated (or comfortable enough) to intervene.

The bystander effect, however, can be overcome. In group situations, if one person breaks ranks and offers to help, others will gauge this new social norm and quickly join in to help as well. Models of pro-social behavior have been shown to facilitate further pro-social behavior among those who witness it (Bryan and Test, 1967; Rushton and Campbell, 1977; Schnall et al., 2010). What this means for vegan advocacy is that creating a social norm of helping other animals is critical. Humans are social creatures who experience immense pressure to act and think like everyone else. If someone breaks ranks and behaves pro-socially, this encourages others to reconsider prevailing speciesist social norms. This disruption could inspire a reinterpretation of veganism and Nonhuman Animal rights activism as a desirable pro-social behavior.

Violence

Anti-social behavioral norms can also manifest in group settings that value pro-social goals. For much of history, violence has been integrated into advocacy repertoires, especially those associated with grassroots movements dominated by male-identified young people. Men are often raised to deal with their problems through violence, so applying this technique in social movement spaces is a natural progression. It is carefully repackaged as heroic, brave, liberatory, and admirable (as many problematic patriarchal practices are). Despite the glory and grandeur, one fact remains: violence does not often work. Indeed, Regan has identified violent tactics as one of the primary barriers to Nonhuman Animal liberation (2004a, p.235; 2004b, p.188). I define violence as *any form of intentional physical or emotional harm enacted on another person or persons*. This would include a physical attack, an emotional attack, property damage, and other forms of terrorism. Posting flyers on a college campus promising a reward to anyone willing to report the home addresses of students engaged in university vivisection is an act of violence. Beating (or threatening to beat) someone with a baseball bat for hurting other animals is an act of violence. Bombing a research facility is an act of violence. Staking out a researcher's home (especially if there are children in the home) is an act of violence. Proclaiming that anyone who wears animal hair should be raped is an act of violence. "Reenacting" scenes of rape, sexual assault, and torture on women as a "metaphor" for speciesism is an act of violence.[14]

Advocates often reframe the meaning of violence in order to legitimate tactics that others have identified as harmful (Best and Nocella, 2004, p.25; Elise, 2013, pp.38–40). As an example, one common appeal is that burning down empty laboratories is not an act of violence. The argument is that the building is empty; therefore, the only hurt caused is to the industry's profits. As someone who has had my own home burned down by arsonists (it was uninhabited at the time), I can assure readers that there is really only *one* interpretation of such an act. These activists may see themselves as freedom fighters, but the public views them in the same light as they do other arsonists: unstable criminals who pose a threat to public safety. Burning buildings is an act of violence because of the fear that it creates (to owners as well as neighbors), the danger it poses to the surrounding community should the fire spread, and the certain death to any free-living Nonhuman Animals who have taken up residence in the building.

Breaking into facilities to liberate Nonhuman Animals is also problematic as a tactical and ethical matter. In the vast majority of cases, freed Nonhuman Animals will simply be replaced (if not by the targeted facility itself, then by other facilities in the industry that take up the slack to meet the unchallenged demand). Additionally, illegally entering a building and causing damage (either by breaking equipment or by removing property/Nonhuman Animals) is also likely to be interpreted as violent. Breaking and entering is generally experienced as threatening and frightening to owners. It is not likely that they will pause to consider the good intentions of the burglar. Many professionalized organizations practice direct action of this sort, which does legitimize it to some extent. However, the primary goal of professionalized organizations that engage open rescues is to obtain footage to use in their campaigns for fundraising. Regardless of intentions, the owners of the compromised facilities will interpret these actions as a threat. The sharp rise in "ag-gag" laws that criminalize whistleblower activity in Nonhuman Animal industries only reinforces the futility of such an approach.

Another argument in favor of these tactics posits that violent behavior directed at Nonhuman Animal exploiters is an act of self-defense on behalf of the Nonhuman Animal victim. No one would suggest that bystanders stand idly by while a dog is beaten, but what should be done about socially sanctioned forms of suffering? Should activists lurch after "hunters" in the woods with baseball bats? Would it be advisable to telephone the homes of slaughterhouse workers with threats? These tactics would be a fast-track to prison, and anti-Nonhuman Animal rights sentiment would only be aggravated. These speciesist practices, as gruesome as they may be, are considered normal, socially acceptable, necessary, and sometimes enjoyable. Violent interference will not be viewed favorably in a speciesist society. Research supports this opinion. A study of over 300 social movements demonstrates that nonviolent movements are not only more likely to succeed, but are more likely to have *lasting success* in comparison with violent movements and revolutions (Chenoweth and Stephan, 2011, p.10). The logic is simple: nonviolent civil resistance is less risky and more attractive. An attractive movement solicits more recruits and more resources. More recruits and more resources translate to increased success.

In a publication with the *Journal for Agricultural and Environmental Ethics*, I explore the role of violence in both human and nonhuman abolitionist movements (Wrenn 2013c). I posit that neither have been especially successful. The human abolitionist movement is an especially useful parallel, as African captives were considered property/nonpersons and also faced insurmountable institutional barriers. Violent resistance *did* happen, but more often than not, those collectives met with swift and heavy repression. Violence also tended to fuel stricter constraints on slaves (and abolitionists).[15] For the most part, violence only succeeds in inviting further violent resistance and retaliation, especially within a societal infrastructure designed to protect and maintain oppressive structures at all costs. A violent strategy is largely futile, as "the state has enormous resources (intelligence, surveillance, labor power, and weaponry) to counter successfully such a campaign" (Nibert, 2013, p.271).

Lovitz (2010) has warned that increased state repression that results from violent tactics is "muzzling" the movement and discouraging activism of all types, violent or not. Without a critical mass in support of the social change, it will be nearly impossible to achieve. In the unlikely event that a violent movement succeeds, it will be unstable and highly vulnerable.

Normative violence may also be off-putting to a movement that has historically attracted women, meaning that the movement's tolerance for illegal tactics, harassment, and vandalism may begin to alienate its largest demographic. Violent and illegal tactics are not only off-putting to many women, but also to many people of color, who have long been discriminated against by the criminal justice system. While engaging these tactics is dangerous for anyone, the white men who are disproportionately drawn to them are privileged with the relative leniency afforded by their racial identity. For white-identified activists who do not escape prosecution and punishment, they are nonetheless generally privileged with access to resources and networks that are less available to people of color. Violent tactics, then, are not universally accessible, but they are specifically suited to white masculinity. Whether useful or not, as Hall explains in her 2006 publication *Capers in the Churchyard: Animal Rights Advocacy in the Age of Terror*, violence is *antithetical* to the goal of peace and equality advocates wish to realize. Feminist Marti Kheel (2006) agrees, suggesting that these tactics only replicate the mechanisms of patriarchy. Using the tools of oppression (force, domination, coercion, terrorism, and violence) afforded by powerful forms of privilege (whiteness and maleness) to dismantle oppression only replaces one oppressive structure with the other.

4
Reconciling Gender and Rationality

While ineffective tactics have beleaguered the Nonhuman Animal rights movement, the reign of sexism and pornographic exploitation is equally disastrous to liberation efforts. The Nonhuman Animal rights movement comprises primarily of women (Gaarder, 2011, p.11),[1] and yet it continues to operate according to patriarchal norms. Just as industry-friendly welfare reform deflects movement resources from recruiting potentially thousands (if not millions) of new vegans, patriarchy-friendly tactics that bank on degrading women reduce the potential of the movement's female majority. If the millions who consider themselves "animal lovers" were to step back from the irrationality of welfare reform and single-issue campaigning and commit to political veganism, real change would be at advocates' fingertips. If the millions of *women* were to escape the irrationality of patriarchy and become full citizens both in society and social movements, it is likely that systems of oppression would crumble. In other words, the movement's greatest source of people power is currently immobilized, as female activists are so often stripped or silenced. The movement must liberate its women before it can liberate other animals.

Two major issues complicate the full utilization of the large female demographic in Nonhuman Animal rights advocacy spaces: the degeneration of feminist mobilization and the exclusion of feminism from the discourse of rationality and science. Both can be sourced to the patriarchal assault on feminism. Science – an institution with a sordid history of oppressing women – continues to chip away at feminist gains by either ignoring women-specific issues or delegitimizing them. On the other hand, the feminist movement itself seems to have lost its radical agenda, leaving itself ripe for patriarchal infiltration (Dines, 2012; Levy, 2005). The rise of third-wave feminism, the illusion of post-feminism, and the popularity of "choice" feminism derail feminist goals that are still very much relevant, even in today's supposedly more "egalitarian" society. This chapter will demonstrate how these ideological derailments manifest in Nonhuman Animal rights spaces as well.

Individualism, feminism, and Nonhuman Animal rights advocacy

The general attitude of indifference to feminist concerns in the Nonhuman Animal rights community likely reflects normalized attitudes of sexism in larger society, women's internalization of normalized sexism, and perhaps even a simple hesitancy for the movement to admit weakness. Indeed, the notion that sexism could exist in a movement that is comprised largely of female-identified advocates seems almost inconceivable as a matter of common sense. If sexism is not thought a problem and if feminist critique is considered irrelevant in a society that is still very much oppressive toward women, then these conditions are indicative of post-feminism ideology. Post-feminism is a concept that presumes that the core problems of sexism have been addressed (or are being addressed) and that feminism no longer holds any direct relevancy. Those adhering to post-feminist ideology may react to feminist critique with skepticism or incredulity.

In association with this post-feminist view, there is also the complicating presence of choice feminism, which, in some ways, represents a neoliberal and patriarchal co-optation. Anita Sarkeesian addresses the resulting consequences in a 2015 feminist panel, *All About Women*:

> Choice feminism posits that each individual woman determines what is empowering for herself, which might sound good on the surface, but this concept risks obscuring the bigger picture and larger fundamental goals of the movement by focusing on individual women with a very narrow individual notion of empowerment. It erases the reality that some choices that women make have an enormous negative impact on other women's lives. So, it's not enough to feel *personally* empowered or be *personally* successful within the oppressive framework of the current system. Even if an individual woman can make patriarchy work for her, it's still a losing game for the rest of the women on the planet. The fact of the matter is that some choices have ramifications beyond ourselves and reinforce harmful patriarchal ideas about women as a group and about women's bodies in our wider shared culture. And because of how systems of oppression

intersect and compound one another, it's women of color, indigenous women, women living in the Global South, women with disabilities, queer women, and trans women who bear the brunt of these ramifications.

Some argue that the third-wave approach has eroded the solidarity of the earlier movement, focusing less on a community of shared interests and goals and more on the interests of the individual (Dines, 2012). Each woman is encouraged to define feminism for herself, often in self-serving ways or in consumption behavior. The result has been a dilution of feminist ideals into something palatable and more easily controlled. While earlier-generation feminists decried the sexual objectification of women and the encroaching pornification of mainstream society, feminism today is increasingly associated with the individual woman's "freedom" to express herself sexually. Self-identifying as a "slut" has become a badge of honor, consuming porn has become "empowering," and dressing in revealing clothes for the male gaze has become "liberating." This façade of liberation serves to benefit a patriarchy that could have otherwise been threatened by a powerful female movement, a patriarchy that now enjoys a generation of women who have been convinced that taking charge of their own exploitation is a feminist act.

Even with the cooperation of women, however, the sexual objectification of women continues to reinforce a system of oppression. The subordination of women is foundational to systems of inequality (MacKinnon, 1989, p.3). Women may have internalized their behavior as an *individual* "choice," but the consequences of this exploitation speak to women as a *group*. For instance, research warns that, as a result of inhabiting an objectifying culture, women become predisposed to substance abuse, eating disorders, and depression (Szymanski et al., 2011, p.19). Women also begin to self-objectify and subsequently experience lower levels of self-efficacy and social activism (Heldman and Cahill, 2007). A celebration of agency for some is the aggravation of structural oppression for others.

Indeed, as Sarkeesian notes, the negative consequences of post-feminism do not affect all women equally. It is more often less privileged women who suffer for this so-called liberation. Women of color and other poor and disadvantaged women are disproportionately affected by sexual assault and violence[2] and are thus the most affronted by a feminist movement that rejects solidarity and repackages patriarchal domination as female liberation, personal choice, and consumption. Poor women and women from abusive homes are those who are far more likely to end up in the sex industry, meaning that society's exaltation of "sluttishness" and "sexual liberation" further entrenches female objectification and disadvantaged women's susceptibility to harm at the hands of clients and johns. But prostituted women are not the only ones affected by these trends. There is an epidemic of sexual assault, violence, and murder against women as a group, one that is facilitated by patriarchy and disproportionately felt by women of color and women in poverty. Not only are these women experiencing the bulk of violence, but they are also those with the least social and political power and the least recourse. They are society's most vulnerable. The "power" and "agency" in sexual "liberation" is unequally distributed, and the ramifications are unequally experienced.

Further, disadvantaged women who may actually wish to participate in individualized feminism will find difficulty in doing so. Sexual "liberation" is generally a white privilege. Sexual imagery in the United States is overwhelmingly white, while women of color are portrayed generally to fulfill racist stereotypes about the sexual availability of colonized people and their "animalistic" nature (Collins, 2004, pp.27–30). Female bodies of color are often presented as public property, and there is no individuality or personhood associated with "things" that are understood to be property.[3] The extraordinary level of sexual violence experienced by women of color, coupled with the smaller demand and lesser compensation for their bodies, is also evidence to their difficulty in accessing the "empowerment" of sexual liberation.

Speciesism made sexy

The individualized feminist movement is a project that primarily caters to privileged middle-class women. Again, the ramifications will befall abused women, drug-addicted women, disabled women, and other at-risk women who fall into (or are trafficked into) sex work. These women face the less-than-glamorous reality of sexual exploitation, violence, and misogyny, a reality aggravated by a powerless feminist movement and underfunded social services. These political trends extend beyond the confines of feminist mobilization. As a female-dominated space, these values begin to influence anti-speciesist tactics as well. The Nonhuman Animal rights framework frequently reflects this post-feminist or third-wave approach: either feminist issues are perceived as irrelevant or feminist issues are perceived as old-fashioned and judgmental. The sexual objectification of female advocates is thought to be empowering for women *and* other animals despite the tendency for this practice to aggravate a culture of oppression. The ideology of individualism obscures structural inequality.

As an example, a local Nonhuman Animal rights group in Wisconsin staffed its table at a gay-pride festival with two young women who were naked from the waist up save some cabbage leaves that were fastened to their breasts. Those who donated at their booth were given stickers that read: "I SPONSORED A PUSSY" (Wrenn, 2013d). Supporters of tactics such as these generally do not recognize that sexually objectifying women to draw attention to Nonhuman Animal inequality might be problematic. From the post-feminist perspective, the women had *chosen* to participate and *enjoyed* participating. The tabling event also featured one nearly naked male volunteer. Occasional male participation of this kind derails feminist criticism, as male presence is leveraged as evidence of a post-feminist world where men's and women's bodies are considered interchangeable. Individual choice, personal empowerment, and gender "blindness" can dominate campaign rationale.

PETA, too, rejects the possibility of sexism in its advocacy. In an interview with the feminist publication *Bitch Magazine*, PETA's Associate Director of Campaigns Lindsay Rajt explains that women *choose* to stand on street corners in pasties, panties, and body paint (Mirk, 2015). Participation of this kind is framed as an *individual* way in which women can help Nonhuman Animals, and women "feel good" doing so. Indeed, Rajt responds to feminist criticisms of PETA's campaigning as oppressive: "I don't think it's a feminist thing to do to turn to another woman and tell her what she can and can't use her body for." PETA is framed as a vehicle for women's personal choice, and a "thoroughly feminist organization."

The rhetoric of the "individual" easily obscures patterns of oppression. The feeling of individual "empowerment" that is used to legitimate sexually objectifying advocacy is likely seen as an important source of motivation for activists. Indeed, many organizations have absorbed this approach first popularized by PETA (Wrenn, 2015, p.2). Advocacy is framed as a personal benefit to the young woman. She can help other animals by displaying her body, she can feel good about herself (in other words, "empowered") by validating herself in a society that values women according to their sexual availability, and the organization benefits by fundraising through her display.

LUSH Cosmetics, a vegetarian luxury bath and body company, operates an advocacy organization to end cosmetic testing on Nonhuman Animals. It also campaigns for other Nonhuman Animal rights and environmental issues like fox "hunting" and oil dependency. Several of its tactics make use of its female employees' bodies. In one street demonstration, a woman volunteered to wear a nude bodysuit and endure ten hours of simulated (and some real) torture at the hands of a man costumed as a vivisector. She was dragged by her hair, her mouth was forced open with a metal clamp, she was force fed, she was injected with saline needles, her head was shaved, and she had wires and cables attached to her scalp. All of this took place in the storefront for an audience of mall shoppers. LUSH insists that a woman was intentionally chosen to portray the lab animal because women are the primary purchasers of animal-tested cosmetics (Omond, 2012).[4] This suggests that LUSH may be drawing on a history of male-on-female violence to scare or shame customers into supporting its cause (and presumably into purchasing its animal-friendlier products).

Australian-based advocacy group Animal Liberation Victoria at one time regularly used female bodies to simulate graphic scenes of violence (Gawthorne, 2008, pp.72–4). In one demonstration, a woman was tied to a mock vivisector's table. She was splashed in fake blood and naked, covered only by a sheet. In another, the same woman appeared nude on a white sheet, curled into a fetal position, and completely soaked red with fake blood (to mimic the Japanese flag in protest against Japanese whaling) (Hastie, 2008). In another demonstration, the same woman lay underneath a replica cow statue in a public square. She suckled a teat to protest the consumption of cows' milk. In Hawthorne's book on effective advocacy for other animals, he comments on the stunt: "There's nothing like a strange visual to gain attention" (2008, p.77).

Vancouver Orphan Kitten Rescue Association entered a float into a local gay-pride parade that featured live pole dancing by female "pole kittens" who volunteered from Polarity Pole Dance Performances (Victoria, 2013). The float was flanked by swarms of nearly nude women marching alongside. A couple of women were holding signs that featured pictures of the cats available to rescue, but in the pictures later shared on their social networking site, the cats are barely noticeable in the hullabaloo of the mobile pole dancing stage (Wrenn, 2013e).

The Israeli Nonhuman Animal rights organization 269 Life, once staged a public demonstration that combines female nudity with graphic violence in protest of dairy production, which was videotaped and later published on its YouTube account (Grinberg, 2013). In the video, a group of women huddle on the sidewalk, one of whom is cradling a baby. Three men dressed in black and wearing ski masks enter the scene and pull the woman and baby away from the others. The baby is then taken from the mother, who then begins screaming. They place the baby in a small enclosure on the ground (meant to represent a calf hutch). The mother is in hysterics and desperate for her child (who, incidentally, is a real, live infant). The assailants grab her and forcibly remove her blouse, exposing her breasts. One man grabs a breast and attaches a milk pump. As he pumps her, blood streams down her chest and she screams. When they are done, the three men push her down to the sidewalk and beat her before placing a lead around her head and dragging her by the neck to a waiting van.

PETA, PETA UK, and PETA France often stage public demonstrations against foie gras consumption, which characteristically feature women acting as the avian victim and men as the assaulter. This role assignment is important: ducks killed for foie gras tend to be male, but women are the natural representatives given their similarly devalued status. Publicity photographs abound in various internet news sources that document young female demonstrators' reenacting the pain and threat of death faced by ducks in the industry. The woman's entire body is either bound with rope or she is forced on her knees by a man above her, who pushes her head down. In one photograph, a bound woman lies face down in a pool of vomit and blood, apparently "dead" from the mock force feedings (Lepic, 2012). In a photograph from another demonstration, a woman stares fearfully into the camera, her hands tied behind her back, as she is being force-fed from a large tube that the man above her is holding (Hutchinson, 2013). The similarities between this frightened young woman on her knees in front of a male aggressor and "gagging" gonzo porn[5] are distinct. In some demonstrations, fake blood trickles from the over-stretched mouths of the female victims (Usborne, 2013). Engaging female volunteers to portray victims of violence, often in a sexualized manner, seems to be endemic to tactical design across the movement. Organizations pull on clear social scripts of misogyny and sexism in order for the campaigns to make sense to the audience. It is disingenuous to frame participation of this kind as empowering for women or other animals.

Kim Socha rightfully observes that "exploiting women is an unethical and callous way to market animal liberation" (2013b, p.58). More than unethical, it is also ineffectual. Importantly, there is currently no evidence to suggest that this type of advocacy is effective in promoting veganism and anti-speciesism. Recall that empirical research has shown that sexualized images of women *reduce* support for Nonhuman Animal ethics campaigns. This type of advocacy perpetuates because PETA, the largest and most successful organization (if success is defined by longevity, donations, and membership), has legitimated sexual objectification as a normal and acceptable tactic for Nonhuman Animal liberation efforts. Other organizations and advocates follow suit because this approach has become a taken-for-granted norm in Nonhuman Animal activism. It is done because it has always been done that way, at least in the recent memory of the modern movement. It has become a comfortable, familiar approach.

Vegan pornography

In an opinion piece for *Pacific Standard*, McWilliams writes: "If attractive women and men want to use their good looks to make the world a better place for animals, I'm willing to step aside and let them pose with seduction until their hearts are content" (2013b). These tactics, however, involve more than the content of individual activists. The price of posing with seduction falls squarely on women as a class of vulnerable persons. Furthermore, this price is unequally distributed among women. Recall that women of color, poor women, and abused women are especially burdened. Again, as of this writing, there is no research of which I am aware that demonstrates a correlation between sexually objectifying female-identified volunteers and increased anti-speciesist attitudes, but there *is* copious evidence to support the link between the sexual objectification of women, increased and *normalized* sexist attitudes, and violence against women (Dines, 2010; Dworkin, 1981; Szymanski et al., 2011). Sexual objectification strips women of their personhood. They become commodities and resources for the convenience of those in power. In this way, the experience of women is not unlike that of other animals. Given the similarities of their oppressed states of being, it is unclear how the aggravation of women's objectification could ever seriously challenge the objectification of Nonhuman Animals (Glasser, 2011; Hall, 2010, pp.237–43).

Pornography is a highly contested term that is generally taken to mean the domination, degradation, and humiliation of the feminine for male pleasure and male consumption in the service of reinforcing male supremacy (Jensen, 2007, pp.51–9). Catharine Mackinnon and Andrea Dworkin define it as a matter of civil rights: "Pornography is a form of discrimination on the basis of sex. [...] Pornography is sexually explicit subordination of women, graphically depicted, whether in pictures or in words" (1997, p.427). Pornography, then, is more than nudity and sex. It reaches beyond sexual objectification, existing as a form of systemic violence. For this reason, pornography's domination over the landscape of Nonhuman Animal rights advocacy is unscrupulous. Women's bodies are put on display for public consumption in a way that uses a very paradoxical logic: the movement invites society's privileged to consume and overpower female-identified advocates in order to tap into the language of patriarchy with the hope of persuading viewers to *not* consume and overpower *other* animals.

Importantly, some organizations display women not only for male consumption but for female consumption as well. It is as though the display of sexually objectified vegan women will convince other women – who are placed in competition with one another for men's attention[6] – that veganism is a means to achieve the perfect, sexually desirable body. Photography-based advocacy groups like vGirls|vGuys and Vegan Pinup host pornographic images of women in various degrees of undress and suggestive pose. The claim is that the images are intended to combat the stereotype that vegans are pale, weak, unhealthy, and unattractive (Meinberg, no date; vGirls|vGuys, 2014). The pornification of veganism is likely not coincidental. Because veganism is feminized in a way that challenges male dominance (it necessitates the rejection of patriarchal products and practices produced through exploitation), veganism thus becomes a site of female liberation. To combat the egalitarian potential of vegan feminist liberation, patriarchal institutions have reframed veganism as something sickly and ugly despite ample research that demonstrates the healthfulness and vitality associated with plant-based diets. The Nonhuman Animal rights movement has responded, not by reasserting the feminine power of veganism, but by subverting that power and applying the language of patriarchy: veganism is *sexy*. Vegan women are not portrayed as anti-patriarchal dissenters. Instead, they are actually super-feminized, more voluptuous, and more enticing: "vegans taste better." Not surprisingly, body-policing has become ubiquitous to the movement as a result.

No longer a site of radical social change, veganism has become one more space for patriarchal co-optation. The liberation of women and other animals is decentered when veganism is framed as a means of achieving a body that is desirable to men. When a woman advocates for other animals unclothed, veganism is repackaged in a way that removes the threat of feminine power. She is in her underwear or naked. She is alone or nearly alone (never representing a movement, in the age of individualism, she represents only herself). She is vulnerable. She is presented for male consumption. A collective mass of empowered women demanding equality is a threat, but a series of *individuals* who understand "empowerment" to mean standing on a street corner in lingerie while distributing non-dairy ice cream treats is *not* a threat to ogling men. Really, they are no threat at all. Instead, they become another niche demographic of "exotic" women to fulfill the male desire for unusual, unique, and conquerable women. In Portland, Oregon, voyeurs can even visit a vegan strip club where "liberated" plant-based women dance nude under the male gaze, squarely within the patriarchal confines of female objectification. As owner Johnny Diablo describes it to *The Oregonian*, "We're all about love and compassion" (Zacchino, 2013).

The pornification of Nonhuman Animal rights activism is not congruent with abolitionist goals. Violent and sexualized portrayals of women in media negatively influence the social status of women. While advocates who engage in these sexualized campaigns are performing specific gender scripts intended for the male gaze, it is important to recognize that very little control rests with female participants. Media producers are largely male. The Nonhuman Animal rights movement is primarily male-led (Gaarder, 2011, p.87, Kheel, 1985, p.4), meaning that most of the movement's media producers are also male. Men are creating media, which in turn creates culture and meaning. Through this process, patriarchal control is preserved while threats are diminished. The influence of male-led media campaigning has been cited as being responsible for considerable feminist backlash (hooks, 1994; Lindsey, 2011, pp.17–20). Those who create media do not haphazardly collect images and indiscriminately relay what they have captured. Media producers strategically interpret the social world and portray their own version of events. A particular and intentional message is being conveyed.

The anti-feminist media campaign infiltrates activist spaces as well. No longer are women strong warriors for social justice; they are sexually available "lettuce ladies" and "cabbage chicks:" naked, voluptuous, and inviting. The sexual objectification of women in Nonhuman Animal rights media warps their agency. They are reduced to walking advertisements, living billboards, and breathing bait. Instead of leading protests, hosting podcasts, lecturing, writing theory, managing online communities, or creating outreach material, women are instead encouraged to take their clothes off and glue leaves to their breasts, perform strip teases for parades and "gentlemen's clubs," or reenact horrific scenes of rape and murder in street demonstrations. Instead of channeling women into vitally important and rewarding social movement work that maintains their dignity and bodily integrity, Nonhuman Animal rights media grooms new volunteers into associating activism with pornographic performances of female subservience. This is not to say that in a mostly female movement, women have not been performing these integral social movement roles,[7] but those roles go largely unacknowledged and uncelebrated. In an effort to avoid the stigmatization of feminine empowerment, the Nonhuman Animal rights movement presents women's desire for social change within obfuscating patriarchal packaging. The movement speaks the language of male supremacy with the irrational expectation of ending oppression by capitulating to oppression.

As another example of this strategy, PETA protested the 2013 National Buffalo Wing Festival by issuing a press release that urged the festival, not to spare the chickens per se, but to "keep pregnant women out for the sake of their sons' sex organs." Before any mention of chicken suffering, PETA builds a case for penis protection, citing scientific research linking penis size to chicken consumption: "consuming poultry while pregnant may lead to birth defects *in utero*, including smaller-than-average penises for newborn boys. I think we can agree that embarrassment and insecurity are no *small* matters" (PETA, 2013). But, according to PETA, the stunting of penis growth from chicken consumption is not just a matter of male ego; it is hurting women as well. Rajt, warns that "evidence indicates that heterosexual women's sexual satisfaction depends in part on their partner's penis size."

There are a lot of reasons not to consume the flesh of chickens. The practice is devastating and unjust for the chickens exploited and killed. It is also hugely detrimental to human health and the environment. PETA only briefly alludes to these issues, instead choosing to frame veganism as a means of ensuring large penises for unborn baby boys and the sexual satisfaction of their future intimate partners.[8] Presumably, the language of social justice is not expected to resonate as well as the language of masculinity. PETA's androcentric approach prioritizes men's egos and treats both chickens and women (mothers and future sex partners) as secondary subjects. Such a framework necessarily excludes many homosexual women. It also incorrectly suggests that penile penetration is either the most normal or superior sexual act. By normalizing the male experience in sexual intercourse, the female experience is pushed aside as secondary or unimportant. A feminist perspective might suggest that clitoral stimulation is the embodiment or epitome of sexual intercourse rather than penile stimulation, but PETA's protest speaks primarily to patriarchy. Penis size is linked to masculine power, a power reserved for men and denied to cis-women (and many transgender and intersex individuals). By implying that men can have larger penises (and thus more power) by adopting a vegan diet, PETA is reinforcing male supremacy as normal, natural, and desirable.

Androcentric advocacy is also present in its British billboard, depicting a shocked and wide-eyed looking woman covered in a chunky white substance that reads, "Some bodily fluids are bad for you. Don't swallow. Ditch dairy" (Sabin, 2014). The message is a pun that references the practice of swallowing ejaculate following oral sex, while the image simulates a popular sex act in pornography that involves men ejaculating on women's faces. Otherwise known as the "money shot," it is an act that sexualizes the subjugation, dehumanization, and humiliation of women for the gratification of men (Jensen, 2007, p.69). Linking sex with domination is a dangerous recipe for a movement operating within a rape culture. Instead of working to dismantle systems of oppression through social justice claimsmaking, these male-centered tactics reinforce that oppression by prioritizing male sexual prowess and by pandering to patriarchy. It is this same deference to male sexuality that has facilitated large-scale violence against women and other animals. By paying homage to male dominance, the Nonhuman Animal rights movement erases from view the structural oppression against feminized and vulnerable social groups.

The Nonhuman Animal rights movement accommodates a very muddled feminist philosophy. Sexism is a serious problem at the societal level, and this seems to have seeped into social justice movements, standing in direct conflict with their anti-oppression ethos. A strong feminist theory must be integral to a rational approach to Nonhuman Animal liberation. Because women comprise the majority of the movement and act as an important base of power, creativity, and innovation, it would certainly be irrational to ignore the structural inequalities that inhibit female potential. Strangely, though, the importance of feminist theory is rejected not only in many mainstream advocacy spaces but also in some vegan rationality spaces. Feminist studies are sometimes thought to exist outside of evidence, representing only a philosophical perspective. Unfortunately, in a male-led movement, it is to be expected that male-led science is favored. On one hand, the movement's sexism hinders women's potential in relegating them to sex objects, while, on the other, feminist theory is devalued in favor of the masculine rhetoric of reason and rationality.

Patriarchy and the production of knowledge and reality

A rational approach to Nonhuman Animal rights will necessitate an eradication of tactics that sexually objectify women. Objectifying women is empirically ineffectual but also counterintuitive as a philosophical matter. It is also possible that these tactics facilitate a culture of misogyny and erode the status of women. However, a rational approach to advocacy must also consider how science and rationality are institutions of social control that have also posed a threat to the well-being of women and other animals. They can also work to devalue disabled groups who may not meet up to a socially constructed standard of rational thinking in a world that privileges the able bodied. Applying rationality to social justice spaces, then, must be done with the utmost care and with a recognition that the rationality project is itself not impervious to irrationality. Just as rationality can sour social change organizations (as was explained in Chapter 2), it also threatens social change values.

As a patriarchal space, the Nonhuman Animal rights movement generally values the masculine and devalues the feminine. While considerable claimsmaking of the late 19th century and early 20th century insisted on science and evidence as foundational to Nonhuman Animal rights efforts, there is reason to believe that this position may have represented the male-led movement's attempt to avoid the stigma of association with women's suffrage efforts (Leneman, 1997, p.281). Many female activists identified feminism and vegetarianism as politically congruent and were actively involved in both movements. Compounding the public's distrust with women's empowerment was the discrediting anti-science position taken by some feminists who advocated for other animals, notably Francis Cobbe (Mitchel, 2004, p.278). Already a movement "tainted" by feminine associations, the Nonhuman Animal rights movement may have been seeking to avoid the anti-science position that was also associated with women's campaigning. In other words, the Nonhuman Animal rights movement's early support for rationality may represent an intentional distancing from feminism. Therefore, rational Nonhuman Animal rights advocacy must be cognizant of how epistemologies of rationality act as a double-edged sword. Rationality can hurt as much as it helps depending on the intentions and awareness of those who wield it. It is important, then, to acknowledge its history of use in a patriarchal society and to recognize its subsequent limitations before it can be appropriately applied to advocacy. This is *especially* so in a movement that is mostly female-identified.

Both culture and knowledge are created by those in power. Under a patriarchy, it is men privileged with power who are then privileged with the ability to create social reality. Men are the lawmakers, the law protectors, the researchers, the professors, the media creators, the CEOs, and the politicians. Men dominate all areas of institutional power and knowledge production. Knowledge is male (Smith, 1990, p.13) (and white for that matter) (Collins, 2013, p.101; Zuberi and Bonilla-Silva, 2008). Men are socialized to see themselves as knowers, and everyone else is *also* socialized to view men as the knowers. Language is an important manifestation of this male supremacy, as it has the ability to shape culture and create meaning. Words, labels, and definitions can empower and include some while ostracizing and excluding others:

> men have the power of naming, a great and sublime power. This power of naming enables men to define experience, to articulate boundaries and values, to designate to each thing its realm and qualities, to determine what can and cannot be expressed, to control perception itself. (Dworkin, 1981, p.17)

Men, with the power to name, have named the hard sciences the one true science, and the "rational" (in other words, *male*) experience as the one true experience. What is perceived to be true, real, or objective must necessarily be perceived through the masculine scientific lens (Smith, 1990). Sociologist Patricia Hill Collins notes that society's elite produce "theory," while everyone else simply engages in mere "thought," "folk wisdom," or "raw experience": "elites possess the power to legitimate the knowledge that they define as theory as being universal, normative, and ideal" (1998, xiii). She urges readers to recognize how taken-for-granted views of "truth" are shaped and limited by the possession or absence of power.

Not only is feminism as a field of study dismissed as inherently unscientific, but male supremacy has demonized the very word. As a result, the "F Word" is almost an insult. Women become alienated from their own culture. They are encouraged to abandon woman-centric approaches and absorb and celebrate androcentric norms and ideals. The male perspective becomes the default for "legitimate" knowledge and values (Vance, 1993). Social control is at its strongest when an oppressed group rejects its own values in favor of that of the oppressor: it is cultural genocide, colonization, and domination. The masculine approach to knowledge and truth is held up as the ideal to which all others should work to achieve. In order for the oppressed to be heard, they must conform to these standards. Ideas must be framed in "the language that is familiar and comfortable for a dominant group" (Collins, 2000, viii). This translation leaves marginalized ideas vulnerable to misinterpretation and co-optation.

They are also ripe for the picking. Researchers have coined a term for the male appropriation (and theft) of female ideas in the sciences: the "Matilda Effect." Following successful collaboration on a scientific project that results in the production of knowledge, those individuals who enjoy more social status will gain more of it from the collaboration, while those who have little social status will *lose* more of what little they have (Rossiter, 1993). Many important advancements in science were first developed by women to the benefit of privileged male scientists and scholars.[9] Despite the critical role that women play, it is *men* who enjoy the credit and acclaim for those ideas once packaged in a masculine framework and presented by the more credible male authority. Women's knowledge and contributions have been absolutely essential to many great scientific and social developments, but their participation is often downplayed, ignored, or forgotten. Male knowledge is also seen as the "natural" state of things. "Rationality" as it is understood in the masculine sense is seen as the only accurate account of reality that speaks for all and applies to all.

Power, politics, and science

Again, if social change actors hope to apply rationality to their advocacy, they must be cognizant of how rationality is embedded in gender oppression. Power rests in the ability to create meaning from the social world, and that meaning works to reproduce power (Bourdieu, 2005). It is not just the ability to create meaning that is relevant but also the power to create meaning in a way that is considered authentic and legitimate. Any opposition to this power to name and create meaning is susceptible to defamation and active marginalization. It is not that feminist theory lacks evidence; it is that feminist theory challenges a patriarchal system of power and male privilege. Those who reject the importance of critical feminist theory are often concerned with a utopian notion of scientific "purity," or "objectivity." It is as though the only real and valid knowledge that can be discovered is through the disciplines of physics, mathematics, biology, neuroscience, and so on. This androcentric view of rationality deems that the only reality is that which can be measured through quantification. It is no coincidence that the types of sciences that are deemed legitimate are also those dominated by men.

To strip from vulnerable populations the ability to interpret reality is to incapacitate them. To recognize the experiences and interpretations of those in power as the only valid incarnations is to coddle bias in a dishonest effort to reproduce inequality. A rational society not consumed by exploitative hierarchies of power might triangulate different ways of knowing in order to construct a more comprehensive understanding of the world. For this reason, Mary Midgley (2003, pp.37–41) argues that there are "many maps, many windows" to the pursuit of knowledge.

Critical of the scientific preoccupation with reductionism, she advises scholars to instead adopt scientific pluralism. The sexual politics of science will necessitate for social change workers an immediate suspicion of claims to universal knowledge.

The problem with objectivity

Writing on the nature of knowledge production, Paulo Freire insists: "To deny the importance of subjectivity in the process of transforming the world and history is naïve and simplistic. It is to admit the impossible: a world without people" (2006, p.50). So long as science is created by humans and conducted by humans (including computers and analysis programs, which are designed by humans), science is *never* value-free, though many scientists insist that it can be or should be. Importantly, science tends to be heavily entangled with economic interests. Even seemingly humanitarian pharmaceutical science that seeks to cure deadly diseases is often done in the interest of drug companies and the powerful industries that cause the diseases in the first place. Billions of dollars fund cancer research, for example, but pitifully little funding goes into preventative strategies such as improving access to good nutrition (Campbell, 2006, pp.249–50). Capitalist ventures have more to gain from supporting the science of cures and medications than prevention efforts.

Science is often utilized as a means of legitimizing ideology and inequality. The history of scientific inquiry has a sordid past regarding the exclusion of minorities and the justification of oppression. Science is often used to weigh in on the political. Take, for instance, the "debate" over global warming. While the scientific community almost universally agrees that the earth is heating up, that climate is changing, and that this is a direct result of human activity, many conservative groups have been funding a handful of rogue scientists who interpret the data in a way that suggests otherwise. While research shows that the consumption of Nonhuman Animal products is dangerous and deadly and that a plant-based diet is optimal for human health, scientific studies are commissioned by the flesh and dairy industries to fudge this reality. Yes, the scientific method is designed to remove bias, but 58 per cent of Americans do not believe global warming is related to human activity, and 31 per cent of Americans do not believe in global warming at all (Clement, 2013). Almost 98 per cent of Americans regularly consume Nonhuman Animal flesh, dairy, and eggs (Vegetarian Resource Group, 2011).[10] Dr. T. Colin Campbell documents the struggles with advocating sound nutrition science in his 2006 publication *The China Study*, demonstrating that industry influences are thorough and formidable. With enough political pressure and funding, science can "prove" just about anything, or at least encourage considerable support.

Science is a tool. It is a socially constructed institution that is intended to socialize and maintain existing power structures. Much like the media, the family, the educational system, organized religion, and other institutions, science is part of the project of patriarchy. The scientific method is intended to remove bias in procedure, but most lose sight of just *who* is able to earn the qualifications to conduct science and *whom* that science is done for. The story of science demonstrates that it is generally men who are encouraged to enter the sciences, it is generally male-dominated institutions that fund that science, and it is generally patriarchy that benefits from science. Science's interest in objectivity also reflects the anthropocentric and androcentric belief that humans can stand "outside" of nature when observing it, a concept that reinforces the arbitrary separation between humans and nonhumans and the subsequent stratification of species (Birke, 1994, pp.73–85). Objectivity cannot exist without otherizing. For that matter, "objectivity" tends to be a ruse for male subjectivity. That is, because patriarchal power structures benefit men, the ways in which male-identified persons see and experience the world are considered rational, evidence-based, and legitimate, while the opposite tends to be true of feminized groups (Tomm, 1987, pp.1–5).

Scientists are also influenced by their social environment. They choose what to study based on physical ability, funding, the popularity of the subject, the need for the data, and so on. Bias is unavoidable. The scientific method is designed to reduce bias, and in many cases (especially in laboratory settings), it can be reduced considerably. Yet, bias remains omnipresent in human conception and interpretation. Some scholars have even suggested that subjectivity is even desirable (Smith, 1990, pp.22–8; Vance, 1993, pp.135–40). The tendency to objectify subjects of study and to reduce phenomena into abstractions risks losing meaning (Midgley, 2008, pp.30–41).

Science and oppression

At this point, it should be clear that the scientific discipline is not without its problems. While science purports to value objectivity, the reality is that even scientists are products of their society and are never able to fully escape the associated biases. Sociology, for instance, is highly interested with social inequalities, yet speciesism remains relatively unexplored and oftentimes outright rejected as a legitimate area of interest (Peggs, 2013). This is not to say that Nonhuman Animals are not social actors in human society. Nor is it to suggest that other animals are incapable of experiencing social injustice. Sociologists, as scientists who interpret "reality" and construct knowledge, have declared, based on their own socially influenced prejudice, that Nonhuman Animals are categorically "different" (in other words, "lesser") and inconsequential. The illusion of objectivity obscures patriarchal interests with a veil of neutrality. Knowledge that works in the service of privileged interests is deemed value-free, whereas knowledge that works to dismantle systems of oppression is generally labeled as biased. Nonhuman Animal rights theory is no exception, as it tends to privilege male "science" over female "non-science" (Luke, 1995).[11]

Over the centuries of Western "progress," scientific institutions have tended to grant attention first to those who are considered of consequence (in other words, those who enjoy social power) and to gradually open the circle of concern in response to changing social values. Of course, vulnerable groups like women, disabled persons, persons of color, and other animals, have been horrifically exploited as test subjects in pursuit of said progress (Gruen, 1993, pp.65–90). While science certainly may have a part in determining positive social change, science will more often work to reinforce a pre-existing socially constructed reality. Like religion, education, and politics, science is an ideological instrument largely concerned with legitimizing the prevailing social order. Science has been used to differentiate the "other" since the inception of the American nation (Hammonds and Herzig, 2008), but the creation and reinforcement of race and gender differences made possible by the legitimizing language of science continues in modern times. For instance, sociobiology and the study of genetics and evolution are often used to support social inequality and oppressive ideologies.

Contemporary science is still very much gendered, and the scientific community continues to be a white-centric, male-dominated institution. According to a 2013 survey conducted by the National Science Foundation (2015), only 30 per cent of the science and engineering workforce was female-identified and only 30 per cent identified as persons of color. Gender socialization plays a predominant role in this segregation, but the scientific community itself is partly responsible for its reluctance to embrace diversity. Gross and Levitt (1994, p.131), for instance, argue that "multiethnic perspectives" brought in from affirmative action programs have little to offer science, insisting that the only discrimination that exists in the scientific community is against *white males* (p.110). Gross and Levitt demonstrate a post-feminist and post-racial position in suggesting that discrimination is no longer practiced nor condoned in the sciences. Science, in purporting to be wholly objective and value-free, is presumed to be exempt from the lowly prejudices of lay society. But scientists are still humans, of course, and thus apt to err. Gender status in particular will impact how one perceives discrimination. Research shows that women are more likely to recognize discrimination than are their male counterparts (Ecklund et al., 2012). One's gender, these researchers explain, overrides one's status as a scientist. Regardless of discriminatory behavior, male and female scientists conduct their work and their interactions in gendered ways, just as any humans would in this gendered society.

When scientists themselves cannot recognize how they, too, are prone to discrimination, it is evidence to the fallibility of the scientific discipline as well as the fallibility of humans. All humans are prone to bias, and the refusal to recognize this bias demonstrates the weakness present in even the most advanced scientific training. In not acknowledging personal shortcomings and impartiality, scientists allow extremely influential social systems to go unexamined in their research. This oversight can significantly skew results.

Feminist science

The scientific discipline has traditionally been used to reinforce the power of the privileged and to legitimate inequality. However, science differs from other tools of social control in one important aspect: the value of objectivity. True, science has oftentimes failed to achieve objectivity, with terrible consequences for vulnerable populations over the centuries, but at least science welcomes debate and opposition. It is here that feminism and scientific values might be reconciled for a rational approach to Nonhuman Animal rights. Both feminism and science theoretically seek to validate the experiences and opinions of everyone equally. These perspectives are, for the most part, compatible. Science, however, also demands accountability and evidence. Some experiences and opinions are simply impossible to validate. For instance, feminist sociology may seek to measure sexism in describing the gender ratios of important institutions, the wage gap, and health discrepancies between women and men. It may even seek to measure more nuanced forms of sexism in everyday interactions, such as male dominance in conversations and their tendency to take up more physical space. Yet, the intricacies of sexism and other forms of oppression are so complex that the entire picture could never fully be encapsulated. A *complete* picture may never be formed, but researchers can often fill in enough blanks to get a relatively *clear* picture.

Feminism can improve on science by challenging the hyper-focus on objectivity. While some things are "out there" and are able to be observed and measured, for us as cognitive beings, much of what is "real" to humans is actually subjectively experienced. Subjectivity is that which cannot be fully shared with others, that which can never be truly observed by others, and something that can never be completely measured. In other words, it is something that must be relayed by experience and narrative. Researchers can compensate by relying on outwardly measurable variables like verbal description. Respondents may lie, but scientists can supplement their narratives by examining objective social phenomena to support the data provided. Indeed, there are a number of methodological "tricks" that scientists utilize to increase the validity of qualitative data. These strategies include the manipulation of question wording, probing, personalizing the interview, or the utilization of focus groups. They may also supplement with surveys, historical analysis, fact-checking, and observation in the subject's environment. Ultimately, experiences will always be bound to the subjective. Researchers rely on the subject to convey the experience, and the researcher uses their own subjectivity to interpret that data. Humans are tools of measurement.

Scientific values *do* purport to demand neutrality and accuracy, and this is something social change actors can work with. By increasing female representation in the sciences (which will require encouragement and mentorship from an early age) and by taking an honest look at how bias is, for better or worse, inherent to science, advocates may be able to liberate science from its patriarchal barriers. Instead of upholding inequality, science can act as a prime contender in the fight for egalitarianism. Putting scholarship in the service of social justice should not be equated with the introduction of data-fuddling bias, because science always has an intended purpose. Advocates can make that purpose positive and transformative.

Social change workers who hope to apply rationality to their efforts cannot see bias as defeat. Instead, science that serves social justice should be seen as an application to questions that matter, questions that need answering, and questions that, if answered, have the potential to benefit society. *All* science is done with some interest in mind; *all* science is more or less biased. Knowledge is not simply "discovered"; it is *constructed* with some purpose in mind. Knowledge is embedded within narratives. Generally, it is the narratives of those in power that rise to importance, meaning that women, Nonhuman Animals, and other marginalized groups are silenced (Vance, 1995).[12]

Feminist scholars have argued that scientific values have tended to operate as a disguise for *patriarchal* values. Advocates should therefore be careful to apply these values in a way that transcends their long association with oppression. In doing so, scientific values can be resurrected and applied toward effective persuasion, analogies, tactics, and decision making. These values should *not* be used to aggravate gendered power differentials. That is, they should not be used to elevate men and exclude or devalue women and other feminized groups. Wielded appropriately, science can be a benefit to egalitarianism rather than an impediment to it.[13]

A feminist-positive approach to rationality in Nonhuman Animal rights

Within the social movement arena, gender inequality could be seen as especially volatile to those liberal movements which advocate equality and work to dismantle oppression. A movement that is co-opted with ethical and tactical compromise and illusionary female agency is not likely to achieve the radical change needed to eradicate injustice. The feminist movement, co-opted by the neoliberal notion of the individual and the patriarchal notion of liberated sexuality, has in many ways stagnated as sexual objectification becomes mainstream and radical feminist critique is viewed as an overreaction. The Nonhuman Animal rights movement becomes quite disoriented when it seeks to make Nonhuman Animal suffering sexy. Transformative collective action is betrayed by the enlistment of "empowered" female *individuals* in vegetable lingerie who seek to assert their personal identity and "agency" by performing oral sex on cucumbers or handing out crass stickers about their "pussies" in the name of anti-speciesism. There is nothing rational about combating the objectification of the underprivileged with the self-objectification of the slightly more privileged. Neither is it rational to dilute a *collective* in favor of *individual* "empowerment." A rational approach will necessitate a mass mobilization and a rejection of co-opted tactics. It will require the serious inclusion of women, not the patriarchy-friendly inclusion of volunteer sex objects.

Feminist sensitivities

The rational approach to Nonhuman Animal rights acknowledges that men and women exist in fundamentally different subcultures based on differences in gender socializations and subsequent differences in opportunity and access. Men and women experience differing amounts of social power. They are raised differently, they are treated differently, and they understand their world differently. There are different priorities, different necessities, and different challenges. Feminism is not concerned so much with erasing differences, but rather it is concerned with erasing the devaluation of difference. Recognizing the fundamental differences between "women" and "men" as socially constructed gender roles is not to resurrect biological determinism (indeed, feminism is inclusive to a variety of sexes, genders, and orientations). Nor does it seek to aggravate those socially constructed differences. Sensitivity to feminist experiences is urged because the *consequences* of this social construction are real. The negative consequences of reproducing harmful gender norms especially affect about 80 per cent of the Nonhuman Animal rights movement's activist base. For a movement that is already deeply patriarchal, a demand for rationality, science, and evidence (concepts generally reserved for men to the exclusion of women) could easily work to reinforce male-power and further devalue female activism.

Therefore, a rational approach to Nonhuman Animal rights *must* be inclusive of feminist principles. Criticizing Nonhuman Animal rights theory that "is developed within a framework of patriarchal norms, which includes the subordination of emotion to reason, the privileging of abstract principles of conduct, the perception of ethical discussion as a battle between adversaries, and the presumption that ethics should function as a means of social control," Brian Luke warns that vegans ignore the interconnectivity of masculine and feminine ways of knowing and advocating (1995, p.292). In a movement that is comprised mostly of women and seeks equality, maintaining a patriarchal social movement structure is inherently irrational. It does not stand to reason that advocates can dismantle oppression in the larger society when its own community protects that same oppression. A patriarchal social movement structure is also irrational if it discounts the power, creativity, and potential for innovation in its largest demographic. When 80 per cent of the movement's force is relegated to drudgery work, leaving theory and tactical development to an elite few, it is encumbering itself.

The rationality of egalitarianism

Social change actors should consider that equality is, on its surface, not a rational goal for those who would stand to lose their privilege. Egalitarianism, then, must be reframed in a manner that incorporates the interests of vulnerable groups fairly, but also entices those who already enjoy considerable social power. At the societal level, prejudice and discrimination are fundamentally irrational. Speciesism, patriarchy, and other systems of oppression tend to benefit a select few, but the procurement of this privilege involves the exploitation and subjugation of a disproportionately larger mass of people. Marx predicts that this volatile situation creates a great potential for revolution. Eventually, he supposes, the oppressed will develop a class consciousness and rise up to demand equality. Of course, this revolution is thus far unrealized. Oppressive social institutions draw much of their strength from an ability to self-legitimate and reproduce power. A primary support for these processes is the individual internalization of institutional power. This results in a self-disciplined population that controls itself and is either reluctant to or unable to recognize its oppression (Foucault, 1977). Even social movements have been co-opted by the state and elites. As explained in Chapter 2, the non-profit industrial complex ensures that organizations renounce their power and privacy in exchange for funding and acceptance, a trade that encourages self-policing and ultimately pits groups against one another in competition for scarce resources. Radical collectives are excluded and left to perish in the elements, facing resource starvation and state repression.

Indeed, society's elites have been very successful in establishing institutions of social control and suppressing the ability for social change and even the *desire* for that change. For these elites, there is substantial benefit at stake, meaning there is intense pressure to maintain structural and ideological control to protect the system of inequality that benefits them. A hierarchy of oppression is good news for a few persons and groups of privilege, but prejudice and discrimination are ultimately incompatible with a rational liberal state. A system that maintains power for some by removing opportunity and voice from the majority of the population is a system in which diversity, creativity, innovation, and the power in collaboration and cooperation are ultimately stifled. Despite hugely powerful methods of social control, the stresses of inequality will always feed dissention and civil unrest. Unchecked oppression creates a level of exploitation that is ultimately self-destructive.

A capitalist, male, elite-driven society may have difficulty recognizing the value in egalitarianism, but the scientific discipline, for the most part, recognizes the value in equal opportunity and diversity of both experience and background. As it is closely related to capitalism and patriarchy, science will still have trouble extrapolating values of egalitarianism from its long tradition of oppression. This is somewhat ironic, as it should be evident that science languishes when it is primarily conducted by that very small percentage of the population who enjoys the privilege necessary to participate. Many of the male elites who dominate science may defend their ability to speak on behalf of society, but a considerable number of scientists and feminists question the validity of such an approach. Equal opportunity and female representation in the sciences is critical for sound science.

Inequality is ultimately irrational. While it may be "rational" for elites and other persons of privilege to maintain systems of inequality for their immediate gain, these systems are ultimately unsustainable (Stiglitz, 2012). A predatory system that protects and privileges the few at the expense of the many actually impedes efficiency and growth. Inequality weakens the economy, increases political tension and upheaval, and erodes a sense of community. On the global scale as well as the national scale, inequality has been disruptive and is leading toward environmental collapse. As demonstrated in Chapter 2, inequality reduces efficiency at the social movement level as well. Careerists in the Nonhuman Animal rights industrial complex (many of whom are men and most of whom are white) certainly benefit from the inequality that protects their positions, but the movement in general benefits from maintaining inequality in regard to fundraising and bureaucratic growth. The logic of organizational growth, however, is often at odds with effective liberation strategies.

Social inequality supports the non-profit system. The non-profit industrial complex creates a situation in which movement organizations are dependent upon the support and funding provided by society's most socially and economically privileged. Non-profits are deterred from pursuing serious social change by professionalizing; plans for radical societal restructuring repel their conservative funders. By operating under masculine approaches to collective action and by ascribing to white normativity, professionalized organizations are able to draw on resources that would otherwise be unobtainable. If the movement were to prioritize women, people of color, Nonhuman Animals, and other less attractive groups, for instance, perhaps many important funders would cease their support.

On the surface, then, maintaining social movement inequality may seem rational as a matter of organizational survival for those reliant on bureaucratic growth and financial support. In the long run, however, it is ultimately inefficient for a movement to alienate the public and its constituencies from oppressed groups, its largest demographic of potential support. If the Nonhuman Animal rights movement really seeks to achieve social change, relying on the benevolence of elites with conflicting interests will not accomplish it. Elite support works to adulterate social change efforts by actually *replicating* the inequality that benefits those elites. If advocates were to challenge oppressive ideologies that taint collective action efforts, they could significantly expand their reach. Minorities may not be able to grant millions of dollars, donate an estate, or lend celebrity support, but they will ultimately wield the greatest power through sheer numbers and their variety of skills. A handful of privileged persons who pour money into professionalized non-profits (which, in turn, fund repellant, sexist tactics) will not have anywhere near the impact of several million people recognizing their own power by going vegan, joining grassroots efforts, and creating their own community mobilizations.

The arrogance of science has always been its greatest weakness. The moment that scientists presume an answer solved and shut the door on alternative interpretations or contending evidence, bias triumphs and the scientific method ceases to function properly. When scientists insist that there is only *one way* of exploring reality, they have erected blinders that reduce their view to a space so narrow that the results of their research cannot be trusted as reasonably valid. Similarly, advocates need to look beyond androcentric ways of knowing in their advocacy for other animals. The Nonhuman Animal rights movement needs to appreciate how women can contribute to social movement mobilization beyond the presentation of their naked bodies for the male gaze. A rational approach to advocacy on behalf of other animals must be an intersectional one.

To put science and rationality in the service of social change, activists would do well to emphasize three points. First, science should be embedded within critical feminist theory. Because institutions of rationality have historically been used to create, aggravate, and naturalize systematic violence against vulnerable populations, it is important that this history be acknowledged and transcended. A conscious and reflexive application of rationality will be required to accomplish this. Second, inequality is irrational. That is, inequality might be superficially rational for those who benefit from it, but because it disenfranchises large groups of persons (both human and nonhuman), it is ultimately restrictive, inefficient, and unsustainable, and it erodes quality of life (Bone, 2010). Social psychological research demonstrates that human predispositions toward irrational behavior have *normalized* many of these problematic structures (Ariely, 2008, xx). However, as social animals, humans are also wired for many moral, cooperative behaviors (Bloom, 2013; Harris, 2010). *This* is the science advocates should embrace: the science of equality. Finally, mobilizing a large and diverse group of activists and resonating with a large and diverse body of constituents will be essential for effective, lasting, and large-scale social change work. The next chapter expands this requirement beyond the gender variable and argues that incorporating the interests of people of color will also be essential to a rational, effective approach to abolition.

5
Problematizing Post-Race Ideology

In the previous chapter, the objectification of women in Nonhuman Animal rights spaces was argued to be ineffectual and theoretically counterintuitive. This chapter will extend this critique and address the perpetuation of race and ethnicity bias in social movement mobilization. A rational approach will necessitate a serious acknowledgment of racialized differences and discrimination. Harper (2010a) notes that Nonhuman Animal rights advocacy generally operates according to post-race ideology (the notion that race is no longer a significant variable), which likely reflects the white majority of its membership. This chapter will extend her critique and build a case for a race-sensitive vegan abolitionism. A rational approach to Nonhuman Animal liberation must be cognizant of continuing racial inequality to achieve effectiveness and theoretical consistency.

The invisibility of race in Nonhuman Animal advocacy

In 2013 a group of Israeli advocates launched "Non-Humans First!" – a campaign that boasted the international support from several organizations and prominent activists. It is a project that seeks to prioritize the needs of Nonhuman Animals; they are thought to be in a "state of emergency." Humans, they argue, can fight their own battles; Nonhuman Animals need advocates' undivided attention. In the declaration, they insist: "No tactical idea should be excluded from the discussion based on its conflict with human rights ideology."[1] Indeed, they suggest that human "ideologies and interests" have no place in advocacy on behalf of other animals.[2]

Vegan Soapbox, a popular activist blog operated by a Vegan Outreach volunteer, followed up on this campaign with an essay suggesting that human rights advocacy and nonhuman rights advocacy are fundamentally incompatible: "There's not enough time in the day to work on all issues that need attention. There is not enough money in the movement to work on all the issues that need attention. We have to choose. We have to focus" (Vigneault, 2013). This sentiment appears to be a common one, with many advocates believing that intersectional advocacy work is a drain on resources or that human oppression is distinct from that of other animals. The Nonhuman Animal rights movement is predominantly white, middle-class, and well-educated (Maurer, 2002, pp.8–11; Socha and Blum, 2013, p.4). The incredible privilege afforded to most Nonhuman Animal rights advocates influences what tactics and theory are prioritized and what at-risk groups are designated as worthy of attention. Because activists with relative privilege are not pressed to recognize the suffering of other humans, they oftentimes reject the need for human rights advocacy and may even portray it as existing in direct conflict with vegan outreach.

Veganism, as a political project, is a white and Western conception. The history of the anti-speciesism movement is largely understood to have been developed by white men in the 19th century, and it later progressed by the white male theory of ethicists such as Singer, Regan, Ryder, Francione, and others. Indeed, the term "veganism" and the modern vegan movement are attributed to British white male Donald Watson (Marcus, 2011, no pagination; Phelps, 2007, p.165). While it may be true that veganism as a *political* movement is largely attributable to Western whites, this widely accepted history of veganism, for the most part, ignores the contributions of people of color who have been adhering to plant-based diets for thousands of years.[3] Indeed, approaches to veganism that are bound to the traditions and cultures of people of color are largely deemed illegitimate (Harris, 2013). Instead, whites are credited with "inventing" veganism, while the experiences of people of color are diminished with white-centric claimsmaking, a history of Western colonialism, and ongoing institutionalized discrimination.

Racist repertoires

People of color are largely excluded from the vegan community, but they also serve as "scapegoats" for advocacy organizations that seek to otherize Nonhuman Animal exploiters to create a community of members and donors who see themselves as saviors and "good guys" (Yarbrough, 2013). Demonizing people of color makes for easy advocacy in a discriminatory social environment that already views them as lesser. It allows for easy victories for organizations to campaign behind. For instance, Nonhuman Animal rights organizations often utilize undercover video in slaughterhouses and other exploitative industries to document egregious "abuses."[4] These videos are used to press charges against the employees involved, and the organization can then promote the "victory" with heavy encouragements for members and other viewers to donate. Employees are criminalized as abusers, and organizations claim that Nonhuman Animals are thus rescued following this intervention. In order to continue criminalizing said abusers, the organizations request more money from constituencies.

Campaigns of this kind are not race neutral. The people employed in birds' eggs facilities, slaughterhouses, and other industrialized Nonhuman Animal enterprises are disproportionately people of color, illiterate and impoverished persons, undocumented workers, and nonnative citizens. The working conditions in these facilities are especially dangerous. "Meat" processing has rates of injury and illness that are some of the highest of any industry. In 2003, about 11 such cases were reported among every 100 employees (Kandel, 2009, p.9), a number less than half that of just a decade earlier (US Government Accountability Office, 2005, p.26). These numbers are much lower than actual cases, as the industry is notorious for suppressing reports (Human Rights Watch, 2004, p.4; Schlosser, 2001, p.174). There is considerable pressure on the industry to tamper with the numbers, as the jobs are so incredibly dangerous. Obscuring injury and illness is accomplished with false recordkeeping, intimidation, low rates of employee literacy and language fluency, and fear of penalization, termination, or deportation.

Employees suffer injuries related to repetitive motions, prolonged exposure to high or low temperatures, slips in moist conditions, bruising from machinery and struggling animals, deep cuts, disfigurement, amputation, burns, and respiratory ailments from exposure to chemicals and pathogens, and many are even killed (US Government Accountability Office, 2005, pp.21–4). Workers are sometimes physically enslaved when they are held against their will over several days and nights in the facilities. Women experience extremely high rates of sexual harassment, sexual assault, and rape (Bergman, 2013). The nationwide average monthly turnover rate for all industry is only 3.1 per cent (US Bureau of Labor Statistics, 2013), but it can be as high as 6–8 per cent for "meat" processing plants (Stull and Broadway, 1995, p.69). In the first year of operation, "meat" plants average a turnover rate that exceeds 200 per cent (Broadway, 2000, p.39). Thereafter, these plants maintain extremely high turnover rates. Between 72 and 96 per cent annual turnover is thought acceptable (Stull and Broadway, 1995, p.69). This instability is thought to work to the industry's advantage, as the workers' ability to organize for better working conditions and pay are significantly reduced (Schlosser, 2001, p.161). Employers also avoid having to disperse expensive benefits, which are allotted only to those who are employed for a certain length of time (Stull and Broadway, 1995, p.70).

Clearly, these are not exactly pleasant working conditions; employees working in Nonhuman Animal industries are almost as oppressed as the Nonhuman Animals themselves. It seems cruel to target these vulnerable and suffering humans for the sake of organizational fundraising. For that matter, such an approach is contradictory to anti-oppression work. Hall explains:

> ... locking up people for handling their animals improperly doesn't change the world. It reinforces the idea that cages and control are the answer to life's problems, while missing the real issue—that we think it acceptable to be the keepers of other animals—and suggests that everyone should just listen to experts to learn how to properly keep them." (2010, pp.33–4)

Campaigns that target the extremely vulnerable employees of slaughterhouses, dairies, piggeries, and many other speciesist industries are not only racist and classist but also theoretically counterintuitive.

Nonhuman Animal advocacy tactics that target industry employees individualize Nonhuman Animal exploitation and relieve viewers from feeling immediately responsible for the industries existing in the first place. Rather than encouraging viewers to consider how their food, clothing, and entertainment choices support and perpetuate these oppressive systems, and rather than framing Nonhuman Animal oppression as *institutionalized* and *systemic*, they are persuaded to view violence against other animals as something done by "those people." It is violence that can be "fixed" if those people could only be disciplined, punished, and rehabilitated. The white-led Nonhuman Animal rights movement thus exploits members of disadvantaged groups to appeal to a privileged white constituency. In doing so, the suffering of vulnerable humans and the *systems* of oppression that hurt humans and nonhumans alike go unseen.

Empty rhetoric

Professionalized organizations have not performed well in the pursuit of disrupting oppression, but the abolitionist faction[5] of Nonhuman Animal rights activism, despite its long history of cooperation and appropriation, also appears to have a relatively incoherent understanding of racial inequality and anti-discriminatory efforts. Pandemic racial and ethnic insensitivity is rooted in the movement's history. Nonhuman Animal rights activism grew with the anti-slavery movement of the 18th and 19th centuries, with many early theorists advocating for the abolition of nonhuman slavery via the rhetoric of human anti-slavery efforts. Today, that tradition continues in modern conceptions of vegan abolitionism (Wrenn, 2013c, pp.178–81). In Francione's debate with Robert Garner, Francione explains:

> The rights position as I propose it maintains that [...] we cannot make meaningful distinctions between the quality of sentient experiences between humans and nonhumans that would justify imposing any pain and suffering on nonhumans incidental to our use of them as our resources, any more than we can make such distinctions between or among humans for the purpose of justifying slavery or otherwise treating humans exclusively as resources. (2010, pp.24–5)

Francione positions the modern vegan abolitionist approach within the framework of human emancipatory efforts. In doing so, he is careful to recognize the intersectionality of human and nonhuman oppression. His abolitionist theory argues that Nonhuman Animal exploitation is just as morally unjustifiable and irrational as human exploitation. Indeed, he is often outspoken against human rights violations, insisting that respect for human struggles is as important to Nonhuman Animal rights advocacy as anti-speciesism.

Nibert (2002; 2013), too, has centered intersectionality in his theory of Nonhuman Animal liberation, arguing that human and Nonhuman Animal oppression are not only related but indeed entangled. Nonhuman Animal oppression cannot be abolished so long as human oppression goes unchecked. Nibert argues that human and nonhuman oppression emerged almost simultaneously thousands of years ago when humans abandoned egalitarian, communal gathering and adopted a "hunting" economy. The two oppressions continue to reinforce and aggravate one another today (2002, pp.21–4). Sociologists point to the mode of production as the impetus for the shaping of social structure, a structure that subsequently systematizes the exploitation of vulnerable groups. Dismantling oppressive structures will be necessary to help Nonhuman Animals, but included in this process is the need to emancipate suffering *humans* as well.

Vegan abolitionism, then, *in theory* supports an intersectional approach, one that rejects violence against humans and seeks emancipation for all sentient beings, human and nonhuman alike. Unfortunately, *in practice*, it seems that vegan abolitionist rhetoric too often falls flat. By way of an example, in September of 2013, Harper, who spearheads the discourse on white supremacy in Nonhuman Animal rights mobilization and the subsequent marginalization of people of color, hosted her first web conference on "Embodied and Critical Perspectives on Veganism by Black Women and Allies." Several organizations and prominent individuals promoted the conference, including Raw Girl Toxic World, The Curvy Vegan, Crunk Feminist Collective, Healthy Black Women, Byron Hurt, and Carol Adams. It was sponsored by the Food Empowerment Project, A Well-Fed World, VegFund, *T.O.F.U. Magazine*, The Vegan Society, and Vine Sanctuary. Conspicuously absent were the Francionian abolitionist groups. The Black Lives Matter movement of 2014 seems to have created discomfort in white-dominated abolitionist spaces as well. After sharing anti-racism campaigning material in the wake of Ferguson protests, The Abolitionist Vegan Society reports having lost a large number of subscribers on social media platforms. The group also received a number of indignant correspondences from readers who insisted that the focus remain on Nonhuman Animals. One volunteer even disassociated in protest.[6]

Nonetheless, abolitionist groups routinely post information about human-inclusive anti-oppression issues on their promotional material and social networking sites and frequently engage intersectional rhetoric in their advocacy. People of color appear to be included in the abolitionist framework when it works to further an argument, but they are ultimately excluded from abolitionist priorities and outreach efforts. Where it really matters, abolitionist theory can fail to deliver. Human emancipatory language creates a veneer in abolitionist spaces that masks a general lack in emancipatory *action*. There is very little cooperation with communities of color, outreach remains focused on privileged communities, and the abolitionist faction remains unsurprisingly dominated by whites. Harper and Ornelas (2013) refer to this phenomenon as "tokenizing." That is, Nonhuman Animal rights organizations may claim interest in dismantling systems of oppression against humans as well as nonhumans. In practice, however, they continue to operate according to white-centric, exclusionary tactics and claimsmaking. *True* intersectionality requires meaningful *action*.

This shortcoming has been documented in the feminist movement as well (Davis, 1983; hooks, 2015). Indeed, Black feminism is credited with developing the sociopolitical concept of intersectionality to address the complications presented by race and other identities that typically went unacknowledged in mainstream feminism. Collins explains that people of color are just as easily excluded from groups that "talk the talk" as they are from mainstream discriminatory society because these groups are so often hesitant to "walk the walk." She explains: "Another pattern of suppression lies in paying lip service to the need for diversity, but changing little about one's own practice" (2000, p.6). In fact, empty rhetoric may be just as detrimental as none at all. Advocates and organizations can point to their intersectionality claimsmaking and insist that they are indeed involved in inclusivity efforts and anti-oppression work. The meaningless slogans work to deflect criticism. The ideas are there, but the discourse is empty and social change stagnates. Real anti-oppression work will entail tactics that *include* rather than *exclude*.

As another example, abolitionist groups often publish food recipes with the intention of recruiting new vegans. The recipes are promoted as "cheap" and "easy," with the suggestion that anyone who believes that veganism is anything but must be intentionally resistant. These recipes often feature expensive and difficult-to-locate ingredients like tofu, nondairy milks, vegan "cheese," pure maple syrup, tempeh, olive or sesame oil, nutritional yeast, tamari, flax seeds, and Bragg's Liquid Aminos. Regularly purchasing many of these ingredients for everyday meals would break the bank for the millions who live near or under the poverty line. Recall from Chapter 3 that vegan food can be important for creating attitude or behavior change, but only if it resonates with the needs and interests of the audience. Too often, recipe campaigns fail to acknowledge that many of America's poor and persons of color live in food deserts where fresh water, fruit, and vegetables are difficult to locate, much less tofu and real maple syrup. Most food deserts are located in urban areas with high populations of people of color or in rural areas with high populations of Native Americans, Hispanics, and poor whites.

The scandalous release of the white-authored *Thug Kitchen Cookbook* (2014) also lends evidence to the cultural privileges of white vegan leaders and the movement's narrowly perceived audience. The project's appropriation of African American culture has been criticized as a form of minstrelsy and Blackface, with protest successfully shutting down some book launch events. The book, however, receives considerable support from a post-racial, white dominant Nonhuman Animal rights movement. The debates that ensued create considerable hurt and pain for people of color who are all too aware of the violent realities of a so-called post-racial America, a society where "thug" labels are used as powerful justifications for oppression (Harper, 2014). African American vegan chef and activist Bryant Terry (2014) explains in a piece for CNN that, being about more than cultural appropriation, the book also aggravates an inaccurate stereotype of unhealthy African American cuisine that obscures a long history of plant-based eating, much of which is linked to experiences in American slavery and sharecropping. Still, white readers do not seem to get it. *LA Weekly* reports: "Some Thug Kitchen fans and several food writers have wondered why everyone can't just focus on the food and not the politics" (Rashkin, 2014). This is what Harper has referred to as the *white normativity* of vegan outreach. Because the Nonhuman Animal rights movement is predominantly privileged (white and middle- to upper-middle-class), most advocates operate according to a white worldview. White-identified advocates might not recognize or may even reject that "thug" imagery remains closely tied with racial oppression. "Thug life" may be quirky and edgy for some but oppressive and deadly for others.

Again, white normativity in the movement also takes for granted access to fresh produce, exotic ingredients, and natural products. It often does not register that large chunks of society do not enjoy this basic privilege. This problem is evidenced in a *Vegan World Radio* interview with Francione (2012c), who states: "I mean you can get fruits, vegetables, and beans, and grains just about any place on the planet.... [T]his idea that [...] a vegan diet [...] is inaccessible to people is nonsense. [...] A healthy vegan diet is easily accessible to [...] everyone. [...] So it's easy to do." While plant-based staples do tend to be much cheaper, whether or not they are *available* is another matter altogether. At least 23.5 million Americans currently live in a food desert (US Department of Agriculture, 2009, pp.1–2). Again, it is a highly racialized issue, in which food deserts and food insecurity disproportionately impact communities of color (Elsheikh and Barhoum, 2013).[7] This is to say nothing of exploited third-world countries, many of which export food while their citizens face malnourishment and starvation (McMichael, 2008, p.108).

As another example of how white privilege obscures vegan outreach efficacy, a Humane Research Council (2011) study finds that most vegan outreach literature is written beyond the 11th grade reading level. Some even reach beyond college reading levels. This is disconcerting when one considers that the average US adult reads at just a 9th or 10th grade reading level. While Francione's "Animal Rights: The Abolitionist Approach" pamphlet is not included in the study, its heavy philosophical language suggests that it likely reads beyond the college level as well. This is something that should concern advocates interested in reaching the largest possible demographic. Literacy and education, like food access, also varies according to race, class, and nationality (Duncan and Murnane, 2011). Poor persons, persons of color, and non-native persons are all especially disadvantaged in educational access and literacy. The ideology of vegan outreach reflects white normativity, but it might also be true that the *language itself* works to exclude vulnerable groups.

Moral relativism and ideological colonization

It is unfortunate that Collins' critique of the exclusionary practices of white feminism appears to apply to Nonhuman Animal rights advocacy as well. Vegan advocates claim to value diversity in their ranks and in their constituency, but they have largely failed to employ these goals. The rigidity of white-centric, Western vegan theory is largely responsible for this barrier. For instance, wary of moral relativism, which might abscond some speciesist institutions, many abolitionists understand veganism to be a requirement for any community, including the vulnerable populations of developing nations with long histories of colonial exploitation by Western powers. Advocates of this persuasion may insist that Western Nonhuman Animal activists are morally obligated to intervene on speciesist injustices in non-Western regions. Moral relativism – the notion that morals are subjective and are dependent upon context and culture – acts as a powerful distraction for those who are encumbered by white or Western privilege. That is, moral relativism creates a panic over the possibility of some Nonhuman Animals going unacknowledged by social justice efforts. This privilege-induced alarm obscures the ability for social change workers to be mindful of imposing Western interests and ethics on regions devastated by Western expansion. Indeed, many of these regions experience great human and nonhuman suffering, not because of some innate immorality, but because their infrastructures have been decimated by Western capitalist imperialism. Recall that veganism is not a Western creation; it already existed in many cultures prior to Western infiltration. White impositions of morality teeter toward paternalism and can even come to recreate a colonialist relationship.

The vegan desire to police the world is a general reflection of the movement's historical association with the centuries-old project of Western conquest and domination. By way of example, many Nonhuman Animal rights groups target East Asia for what they see as particularly cruel Nonhuman Animal uses. Animal Equality and Last Chance for Animals campaign against dog and cat abattoirs in China (Sky News, 2013), while PETA's antivivisection campaigns often target Chinese laws that mandate animal testing for imported cosmetics (Kretzer, 2014). British musician and activist Morrissey once commented that the Chinese treatment of other animals has convinced him that "the Chinese are a subspecies" (Topping, 2010). Campaigns intended to alleviate violence against Nonhuman Animals in historically colonized regions have the potential to recreate Western imperialism. Animals Asia's "Friends not Food" campaign targets dog and cat slaughter in China, Korea, and elsewhere but does not advocate for the liberation of those species traditionally consumed by Westerners.[8] This is a strange omission given that the majority of Nonhuman Animal exploitation lies in the production of cows, pigs, and chickens to meet the soaring demand for "meat." Incidentally, the association between "meat," wealth, and modernity is often a product of Westernization and is aggravated by expanding Western fast food chains in the region. Animals Asia defends this exclusionary focus on dogs and cats by insisting these species are "inherently different in temperament and physiology to most domestic livestock species" (2012, p.7). It goes on to explain that animals "more commonly raised intensively for food" can be humanely slaughtered but dogs and cats cannot. The majority of the organization's staff (approximately 68 per cent) appears to be white and most of Animals Asia's offices are located in the West.[9] By normalizing Western speciesism in outreach material while simultaneously targeting those species who are beloved by Westerners but objectified in Asian countries, these campaigns work to replicate colonization through advocacy channels.

It is important to recognize that prior to Western infiltration and the rise of the neoliberal globalization, Chinese traditions were relatively inclusive of Nonhuman Animal interests. Chinese diets were primarily plant-based (and still continue to be in many rural areas) (Campbell, 2006, p.69). Additionally, some Buddhist traditions emphasized vegetarianism and opposed Nonhuman Animal exploitation (Phelps, 2004). Today, China hosts the largest percentage of vegans in the world, many of whom are vegans for ethical reasons rather than religious (Magistad, 2013). Nonhuman Animal suffering in Asia is not due to some innate "evil" in non-Western populations. The skyrocketing level of Nonhuman Animal exploitation in China (and other industrializing countries) is more accurately attributable to imposed Western cultural norms, the unrelenting pressure to accommodate capitalism, and the "humanitarian" efforts of international bodies such as the World Bank that have created food dependencies that support Western markets (Wrenn, 2011, pp.12–15). Because the Chinese have been more or less forced to conform to Western global capitalist culture and have been disconnected from traditional ways of life, oppression and suffering have expanded considerably.

Unfortunately, the long history of Western global domination and the associated cultural, political, and economic effects remain outside the consciousness of Western Nonhuman Animal rights collective efforts. These oppressions are by and large omitted from Western historical accounts, and the regions in question are usually geographically distanced and are populated by relatively powerless people who often lack the voice and ability to elicit the needed attention to their suffering. Just as privileged advocates in the United States may wrongly presume that access to healthy food and vegan options are universal to all Americans, advocates are also mistaken to presume that human rights, the ability to organize, and the privilege to extend attention beyond immediate matters of survival are universal advantages that extend beyond American borders. Global inequality complicates efforts to reduce suffering for nonhumans *and* humans. This is well illustrated in a correspondence between Harper (2013a) and a vegan of color living in post-apartheid South Africa who had embraced veganism as a means of decolonization. She reflects on her experiences with the white community's insistence that she frame her veganism as a matter of Nonhuman Animal ethics:

> These were spoiled and entitled people: They would not acknowledge sprawling townships that existed not too far beyond their high electric fences, where people of color still lived in tin shacks and used buckets as toilets. [...] it was altogether inconceivable that they would ever acknowledge that I experienced racism.

All too often, advocates perpetuate the neoliberal, white, and Western notion of morality, one that works to ideologically colonize populations who are already colonized politically, socially, and economically. The West has for many centuries colonized the developing world in search of natural resources, cheap or free labor, and new markets. Now, it seeks to colonize them anew with Western ideals of rights and morality under the assumption that non-Western spaces are inherently devoid of these values.

Neoliberal white morality can easily discourage people of color from joining social justice organizations. Collins writes of the feminist movement: "Theories advanced as being universally applicable to women as a group upon closer examination appear greatly limited by the White, middle-class, and Western origins of their proponents" (2000, pp.5–6). Harper has suggested that the same problem manifests among vegan activists and organizations. When white advocates insist that their morality is the only legitimate morality, it is easily interpreted as an insult to the lived experiences of underprivileged groups who are still struggling for their *own* rights. White-centric vegan advocacy thus becomes oppressive, offensive, and off-putting.

Overpopulation: The vegan solution

The anti-reproduction stance that many vegans espouse demonstrates another disconnect between white privilege and racialized global realities. Persons and organizations of this persuasion argue that the human population exists at dangerous levels and must be controlled. For instance, PETA submitted a proposal to the population control non-profit Population Connection, suggesting that it adopt a vegan program (what it calls "Plan V") to improve the efficacy of birth control (Lupkin, 2013).[10] In the discourse of global population, human growth is considered inherently detrimental to sentient life, ecosystems, and the survival of the planet. In his contribution to *Life on the Brink: Environmentalists Confront Overpopulation*, Paul Watson, founder of anti-whaling group the Sea Shepherd Conservation Society, writes:

> It all comes down to this: there are too many of us and too few of everything else. The solution is more of everything else – except cows, pigs, dogs, cats, and our other domestic animals – and fewer of us. [...] Intelligent and ecologically concerned people cut right to the chase and declare they will have no children. (2012, p.134)

Watson refers to those who can and do abstain from having children as "self-sacrificing" and "biocentrically oriented," while those who do have children are framed as "ecologically ignorant and anthropocentrically arrogant." Those countries he deems to be "overpopulated" he refers to as "less responsible." He is critical of social justice efforts in these areas for fear that they may increase consumption rates: "Alleviating poverty, promoting socialism or democracy, and empowering minorities are noble endeavors but irrelevant to the basic fact that resources are finite and there are limits to growth" (p.135). Instead, he suggests a policy that denies impoverished and "ignorant" families the right to have children.

Vegan procreation, too, is often framed as individual selfishness and inherently destructive. This position defaults to the neoliberal approach to social activism, one that understands social change to be an *individual* action and an *individual* responsibility. The terrible impact of human activity on the environment, however, is not so much an individualized issue but a *systemic* one. The capitalist project has sought to dramatically increase consumption, which has entailed astronomical levels of resource extraction and waste.[11] Products that are long-lasting, reusable, or multipurpose are not good for business growth, so a "throw away" culture is fostered instead. People are encouraged (and often forced) to consume in greater quantities, dispose of their consumptions, and then buy more. The ability to consume is also directly tied to socioeconomic status, meaning that most of the world's population lacks the privilege to consume much of anything at all. Focusing on the individual within this irrational system misses the true nature of the problem. Pushing responsibility on the individual, however, does serve the ideological function of relieving industries, elites, and oppressive systems of their culpability. Instead of working to deconstruct these destructive systems, *individuals* are told to reduce, recycle, reuse, and abstain from reproduction. But social change is not simply a culmination of individual actions. It is a collective endeavor that aims to reconfigure or deconstruct unequal and unjust social structures.

Furthermore, anti-natalism is not post-racial. While social change workers may insist that the campaign to end human reproduction cuts across all races and nationalities, the reality is that population growth is happening in third-world nations with non-white populations (Cohen, 2003, p.1174). The image conjured from the language of overpopulation is that of Black and Brown women in far off lands whose bodies must be controlled. The population control agenda does not promote empathy. Rather, it condones *coercion*, victim-blames, and obscures the oppressive structural issues responsible for those major social problems wrongly attributed to rising birth rates (Hartmann, 1995, pp.3–12). Communities of color and colonized regions have long and painful histories with forced sterilization (Bruinius, 2006; Davis, 2003). Deriving from the work of 19th-century theorist Thomas Malthus, population management is regularly employed as a tool of white imperialism and global capitalist agendas. Malthusian approaches single out population control as a means of alleviating the "problem" of poverty from the state and wealthy elites.

Compulsory sterilization policies have routinely been imposed on indigenous and impoverished women to comply with global lending agencies, such as USAID, that hold requirements for population control (Knudsen, 2006, pp.3–9). Sterilization entails dangerous operations that are often conducted by surgeons with minimal training and large workloads in unsanitary conditions. Many women are psychologically scarred and socially ostracized following the procedure. Thousands of women (and wanted fetuses) have also been injured and killed in the sterilization process. While anti-natalists aim for a universal application of their position, population politics in practice are highly gendered and racialized. Western populations are beginning to decline as birth rates in developed areas fall, so the attention has inevitably fallen on third-world communities of color. These are the same communities that have experienced hundreds of years of Western and white interference and control. Again, that environmental destruction is not so much a matter of population but rather a matter of elite-controlled *systemic* overconsumption and wastefulness. It is not communities of color in poor regions who have access to these behaviors but rather the wealthy, white-dominated "developed" nations. Most critiques of human reproduction are inappropriately post-racial, postcolonial, and even post-feminist. Vulnerable communities and female bodies are targeted as out-of-control regions in need of management by anti-speciesist activists who are fearful that increasing human populations will inevitably lead to more Nonhuman Animal suffering. But this fear is misdirected. Because the Nonhuman Animal rights movement is mostly white, Western, and androcentric, the social realities of women, communities of color, and non-Western regions are often absent from the consciousness of activists and their theory and tactics. This ignorance to difference is a serious shortcoming for any movement concerned with advancing social justice.

Nonhuman Animal advocacy as a project of racism

The Nonhuman Animal rights discourse demonstrates a shallow understanding of race nuance, while campaigns are also framed in ways that reflect whiteness and reinforce racism. Because the movement operates according to a post-racial perspective, there is often extraordinary resistance to critique. By way of an example, in 2013 an abolitionist organization called Free from Harm published a story on a campaign that seeks to end the practice of "live sushi" in Japan. "Live sushi" entails the butchering of frogs, octopi, and other small animals in a way that keeps them alive for the majority of the dining experience to demonstrate freshness. In the video that accompanies the Free from Harm story, a disemboweled and dismembered frog was displayed on a plate of their entrails, still blinking and very much alive as they were slowly consumed. Understandably, those who viewed the graphic footage of the frog's torture and death were outraged and disgusted. Commentators, who were largely white-identified and residing in Western nations, were quick to chastise the Japanese as especially cruel.[12] The Free from Harm story encouraged readers to sign a petition that framed live sushi as "barbaric" and "vulgar" (Capps, 2013).

While this campaign may seem critically important for suffering Nonhuman Animals and the campaigners were surely well meaning, the manner in which it is framed is problematic. First, like Animals Asia's "Friends not Food" campaign, the live sushi campaign targets a group of color (Asians) and specifically incriminates Japanese culture as "barbaric." Second, the campaign initiates a "white savior" response, encouraging the largely white readership to impose on non-white spaces to save Nonhuman Animals. Third, it reflects a colonialist attitude, whereby Western countries feel entitled to intrude in non-Western spaces to instill order. People of color are presumed to be too ignorant, uncivilized, "vulgar," and "barbaric" to be capable of handling their own affairs.

At this juncture, it is important to recognize that the Nonhuman Animal rights movement has historically been an enterprise of white supremacy (Lundblad, 2012, p.78). The Nonhuman Animal rights movement emerged strategically in the era of post-slavery reconstruction in the United States and Great Britain. Although slavery had been abolished, intense discrimination and institutionalized racism persisted. Whites were grappling with the newfound "freedom" of a long subjugated people, who now posed a threat to their power and privilege. Many whites and white-led institutions were extremely resistant to granting basic rights to freed slaves, including suffrage, education, and political office. Many looked for ways to justify persistent inequality and reinforce white superiority. Eugenics, a pseudoscience that espoused important racially bound variations within the human species, was popularized in the late 19th century and early 20th century and became a popular tool for justifying differentiation, segregation, and white supremacy. Locating "objective" differences between the socially constructed races gave "evidence" to the inferior qualities of people of color and naturalized white authority. The ideology behind the eugenics project also influenced perceptions of who can be qualified to engage in Nonhuman Animal advocacy. It was thought that only whites enjoyed the ability to empathize with the suffering of vulnerable groups. People of color were framed as brutes and savages, incapable of extending concern to others. Much of this ideology was bound in the movement to frame African American men as rapists and women of color as both sexually insatiable and subhuman. If people of color are thought to pose a threat to other humans and civil society, surely they cannot care about the suffering of dogs, cats, horses, and other animals of concern to gentrified whites.

The construction of Nonhuman Animal "cruelty" is also closely tied to early colonialist efforts. For instance, as Victorians began to view companion animals as objects of civility and affection (rather than mere objects of resource), cruelty to Nonhuman Animals was seen as an affront on the home. This translated to boundary work between the "home" country of the colonizers and the "savage" worlds of the colonized (Deckha, 2013). On the home front, advocates pushed Nonhuman Animal interests as a matter of "civilizing" the public. Anti-cruelty laws tended to target uses that were prevalent among poor and exploited communities, whereas those uses associated with the social elite were exempted. Indeed, Nonhuman Animal exploitation conducted by the elite (like the killing of foxes, pheasants, and stags on private estates with the assistance of expensive horses and dogs) tended to be framed positively in nationalist and imperialist language. Anti-cruelty laws that passed in the colonies (like those against cockfighting) also worked to differentiate the colonizers from the colonized, reinforce colonial rule, and maintain a boundary of racialized difference. These statutes also created the illusion of benevolent Western "stewardship," which helped facilitate and justify subjugation. For instance, the United States has cited failure to assimilate to "Anglo-Saxon" American customs as a reason for refusing a colony its independence as well as denying citizenship to its colonized subjects of "alien races." In other words, Nonhuman Animal exploitations that occurred within communities of color and colonized regions were framed in a way that justified the oppression of humans (Davis, 2013, p.551).

The "savagery" of communities of color is a stereotype that has continued well into the 20th and 21st centuries. As one example, the American Antivivisection Society launched a campaign in the 1920s against vaccinations, as the development of vaccinations involves considerable Nonhuman Animal suffering (Vaught, 2013). The campaign compared the impure and poisonous potential of vaccines to the poisonous nature of African American jazz culture. Advocates were drawing on a fear of scientific advancement as well as African American social advancement. More recently, the Michael Vick scandal (involving a very famous and wealthy African American football player) sparked a highly racialized discussion of Nonhuman Animal cruelty (Glick, 2013). As an African American man, Vick was easily targeted and readily punished by the US legal system, which disproportionately criminalizes people of color. Many advocates actually animalized Vick for his cruel treatment of other animals. In this way, Nonhuman Animal advocates can successfully maintain a boundary between white as "good" and "normal" and Black as "bad" and "deviant." Tellingly, many are quick to demonize Vick despite their own engagement with equally horrific forms of Nonhuman Animal abuse (primarily in consuming their bodies and secretions) (Francione, 2009b).

Therefore, anti-speciesist campaigns that highlight the "barbarity" of non-white peoples must be understood within the context of a Nonhuman Animal rights movement bound to the project of white supremacy. Advocates must be cognizant of institutionalized discrimination that is responsible for stereotypes that construct people of color as uncivil and cruel. If people of color are framed as animalistic themselves, they will find it difficult to be accepted as equals in the advocate community. Instead, they are alienated from privileged constructions of what constitutes empathetic, responsible humanity. In this way, people of color might thus be relegated to animals themselves in need of white caretaking, if they are recognized at all. Subsequently, they are neither considered fully developed humans nor considered proper subjects for human compassion. They exist in a white supremacist netherworld of subhuman animality. When white-identified advocates deride people of color as a "barbaric" "subspecies" of humans for enacting speciesism in ways that whites have defined as deviant, they are extending this racist and speciesist project. They are conflating whiteness with humanity.

Whether or not Nonhuman Animal advocates agree with these racist stereotypes, their advocacy efforts do not exist in a vacuum. Animalizing people of color has been an effective means of otherizing them and justifying any number of atrocities. Campaigns such as the one to end live sushi draw on a long history of racism against Japanese persons (and Asians in general). Exacerbated white-identified activists often react to these analyses with the accusation that critical race proponents must simply not care about Nonhuman Animals killed in non-white food systems. However, this response falsely pits humans against nonhumans. The fear of moral relativism, preserved by the blinders of privilege, can work to deflect critical reflection and stifle attempts to find solutions.

For at least three reasons, recognizing how particular campaigns can foster racism and hurt human groups does not translate to the abandonment of Nonhuman Animals. First, recall that human and nonhuman oppressions are heavily connected and are mutually reinforcing. For instance, it is known that Nonhuman Animal products are deadly, not only to the Nonhuman Animals exploited and killed to produce them, but also to the humans who consume them and the environment in which all must live. Second, a more encompassing argument for anti-speciesism would include *all* Nonhuman Animal use, without needing to single out particular groups of people. Finally, advocates need not rely on colonialist approaches to promote veganism when they can instead extend support to local organizations who are doing the work in a more culturally sensitive and appropriate means. Therefore, advocates need not ignore the plight of some species entangled with historically oppressed human groups. Instead, they can alter advocacy efforts to be more encompassing. To accomplish this, advocates should first draw on intersectional evidence that demonstrates how Nonhuman Animal products hurt humans, nonhumans, and the environment. Second, advocates can adopt an anti-speciesist approach that speaks to Nonhuman Animal exploitation *in general* rather than single issues specific to certain groups. Third, advocates especially concerned with one form of violence would do well to support activists locally situated in the area of concern. Ostracizing already marginalized groups of people will ensure that the movement will never reach the critical mass necessary to instill large-scale change.

Authentic abolitionism

Thus far, I have been discussing single-issue campaigning in the context of Nonhuman Animal rights (efforts to ban seal slaughter or horse carriages, for example). It has been argued that single-issue campaigning is ineffective because it singles out one group of animals as especially important. In doing so, it detracts resources from other groups, and in ignoring the interests of those other groups, the suffering of the excluded may even appear to be condoned. For example, if an organization focuses primarily on ending cruelty against dogs and cats, no resources go toward alleviating the suffering of cows, hens, sheeps, and others. In prioritizing dogs and cats, the implication is that cows, hens, sheeps, and other animals do not matter or do not matter as much; they are not objects of concern. Most importantly, however, the root cause of cruelty, suffering, and exploitation remains unaddressed: the ideology of oppression.

Single-issue campaigning, however, is detrimental not only to members of certain species but also to members of certain human groups. If advocates prioritize Nonhuman Animals, they are starving disadvantaged human groups. Not only do all volunteer hours and donations funnel into helping Nonhuman Animals, but in focusing only on Nonhuman Animals, advocates downplay the needs of disadvantaged humans. One could argue that Nonhuman Animals are more worthy of attention due to the sheer magnitude and horror of speciesist exploitation and death, but this ignores the most important problem with single-issue campaigning: their failure to address the root problem of *oppression*. As evidenced in the work of Harper (2010b), Adams (2000a), and Nibert (2002; 2013), advocates cannot engage Nonhuman Animal injustice without also examining human injustice. This is because the oppression felt by both groups originate from the same source, operate similarly, and even *aggravate* one another. Advocates need to examine how oppression manifests, how it thrives, and how best to dismantle it. Working sporadically in the social movement arena to extinguish fires as they emerge might alleviate some problems temporarily, but if advocates do not seek to transform the social structure so that the root of the problem is dealt with, the problem will continue to fester unchecked. Not only will it persist, but it will also grow smarter. It will adapt to advocacy defenses, and it will co-opt them.

Like Nonhuman Animals, humans are enslaved, tortured, exploited, and killed in large numbers and in systemic ways. People of color are disproportionately targeted and enslaved in the prison industrial complex, for example (Davis, 2005). Laws are designed to criminalize communities of color, thus ensuring that many of them enter the prison system, where their labor will be hired out to private companies for very little compensation (about 25 cents an hour) (Pelaez, 2013). Families are disrupted, communities are destroyed, and people live in terror of police brutality and racial profiling. Prisoners lose their rights. They cannot vote, they have no freedom, and, if released, they face unimaginable difficulties in obtaining fulfilling and adequate work, if they find work at all. In a phenomenon known as the "school-to-prison pipeline," even disciplinary measures in the public school system disproportionately target children of color (Kim et al., 2010). This interferes with their educational attainment and, subsequently, their ability to access the resources necessary to succeed (or survive). Some schools also press charges on students of color and have them arrested. Students of color are punished more often and more harshly. The children are targeted by punitive measures specifically because of their racial identity, not because of their culpability.

Communities of color are also targeted by dangerous and polluting industries. For instance, Native American communities in the American West are subject to the pollution of gunnery ranges and uranium mining, which leads to severe illness, spontaneous abortions, and birth defects (Thunder Hawk, 2007, p.103). In another example, polluting Nonhuman Animal agricultural facilities are disproportionately located in rural, impoverished areas with high populations of African Americans

(Wing et al., 2000). This environmental racism extends beyond destructive industries and chemical runoff and actually shapes access to food. Recall that food deserts are spaces that are bereft of healthy food choices, and people of color are more likely to live in them (Walker et al., 2010, pp.878–80). Many times, the only options available are processed foods, fast foods, soda, and alcohol. This is often compounded by an inability to travel to locations where healthy foods are available; food deserts are often located in areas that lack adequate public transportation. Furthermore, disadvantaged persons often do not have the time or money to travel outside of their communities for groceries. Many are burdened by ticket costs, gas costs, lack of personal transportation, lack of adequate childcare, or long hours on the job (or jobs). Food deserts are just as deadly as uranium mines as the health consequences of consuming nutritionally deficient foods are so many. Not surprisingly, people of color are disproportionately affected by chronic diet-related diseases (Treuhaft and Karpyn, 2010, p.11). Heart disease, cancer, diabetes, and other illnesses impose a tremendous amount of suffering on vulnerable human populations. Many endure prolonged and debilitating symptoms, and many also die young. Oppressive diets are destroying communities, denying vulnerable persons the basic right to live long and healthfully. Entire communities of color endure unhealthy living spaces that are full of pollution and devoid of nutritious food.

Millions of vulnerable persons in the so-called developed countries are denied many freedoms because they are funneled into prisons, inhabit unhealthy land, and are unable to access nutritious foods. But millions of humans worldwide experience no freedom at *all*. As Harper points out, the Nonhuman Animal rights movement often falsely analogizes slavery as an extinct institution of the past. That is, the movement argues that Nonhuman Animals are experiencing slavery like humans *once did*. Operating under a white-centric, post-racial worldview, white advocates often presume that human slavery is a relic of the past. However, at least 27 million human slaves currently toil across the globe, the United States included (Bales et al., 2009). This number far exceeds that of the transatlantic slave trade era that most in the West are familiar with.

The sum of human suffering remains astronomical. The majority of the planet's population is unable to enjoy basic rights and freedoms. So long as humanity holds only a tenuous respect for human rights, it is questionable as to whether rights for other animals can be meaningfully achieved. A non-intersectional, single-issue approach to oppression (in this case, one that focuses on only Nonhuman Animals) overlooks the systemic inequalities that allow this suffering to materialize. For that matter, ignoring the very real suffering of vulnerable human groups seems especially unethical, even if the condition of Nonhuman Animals is substantially worse. There is no need to place human suffering in competition with nonhuman suffering. Indeed, doing so is disastrously restrictive and counterintuitive to a movement for peace. Such an approach is also quite alienating and acts as yet another unnecessary barrier when alliances are sorely needed to create the critical mass necessary for structural change.

The Nonhuman Animal rights movement has, for the most part, attempted to deconstruct (or reform) oppressive systems *by way of* oppressive systems. Many organizations seek to cooperate with speciesist industries to alleviate Nonhuman Animal suffering, cherry-picking particular abuses or industries to campaign against. Subsequently, the system itself remains unchallenged. Likewise, an increasing number of Nonhuman Animal rights activists attempt to manipulate patriarchy with "sexy" advocacy to undo patriarchal violence against the vulnerable. The movement has also maintained a white supremacist approach to dismantling inequality, a likely result of white leadership and a white majority in both participation and audience. People of color are demonized, tokenized, marginalized, and even animalized. In many cases, they are ignored altogether. Ideologically, white supremacy normalizes violence against the vulnerable, so it is unlikely that white supremacy can be wielded successfully against speciesism. The common oversight among these favored advocacy approaches is a failure to recognize the root of oppression. Ideologies of capitalism, sexism, racism, and, as to be explored in the next chapter, religion impose fundamental blocks to radical anti-speciesist social change. Clinging to oppressive frameworks with the expectation of *dismantling* oppressive frameworks is argued to be irrational and worth reconsideration.

6
The Case for Secular Activism

A critique of irrational social institutions and their role in upholding oppression would not be complete without a discussion of religion. The Nonhuman Animal rights movement has sustained bloated nonprofits, sexism, and racism despite the tendency for these institutions to work *against* liberation efforts. The same may also hold true for religious approaches to vegan abolition. Religion is sometimes a powerful tool for many social movements, and it can certainly offer particular benefits to mobilization and claimsmaking that should not be rejected. However, this chapter will offer an alternative, secularized approach worth considering. Religious ideology often stands in opposition to a scientific, evidence-based approach to anti-oppression work. Many advocates rely on faith as a point of resonance, but faith alone is insufficient for effective advocacy. Indeed, faith has historically acted as an important barrier to social progress. This chapter will discuss institutionalized religion and its relationship with Nonhuman Animal oppression. It is argued that religious tactics are largely inappropriate for challenging inequality, specifically speciesism.

As emphasized in Chapter 4, it remains necessary to keep projects of rationality in check, particularly when vulnerable groups are at risk. Recall that the scientific project has itself been a source of incredible oppression. So, while a case is made for secular activism, it remains imperative that rational activism recognize the double-edged nature of rationality. A rational approach to advocacy must be made accountable, and it must be reflexive. It must be conscious of rationality's own dubious history and its uncomfortable relationship with marginalized communities. Consequently, this chapter will also include a critique of irrationalities that appear in secular claimsmaking.

Religion and oppression

A sociology of religion

Religion, like other major institutions, shapes social structures and interpersonal relationships. For these reasons, the work of sociology's founding fathers – Émile Durkheim, Max Weber, and Karl Marx – take considerable interest in religious institutions. Writing at the turn of the 20th century, Durkheim's ethnographic work emphasizes that religion is a social construction: "religion is something eminently social. Religious representations are collective representations which express collective realities" (2012 [1915], p.10). Religion, he suggests, creates a framework for understanding the social world. Likewise, Durkheim sees religion as an internalized mechanism of control. Religion ensures a sense of community and encourages adherence to morality, both of which are needed for the smooth functioning of society. Religion gives society a shared understanding of what is good and what is bad; it distinguishes from the sacred and the profane. It sets boundaries.

Religion, then, manifests across all cultures because it suits some societal need. In analyzing the various religious sects, Durkheim determines that different religions performed similar functions for human society in general, but also specific functions for individual cultures. Histories, traditions, rituals, and narratives are sculpted by the culture in which they are embedded and religious beliefs work to legitimate them. The rich tapestry of social supports that are created to protect and sustain religion effectively erase the human hand involved. As with all successful social constructs, religion and other socially constructed practices come to be understood as both normal and natural.

Durkheim also explores the possibility of achieving these social goods through nonreligious means, particularly so as society had begun to secularize. Religion, he argues, reflects the power structure of a given society. Religious adherence is a collective effort that works to ensure a sense of gratitude to that society as well as confidence in it. Patriotism, however, might serve the same function. The educational system, too, works to integrate individuals into a modern society and instills values (Wallace, 1973). Religion is one of the many institutions that shape society. Because it is socially constructed, its presence is neither mandatory nor guaranteed.

Similarly, Karl Marx sees religion as an institution maintained by the ruling class that is intended to legitimize the prevailing social structure (Raines, 2002, p.3). While he acknowledges that religion works to temporarily relieve the suffering of a highly exploited mass of people, he also argues that religion is ultimately intended to keep the oppressed complacent with their condition. As with other institutions, religion is thought to reflect the economic mode of production. For Marx, the spiritual is a product of the material world. For instance, capitalism benefits a select few at the expense of the many; this is a volatile relationship that may incite outrage and social unrest. To counteract this possibility, religion is applied as one of many tools of social control manipulated by those in power to reproduce those social arrangements that benefit them. Religion is uniquely powerful in that these arrangements are constructed as *divine sanctions*. When an authority becomes divinely sanctioned, it becomes difficult to challenge. Thus, Marx sees religion as a tool of oppression and ideologically imposed ignorance. However, it also exists as a meaningful expression of suffering and dissatisfaction by those vulnerable to exploitative material conditions (Raines, 2002, p.5). Religion works to obscure social inequality, but it also acts as a venue for expressing objection to these conditions. In some cases, religious activity demonstrates an imagination for peace and justice.

Max Weber, too, understands religion to be entangled with social control. He also sees religion as highly rationalized in its ability to systematize and unify society (Weber, 1993 [1922], p.207). As rationalized entities, religions, like the bureaucracies discussed in Chapter 2, can come to wield immense power over the social and are often manipulated to reflect elite interests. In an analysis of Christianity, Weber suggests that religious variation emerges from economic conditions, access to wealth, and inequality (2001 [1905], pp.3–12). Religiosity works to reinforce particular economic values and work ethics in individuals and communities. These are values and ethics that are congruent with business success in a capitalist economy. A religiously bound work ethic encourages individuals to work hard, strive for success, save and reinvest, obey authority, and happily (or tolerably) go without. The Protestant ethic, he suggests, is especially conducive to economic growth and the legitimization of inequality. The focus on eternal salvation, he implies, fuels behaviors in the earthly realm that facilitate capitalist processes.

Writing in the 19th century and the early 20th century, a time of great inequality and oppression, early sociologists sometimes adopted a critical view of religion as a chief variable in social control, one that sometimes undermines human rights to the benefit of social elites. Today, while critical work continues, sociological inquiries into religion have expanded beyond grand structural theories in a multicultural effort to understand how religion is experienced by believers in positive as well as negative ways (Bender et al., 2013, p.11; Christiano et al., 2008, p.38;

Edgell, 2012). This reflects sociology's interest in how people live and understand their social reality, as well as how that reality affects their behavior and life chances. Though current research is more culturally bound, sociologists continue to recognize the importance of religion as a primary institution of socialization and social control.

Even a pluralistic sociological understanding concedes that religion, like any social institution, exists as potential site of inequality and suffering. For many centuries, religion has been used to oppress, both domestically and abroad. Religion is used not only as a justification for atrocity but also as an excuse for it. Intentionally or not, faith can supersede logic in potentially dangerous ways. For example, writing at the height of colonial expansion abroad and severe capitalist exploitation localized in Western nations, philosopher William James advances "pragmatism" as a solution to ethical dilemmas. He determines that if something is considered beneficial to an individual, then it must be "true" and "good." Things are as they are for a reason. In practice, such an approach would allow for "moral holidays":

> we may, therefore, whenever we wish, treat the temporal as if it were potentially the eternal, be sure that we can trust its outcome, and, without sin, dismiss our fear and drop the worry of our finite responsibility. In short, they mean that we have a right ever and anon to take a moral holiday, to let the world wag in its own way, feeling that its issues are in better hands than ours and are none of our business. (James, 1907, p.50).

In other words, if humanity's script is believed to be predetermined and every action and belief associated with human conduct is essential to playing out this destiny, why should philosophers and ethicists strain themselves over trying moral questions? This mindset remains prevalent today. For instance, as was discussed in Chapter 3, social psychologists have noted a tendency for humans to believe in a "just world." Rather than grapple with the hugely distressing reality of incredible suffering and injustice that characterizes modern society, humans tend to default to the mindset of victim-blaming: these terrible things happen for a reason and they happen to those who deserve them. Likewise, good things are thought to happen to those who have earned them or otherwise deserve them. Such a framework obscures the reality of social inequality and the institutions that maintain and reproduce them. Humans are psychologically predisposed to have "faith" in a morally functional world despite significant injustice. Institutionalized faith only aggravates this quality.

Religion has tended to have a troubling impact not only on *oppressors* by giving them both reasons and excuses to facilitate violence but also on the *oppressed* by coercing them into acquiescence and discouraging critical thought.

Sanctifying speciesism

Sociology has a long history of critical analysis in regard to social control and social institutions, and religion is no exception. A major function of religion is to facilitate particular social arrangements that are often in the service of elites. These elites stand to benefit from the exploitation of not only humans but also nonhumans. Religion has played a very powerful role in normalizing human oppression of other animals. Most organized religions include doctrines that legitimize Nonhuman Animal exploitation. As one example, the conquest of the Americas in the 1500s and 1600s (which entailed unimaginable human and nonhuman suffering) is thought to result from the capitalist pursuit of new markets for the raising of cows, sheep, horses, mules, and other domesticated animals, as well as the pursuit of new resources found from free-living animals who were "harvested" for their hair, feathers, and other body parts (Nibert, 2013, p.60). Many of these conquest projects were led by missionaries and churches that were seeking to "assimilate" indigenous populations and also to profit from their appropriated lands and resources.

The sanctity of Nonhuman Animal use remains prevalent today in all organized religions. Religious ideology generally impedes a serious discussion of Nonhuman Animal abolition. Will Anderson refers to this phenomenon as "religion washing"(2012, p.333). Some advocates have found that the religious use and killing of Nonhuman Animals (which prioritizes ritual and cleanliness over humaneness) can be mediated with the adoption of less frightening and less painful techniques (Masri, 2009; Salamano et al., 2013), but Nonhuman Animals are unnecessarily subjected to exploitation and death nonetheless. Some professionalized organizations have sought to starve or eliminate certain religious practices altogether, as seen in efforts to ban live export (Animals Australia, 2013);[1] attempts to end the mass killing of hundreds of thousands of buffalos, roosters, and goats for the Hindu Gadhimai Festival in Nepal (Asia for Animals Coalition, 2014); and a campaign by United Poultry Concerns (UPC) to replace chickens used in the Jewish practice of kapparot with money (Yanklowitz, 2011).[2] The amount of injustices imposed on Nonhuman Animals in the name of religion rival those committed for secular causes and are too many to recount here. Ritual killing is a high-profile form of oppression, but there are also many Amish communities that operate puppy mills and exploit horses for food production and transportation on busy roads, Hindus who control cows and elephants for ceremonial purposes and tourism, practitioners of Hoodoo and Chinese herbal medicine who use Nonhuman Animals in healing practices, and so on.

Bargaining with oppression

Advocates have many barriers to overcome in their outreach efforts. Nonhuman Animal use is difficult to challenge given prevailing patriarchal ideologies that normalize domination and masculinize Nonhuman Animal consumption (Luke, 2007). It is "manly" to ride "broncos," eat "steak," and "hunt" free-living animals. White supremacist ideologies also impede efforts, as Nonhuman Animal exploitation is sometimes seen as a natural right bestowed upon whites. This was evidenced in the white entitlement to American buffalo populations following colonization, for example. It is also seen in the normalization of cows' milk consumption (whites are the primary racial group that remains lactose persistent) (Gaard, 2013, p.596; Vesa, Marteau, and Korpela, 2000, p.166S) and in the use of Nonhuman Animals in white medicinal traditions. The exploitation of other animals is also supported by the ideology of capitalism. Nonhuman Animals are treated as unfeeling products, consumable items, and resources for economic gain (Torres, 2006, pp.38–56). No doubt, these ideologies are formidable. They all speak to a sense of entitlement that is based in social privilege and elite status. Religion, then, can also be situated alongside racialized, patriarchal, capitalist ideologies of inequality and subjugation. This is because religion, too, often presupposes that some will benefit, and others will submit.

Religious ideology also upholds a social hierarchy that is built on entitlement and is highly resistant to repositioning. Marginalized individuals who manage to see past the blinders of "normalcy" and "naturalness" in social inequalities can theoretically rally for change against patriarchy, white supremacy, capitalism, and institutionalized religion, but they will often find their voices muted, garbled, or punishable. The validity of social justice advocacy is easily expunged if the theistic white patriarchal capitalist system has reason to seek or create justification to deny the need for change. Religion offers a unique additional challenge because faith, by definition, is very difficult to challenge. Faith erects a barrier that is highly impenetrable in that faith is not always based on observable evidence. Patriarchy, white supremacy, and capitalism operate according to notions of biological superiority and economic efficiency, which can be questioned. Indeed, science increasingly provides evidence to undermine the notions that cis-men are smarter and stronger than women, that whites are more evolutionarily advanced than non-whites (or that "race" is biologically real at all) (Tobach and Rosoff, 1994), and that capitalism is rational (capitalism is actually quite vulnerable) (Wallerstein et al., 2013). But how can science counter religion? There is no scientific evidence to suggest that a god exists or that there is any divine plan to the universe. Yet, evidence, or lack thereof, is relatively meaningless to the ideology of faith. This is because faith is largely uninterested in evidence. Devotees are expected to believe in divine rule with or without proof. No amount of contrary evidence can counter faith, because faith can operate irrespective of these qualifications.

This inattention to evidence has not deterred many Nonhuman Animal advocates from maintaining a faith-based approach. Repurposing the tools of oppression to dismantle oppression is a popular tactic. As was discussed in Chapter 5, the white-centric movement has attempted to overcome white supremacist claims to Nonhuman Animals through the use of white rhetoric. For example, veganism is often framed as an individual action that those with means can exercise by shopping at expensive natural foods stores. Furthermore, advocacy organizations are white led, and vegan communities in the West are largely white as well. The movement also draws on a history of white superiority, in which whites are framed as particularly empathetic and people of color are framed as cruel barbarians incapable of caring about other animals. In Chapter 4, it was argued that several organizations have attempted to deconstruct speciesism bound in male supremacy by drawing on the language of patriarchy with sexist displays of naked and nearly naked women presented for the male gaze. Vegans have even used the mechanisms of capitalism to challenge Nonhuman Animal exploitation. People who care about other animals are encouraged to donate. Giving money to organizations is frequently presented as the best thing that humans can do to help other animals. Vegans are encouraged to "vote with their dollar" by purchasing vegan products and shopping at vegan businesses (Wrenn, 2011, pp.16–20). Predictably, vegan outreach efforts are also framed in faith. Just as the movement whitewashes veganism to appeal to white supremacy, sexualizes veganism to appeal to patriarchy, and commodifies veganism to appeal to capitalism, it also consecrates veganism to appeal to religious institutions.

It is unclear that a religious approach to veganism can be useful. For instance, while attempts to package veganism in a manner that appeals to the white capitalist patriarchy have been problematic, they can be reimagined and presented *critically* in a way may be more effective. Increasingly, vegans are coming to understand the importance of diversity in outreach efforts. Feminist vegans are challenging the notion that women should be sexually objectified to advertise veganism. Some vegans are pushing for fair-trade and locally sourced vegan products, while others advocate veganic gardening as an alternative to prevailing capitalist conceptions of veganism. Instead of abetting the ideologies of these oppressive institutions, advocates could alternatively work to dismantle them. For religious barriers, this could mean that a secular approach may be more appropriate. In this way, the attempt to fight the religious exploitation of other animals via religious claimsmaking may be framed as problematic in the same sense that bargaining with white supremacy, male supremacy, and capitalism might also be.

Faith-based outreach

Historically, collective action on behalf of other animals has been tightly linked with religious institutions (Calvert, 2008; Gilheany, 2010). Reverend William Cowherd, a Seventh-day Adventist, was instrumental in the founding of the Vegetarian Society in the mid- 19th century. His church is thought to be the birthplace of British vegetarian activism (Millington, 2012; Phelps, 2007, pp.148–68). Members were asked to adhere to a flesh-free diet, and the church also distributed vegetable soup to the poor. Several unconventional churches and Christian-based organizations advocated against Nonhuman Animal cruelty (Webb, 1998, p.30). Meanwhile, in the United States, the famous Alcott family was struggling to create a vegan utopia in their New England commune that they named Fruitlands. A spiritual project, community residents eschewed all Nonhuman Animal products and labor, even their manure (Francis, 2010, pp.2–3). The Quakers, too, have a long history with vegetarianism and Nonhuman Animal protectionism, even working to combat the rise in institutionalized vivisection (Glaholt, 2012). Philanthropist Henry Bergh, a founder of the American Society for the Prevention of Cruelty to Animals, worked with Protestant Episcopalians, urging them to include animal-positive messages in their sermons (1874, no pagination).

This tradition of religiously bound Nonhuman Animal advocacy did meet with opposition as the Victorian era came to a close. From the inception of the modern Western vegan movement, there have been calls for secularism. In 1948 Donald Watson wrote in an early issue of *The Vegetarian*:

> Vegetarian literature should be secular. There must be thousands of vegetarians, both theists and atheists, who regard most religious doctrine as mythical and unintelligible and who do not, therefore, wish to be associated with it. To introduce it [religion] [...] is a sure way to create disharmony within the movement.

Watson notes that religion plays a very important role in both socializing speciesism and facilitating the institutionalization of Nonhuman Animal oppression as a matter of divine right. This aspect of religion, he argues, is a serious barrier to vegan outreach. "The foundations of the slaughter house," he warns, "are safe so long as this falsehood survives." Opposing the society's incorporation of religiosity in its claimsmaking, Watson suggests that the focus on religion be one of investigation, critique, and open challenge. It appears that this secular basis was a key differentiation between the vegan movement and the vegetarian movement that it left behind. Writing for *The Vegan*, W. S. James suggests that a scientific basis is needed, lest the "bunk and bathos" create "embarrassments and setbacks" and "scare away the intellectually minded reformer for ever [sic]" (1948, pp.6–7).

This position echoes that of Nonhuman Animal rights pioneer and rationalist Henry Salt, who agrees that religious ideology firmly entrenches the oppression of other animals. In 1921 Salt writes:

> Religion has never befriended the cause of humaneness. Its monstrous doctrine of eternal punishment and the torture of the damned underlies much of the barbarity with which man [sic] has treated man [sic]; and the deep division imagined by the Church between the human being, with his [sic] immortal soul, and the soulless "beasts," has been responsible for an incalculable sum of cruelty. (p.213)

Salt's Humanitarian League did sometimes reach out to religious institutions in the hopes of persuading them to abandon practices of Nonhuman Animal cruelty, though Salt bitterly reports that their outreach met with disparagingly little response. He maintains: "From Religion, [...] the League expected nothing and got nothing." (1921, p.216)

Despite Watson's and James' early warnings and Salt's misgivings, the movement continued on with faith as a major underpinning to advocacy efforts. In the 1960s and 1970s, many Westerners were introduced to vegetarianism and veganism through the growing fascination with all things Eastern. The Beatles, for example, famously turned vegetarian after their spiritual hermitage to India. Hare Krishna advocacy, which reached a pinnacle in the late 1960s and early 1970s, also helped to popularize vegetarianism. Like its 19th-century predecessor, the Back to the Land movement of the heady protest years, also framed Nonhuman Animal rights as a spiritual endeavor (Nearing and Nearing, 1973; Taylor, 2005, p.150). The Rastafarian movement, too, advocates vegetarianism for its adherents. Rastafarian ital food emphasizes all-natural and peaceful eating, often rejecting the destruction of Nonhuman Animals for food (Dickerson, 2004, p.36). In 1975, the Jewish Vegetarians of North America formed with "the desire to show that Jewish teachings are most consistent with plant-based diets" (no date). More recently, the Christian Vegetarian Association was established with the goal of promoting plant-based diets as compatible with "responsible Christian stewardship for all God's Creation" (no date). Muslim advocacy groups have also appeared, such as Islamic Concern, which seeks to "promote the Islamic way of leading a humane and compassionate life by treating animals with kindness" (no date).

Throughout the history of Nonhuman Animal rights mobilization, groups have been drawing on spirituality and organized religion to promote the welfare of other animals, an agenda that continues despite the misgivings of early leaders. Many religious (and nonreligious) advocates presume that the language of religion can be used to dismantle the religious oppression of other animals (Kemmerer and Nocella, 2011, pp.1–3; Regan, 1990). However, the notions of stewardship, compassion, and peace utilized in religious rhetoric seem to be inconsistently applied. Without an *objective* ethic, Nonhuman Animals can remain vulnerable even to the practices of religious groups that appear to respect them. For example, a tourist attraction in Thailand known as "The Tiger Temple" houses once free-living tigers who have been "tamed" by Buddhist monks. Because the sanctuary adheres to the Buddhist narrative, rampant abuse and exploitation is permitted by the Thai government (Cohen, 2013).

Because religious ideology tends to legitimize the exploitation of other animals, it will be difficult to reconcile oppressive religious doctrines with potentially liberating religious doctrines. Joe Lynch, for instance, analyzes various theodicies that relate to Nonhuman Animal suffering and finds that, for the most part, "animal pain and suffering were either denied or trivialized, and when finally firmly recognized, God's benevolence was called into serious question. [...] the moral view that takes animals very seriously seems to be at odds with the morality of theism" (2002, p.9). He concludes that theism is largely incompatible with a serious consideration of nonhuman suffering.

Furthermore, if advocates base their outreach predominantly on religious scripture, it becomes a game of "my word against yours." Everyone has different understandings of what humanity's moral obligation to other animals should be based on their own religious leanings. By not grounding the argument for Nonhuman Animal personhood in the science of sentience and the logic of social justice and anti-oppression, Nonhuman Animal ethics get lost in the fluidity of religious interpretation. Inevitably, the positions of those religions with stronger presence and more power (with other structures of oppression such as patriarchy and capitalism supporting them) will enjoy greater legitimacy. For instance, while Jainism is based on vegan values, it is overshadowed by the world's larger religious institutions. For that matter, the flexibility of religious doctrine means that even the devout may not necessarily ascribe to values of nonviolence. Indeed, many Jains are not vegan (Francione, 2009a, p.9). For those religions lacking a strong pre-existing ethic for Nonhuman Animals, the prospect for a successful inclusion of other animals is even dimmer. The battle over ideologies (those that respect Nonhuman Animals versus those that view Nonhuman Animals primarily as resources) becomes a quagmire of competing interpretations, interpretations that are inherently bound to the power of those individuals and groups that promote them. Nonetheless, activists jump into the fray in the hopes of their interpretation finding resonance.

Anthropocentric anti-speciesism

Faith-based outreach inevitably deflects the center of concern from the oppressed to the oppressor. Consider Harriet Beecher Stowe's *Uncle Tom's Cabin* (1852), an activist novel that perpetuates racist stereotypes and white paternalism (Yarborough, 1986). While the book was a hugely influential contribution to the anti-slavery cause, it unfortunately portrays African Americans as simple-minded, infantilized victims in need of white intervention. Abolitionist material geared toward children also denigrates African Americans, positioning white children as stewards over pitied slaves (Keralis, 2012). Oppression, then, is viewed as a misuse of power, not as a system that is problematic in its own right. While Stowe's book was successful in advancing abolitionism, it is also possible that it may have played into the maintenance of white supremacy after human liberation. Indeed, African Americans were only reabsorbed into other forms of enslavement like sharecropping and prisons, systems that are justified by perpetuated notions of Black inferiority.

Religious claimsmaking in the Nonhuman Animal abolitionist movement also tends to prioritize self-interest with the effect of reinforcing human superiority. As an example, Bangalore-based abolitionist group Animal Rights Fund invites members to go vegan as a matter of karma:

> guilt is not something we can get rid of by suppressing it. It is a potent negative force that can cause silent damage. It is our most powerful enemy within. It can fester inside us for a lifetime. Guilt never dies. It is a time bomb that is waiting to explode. See about the destructions in the human life, the number of the clinic and hospital that have come mushrooming. Think again, we don't have to make so many changes in our life just an intermittently changes as really required to follow the vegan lifestyle that will do our consciousness good. Go Vegan. (Bafna, 2013)

This self-interest argument frames veganism as a means of alleviating crushing, parasitic guilt. This framework also obscures the notion that Nonhuman Animals are sentient beings worthy of justice and equality based on their *own* personhood. Religious positions become problematic when they focus on *human* personhood instead.

As discussed in Chapter 1, Francione sometimes draws on Jain scripture and symbolism to advocate for veganism and anti-speciesism. He writes, "We have a moral obligation that we owe to ourselves to be healthy; ingesting products that cause us harm is a form of violence we inflict on ourselves" (2010). While Francione bases the bulk of his theory on secular, evidence-based reasoning, his framing of morality in a religious context might detract from Nonhuman Animals' *own* right to be free from suffering, exploitation, and death according to their *own* personhood. Instead, anti-speciesism as something "we owe to ourselves" is presented as a means of personal gain and personal salvation.

It might be countered that a human-centered approach could be justified if it works to alleviate Nonhuman Animal suffering, but the evidence is not convincing. In 2006, Marie Mika tested the efficacy of PETA's claimsmaking on college students and found that advertisements that draw on religious themes generally fail to resonate, even eliciting a *strong negative reaction*. She suggests that religious claimsmaking fails because it runs counter to commonly accepted interpretations of the Bible, thus forcing viewers to consider their own values and actions as problematic in a way that creates psychological barriers to attitude change. For this reason, appealing to the evidence (evidence that both religious and nonreligious individuals can appreciate) may be more agreeable for most and perhaps a wiser alternative.

Scully's (2002) popular publication *Dominion: The Power of Man* [sic], *the Suffering of Animals, and the Call to Mercy* attempts to reinterpret the Bible and reframes passages to suggest that human domination over other animals is a relationship of stewardship instead. But some research suggests that religion may even create a criminogenic effect, meaning that religious beliefs can be distorted (sometimes purposefully so) to both allow for and even encourage criminal behavior (Topalli et al., 2013). Religiosity can be used as a means of managing a deviant identity in a way that adheres to predominant social values. Divine sanction, then, can be called upon to support and rationalize extremely oppressive behavior. This is essentially a contestation over meaning that cannot be won, because it is ultimately grounded in interpretations of a doctrine based less in fact than in a collection of politically influenced, faith-based interpretations. It is the subjective versus the subjective. With no objective basis, it will remain a war of words with no end in sight.

Fighting fire with fire or water?

In 2012, PETA asked an American megachurch to hang a pro-vegan banner that would read: "Blessed are the Merciful." In a news release, PETA explains that Nonhuman Animals, "depend on humans to show them mercy" (PETA, 2012). PETA chose this particular megachurch because its pastor had encouraged his congregation to forgo "unclean" pig's flesh. PETA thus tries to reframe semi-vegetarianism intended for spiritual purity as potential veganism engaged as spiritual paternalism. Like Barfa's argument for veganism as a means to clear one's conscious, PETA's approach completely detracts from the breach of justice to Nonhuman Animals, instead depicting veganism as an advantage to humans.

The UPC has an ongoing campaign to end the use of chickens in Jewish rituals that is often based on claims to the sentience of chickens and their capacity to suffer. However, the UPC pairs its scientific claimsmaking with religious claimsmaking, and this is where things become muddled. Kapparot, it is argued, runs counter to Jewish values of mercy:

> While the Jewish tradition is filled with concepts, prayers and actions during the Rosh Hashanah-Yom Kippur period that stress the importance of rachamim (compassion and sensitivity), the message of kapparot using chickens to those who take part and view it, including

children, is a lesson of insensitivity to the feelings of other living creatures. (United Poultry Concerns, no date)

In tandem with their religious rhetoric, the UPC created the "Alliance to End Chickens as Kaporos," which reaches out to Jewish religious leaders and organizations with shared concerns for the well-being of roosters and hens. While drawing on the legitimacy of leaders and collectives within the community in question is arguably a much stronger (and respectful) strategy than is PETA's campaign, which remains divorced from the community that it seeks to influence, there is still the concern over dueling interpretations of religious doctrine. An ideology bound to faith is, by definition, generally less interested in evidence. Like many institutionalized prescriptions for human behavior, religion is not immune to change, but the work will not be easy. Furthermore, any progress that is gained from a religious argument for anti-speciesism is still constrained by human superiority, and it is still subject to dismissal should the religious ideology shift out of Nonhuman Animals' favor in the future. Binding an argument to evidence is likely to be a more enduring approach because it is less likely to be undermined by future ideological shifts.

Furthermore, objectively bound evidence is far more universal. It crosses across all cultures and religious practices. Atheists, Hindus, Buddhists, Christians, Pagans, and almost everyone in between will recognize the validity of Isaac Newton's findings on gravity, for instance. While different religious ideologies might ascribe differing explanations for gravity that might compete with Newton's, no one disagrees that when an apple parts with its tree, it falls down toward the ground. Relatedly, while various religious ideologies may have differing reasons for ascribing moral worth to vulnerable human groups like women and homeless persons, it has been largely agreed upon that women, homeless persons, and others are human and sentient. Furthermore, many legal institutions reinforce this objective reality. If advocates were to focus on the objective realities of the social world (apples fall down toward the earth, all members of the human species have a more or less equal capacity for sentience, and *any* member of a sentient species, human or not, has a basic interest in seeking pleasure and avoiding pain and death), it would be a more concrete and farther-reaching approach. Regardless of one's spiritual affiliation, the majority of humanity recognizes that pain hurts and it is a negative thing. Pain is an objective reality. Most recognize that humans are capable of experiencing pain; the task remains to demonstrate that pain is an objective reality for Nonhuman

Animals as well and that this is a bad thing for them. If causing pain and death to other humans is undesirable, so should it be for other animals who share similar capacities for personhood.

Religiosity and social change

Again, religiosity often runs counter to support for Nonhuman Animal liberation. A 1997 study finds that respondents with higher levels of religious association tend to be more opposed to Nonhuman Animal rights.[3] Church attendance also correlates negatively with pro-animal attitudes toward Nonhuman Animal rights (Peek et al., 1997, p.433). A more recent study conducted by FARM finds that the effectiveness of outreach literature hinges on religiosity: those with conservative or fundamentalist religious beliefs are significantly less receptive to a Nonhuman Animal rights message (Monteiro, 2012). Similarly, researchers have identified a correlation between right-wing ideology and greater engagement in speciesism. This relationship is thought to reflect support for the dominant ideologies of oppression and a resistance to social change, whereby anti-speciesism efforts are perceived to be a threat (Dhont and Hodson, 2014, pp.15–16).

Of course, it cannot be denied that religion has been central to many social movements. The Quakers, for instance, were successful in influencing social attitudes regarding other animals and enacting legislative change in regard to vivisection (Glaholt, 2012). Religion can be a powerful source of collective identity, one that is especially suited to facilitating mobilization (Green, 1999, p.153). For some groups, it has also been useful in resisting domination by nurturing an oppositional culture and utilizing sacred symbols to clarify goals (Harris, 2001, p.38). Although many important leaders and tactics of the Civil Rights Era were secular (Gorham, 2013, no pagination), the religious undertone to Martin Luther King Jr.'s mobilization efforts built community and both empowered and inspired people (Marsh, 2005). In the 18th and 19th centuries, the Quaker community spearheaded anti-slavery mobilization through Christian epistemology (Stewart, 1976, p.12). However, the anti-slavery movement eventually faced a schism that separated those who thought the church an important ally from those who thought the church a complacent accomplice to human bondage. William Lloyd Garrison saw the church (and the government for that matter) as guilty in upholding injustice and thus incapable of instituting change. Indeed, many churches actively avoided entanglement with abolitionism (McKivigan, 1999, xv). Garrison relied instead on tactics of moral suasion. In fact, the secular ideologies of universal liberty, equality, and natural rights played an important role in anti-slavery claimsmaking in the early years of the American republic (Mason, 2011).

Religion played a major part in anti-slavery efforts, but religion was also a major barrier to social change in maintaining and legitimizing human inequality. Therefore, the utility of religious appeals largely derives from the group's claimsmaking strength and ingenuity. Whichever group can successfully frame religion in a way that legitimizes their position will earn the privilege of constructing social reality. As evidenced by Grimké's 1836 *Appeal to the Christian Women of the South*, a book which meticulously counters Christian justifications for slavery,[4] this can be a complicated undertaking. And while Stowe also conjures moving religious sentiment for the anti-slavery cause in her 1852 *Uncle Tom's Cabin*,[5] others quickly responded with assertions that "Christian slavery" was the "brightest sunbeam which Omniscience has destined for his [slave] existence" (McCord, 1853, p.120) and that Stowe was like "Satan starting up from his disguise" for writing "fiction" that "distorted or disavowed" Biblical doctrines (*Southern Literary Messenger*, 1852, p.730). These competing claims to the same religious ideology readily manifest because *religion is highly contextual*. Interpretations are embedded in cultural norms and tend to reflect the interests of those in power. Marginalized groups are left with the futile task of reconstructing the symbolic capital[6] of the privileged. In the case of anti-slavery efforts, the wealthy slaveholders who enjoyed considerably more economic and political power[7] could interpret the language of the Bible to reflect their interests. They shaped the identity of the African slave as a subhuman brute thankful for white benevolence.

In meaning contestation, both sides struggle for the right to frame reality in their favor, and in doing so, they often seek to delegitimize and vilify their opponent (Ellingson, 1995, p.109). If a group can link their opponent to the willful subversion of social order, this is a powerful dismissal of their opponent's claims (Bromley and Cutchin, 1999, p.195). Anti-slavery abolitionists denounced slavery as evil and anti-Christian, while slaveholders and slavery apologists depicted abolitionists as arrogant and anti-American. Nonhuman Animal rights activists play the same game, labeling exploiters "cruel" or "evil," while activists themselves are labeled "terrorists." Because Nonhuman Animal use is normalized and because exploiters enjoy considerable social power, these exploiters are able to control the symbolic landscape. Lacking capital of this kind, the movement's accusations of cruelty and wickedness have considerably less impact on large industries and institutions. Media portrayals of vegans and Nonhuman Animal activists are largely negative (Cole and Morgan, 2011a), as the media tends to reflect the interests of the powerful (Shoemaker and Reese, 1996). What is more, the Animal Enterprise Terrorism Act (promoted by exploitative industries with enormous lobbying strength) has codified Nonhuman Animal activism as criminal and unpatriotic (Lovitz, 2010, pp.105–7).

Using the ideological framework of oppression in social justice advocacy, then, is risky business. The cards are generally stacked against the contesting group. Radical social change workers should consider reaching deeper for a more grounded notion of morality, one that exists independent of religious affiliation, culture, or historical era. Some scientists argue that the universalities in human values rooted in evolutionary history can offer objective understandings of morality (Harris, 2010). Many human values (like the condemnation of stealing and incest) are thought to be consistent across cultures because they have been advantageous to species survival. Certainly, as humans have expanded from small social groups to large, somewhat anonymous societies, the survival strategies that were originally intended for close-knit networks might be stretched past efficacy and will need to adapt. However, psychologist Steven Pinker's (2011) analysis of human history does suggest that human societies are becoming less violent overall and that war and crime are on the decline. Sociologists also recognize that as a society develops or modernizes, it tends to shift away from religious values and institutions and becomes increasingly secular (Bruce, 2011, p.56). In other words, a just society can be obtained through secular channels.

Authority and resistance

A central reason why religion becomes problematic for advocating on behalf of other animals is because it resists criticism. Religion becomes an impervious authority that shapes social norms, demands obedience, and avoids examination: "religion, it must be recognized, is the only form of thinking in which bad ideas are held in perpetual immunity from criticism and doing so is considered sacred, which is the act of faith" (Harris, 2007). However, this phenomenon can happen in less institutionalized and secular settings as well.

For instance, Singer has argued that death is not a harm for other animals, and thus, he sometimes promotes higher "welfare" products (Singer and Mason, 2006, p.270). For many Nonhuman Animal rights theorists, this argument is thought to seriously undermine the interests of other animals who will be used and killed. In his 2006 publication,

Torres relates his experiences in expressing his concerns with Singer's welfarist position. He reports having received considerable backlash for criticizing the "father" of Nonhuman Animal rights, a reaction that was related to deference to authority rather than to soundness of argument. Influential personalities can develop an impervious authority that is just as problematic as faith-based authority. This is not to say that the ideas of influential persons are unimportant, but only to insist that all ideas must be subject to healthy skepticism. No person, idea, belief, or claim should be invulnerable. Devotion, be it spiritual or secular, can be devastating to critical thinking, and it works to stagnate intellectual growth and social change. Because humans are fallible, no one person (or group of people) can lay claim to all answers, and claims to "truth" should be suspect. The creation of idols and heroes is certainly important for boosting morale and motivating activism, but the practice can easily backfire when it works to shut down discourse and impede effective advocacy.

On the other hand, it is equally problematic to completely eschew certain ideas, based solely on their source or affiliation. As one example, many abolitionist groups avoid promoting the research of vegan critical race advocates because they are not thought to adhere to Francionian principles of abolitionist theory. Consequently, their hugely important work on white normativity and post-race ideology in the Nonhuman Animal rights movement – theory that is relevant regardless of political allegiances or lack thereof – is overlooked. If the movement ignores the voices of those who are not abolitionist, vegan, or secular, it would be doing itself, and Nonhuman Animals, a major disservice. While the "anything goes" approach is surely not the conclusion to draw (not every idea or theory is valid or sound), advocates would do well to appreciate a diversity of knowledges and skills. Theory should be worthy of its own scrutiny, and it should stand independently of the messenger. Social change workers should be skeptical of authority in a rational approach to outreach. This is not to say that skill, experience, and training are not worthy of consideration, but only to suggest that a position of authority is not a position that grants freedom from criticism. It is common for individuals to exhibit a certain trust and faith in authority figures. It is presumed that their position of authority was earned based on their expertise, though this is not always the case. Oftentimes, authority is achieved through access to structural advantages not made available to those in marginalized groups. Both religious and nonreligious approaches to social change can thus be problematic if they demand faith and they encourage communities to rely on authorities to interpret and dictate what faith should entail.

Respecting diversity

It should be considered that an intersectional, rational approach will come across one important caveat: how can advocates respect diversity among marginalized groups while also advocating critical thinking? At times, the two actions may come into conflict. For example, African Americans are the most religiously devout demographic in the United States (The Pew Forum on Religion & Public Life, 2008, p.40). As was previously mentioned, religion has also been an integral mechanism of the Civil Rights struggle. Religion not only gives solace, inspiration, and hope in a grossly discriminatory society but it also creates community. However, some African Americans have criticized the intense religiosity of their community as representative of cultural colonization. Christianity, in particular, is largely an imposition of white supremacy with the historical intention of controlling slaves and other colonized peoples. "Blackness" is often constructed as the ultimate embodiment of sin and savagery. As a result, there is intense pressure on people of color to overcompensate in their devotion to demonstrate their separation from this "evil" Blackness (Hutchinson, 2013a).

Some part of this process was intentional, a result of the Black community's church-led commitment to politics of respectability (Harris, 2003, p.213; Higginbotham, 1993, p.185). Formulated in the Progressive Era in reaction to extreme structural racism, the politics of respectability not only police African American behavior, but also seek to foster a particular presentation to dominant white society. These expectations can be upheld and expected by whites as well as communities of color. In this way, religiosity intersects with respectability politics not only as a reaction to white supremacy, but also a means of maintaining white superiority. When the dynamic of morality is one that positions people of color as the very epitome of impurity, they are pressured to reject their own identity and seek an unachievable level of perfection.

There is also a gendered dynamic, with women being more religious than men (Walter and Davie, 1998, p.640). As with people of color, this may have to do with the religious construction of women as the embodiment of evil, inherently flawed, and prone to sin. Women, especially women of color, are likely under greater pressure to hyper-perform their devotion in a way that separates them from this identity. Similar processes occur for women who are pressured to reject their femininity and take on masculine traits and patriarchal values to earn social capital (Levy, 2005, p.95). Hilary Clinton, for instance, did not rise to power as a politician by demonstrating feminine power (power that is relational, emotional, and caring). Instead, she achieved political clout because she was able to successfully emulate many masculine forms of power (those related to assertiveness, competitiveness, and even her iconic pant suits). Many women do not aspire to be "girly girls" but rather seek to be "one of the boys." Femininity is associated with powerlessness and masculinity with power, so many women overcompensate with masculine traits to overcome the "handicap" of womanhood. They have to work harder, get more education, and sacrifice more. Alternatively, many women engage in patriarchal bargaining by over-performing their femininity. These women may adopt patriarchal constraints as a coping mechanism and a strategy for survival in an environment that is largely hostile to women (Kandiyoti, 1988). This is demonstrated in the *Girls Gone Wild* phenomenon that sees women *volunteering* to perform sexualized gender roles for acceptance and reward in a patriarchal environment.

Similarly, many people of color have also been indoctrinated with the notion that "Blackness" (or "Brownness") is inherently negative and that whiteness is superior and preferable. To harness the power of whiteness in a white supremacy, many people of color reject, downplay, or compartmentalize their "Blackness" (Fanon, 2008). This might entail use of "proper" (in other words, white Anglo-Saxon) English, dressing white, and overcompensating in educational and employment pursuits. It might even entail the physical attainment of whiteness, as evidenced in the continued popularity of skin bleaching creams. The power of whiteness is so fully engrained into society that people of color will sometimes seek to distance themselves culturally and physically from their own communities and their own bodies. Under a theistic, white, male supremacy, women have to be *more* male, people of color have to be *more* white, and both have to be *more* religious to combat the defeating stereotypes ascribed to them and the institutionalized discrimination that disadvantages them.

This hyper-religiosity is thought by some to be a significant hindrance to achieving social, political, and economical progress for women and communities of color. Atheist theorist and woman of color Sikivu Hutchinson (2013b) suggests, "Because charismatic faith movements thrive in the presence of socioeconomic and political turbulence, black religiosity is flourishing." A preoccupation with performing religion in a way that compensates for the social stigma of color and womanhood means that vulnerable groups can become so focused on this identity that they may be unable or unwilling to give proper attention to how religion may actually be hurtful or hindering. Candace Gorham (2013) furthers that the stakes are so high for some that questioning the validity of religious claims and religious institutions becomes unthinkable. She notes the subsequent potential for severe consequences to African American women's emotional and physical health.

This pressure also creates a need to police any potential defectors. To use the language of Francis Beal (1970, p.112), female-identified atheists, particularly those who are of color, are likely to experience "double jeopardy" when the disadvantages associated with gender, race, and nonbelief intersect. This is not unlike the compounding stigmas associated with identifying as both vegan and female and/or of color. White males who adopt atheism or veganism certainly experience stigmatization as well, but the incredible social power ascribed to white masculinity means that their positions and decisions will be granted much more legitimacy and respect. They are likely to be called into question for defecting from the norm. For the vulnerable, however, there seems to be few incentives for already marginalized groups to further ostracize themselves. Despite the pressure for vulnerable groups to conform to religiosity, however, there is actually a rich history of African American (Hutchison, 2011, pp.101–34) and feminist (Gaylor, 1997) free thought. Atheism poses a challenge to oppressive authority, making it attractive to many involved in social justice work. For some individuals in marginalized groups, atheism is understood to be emancipatory (Fonza, 2013). It is a site of resistance.

Atheist alternatives

Thus far, I have argued that religion is often used to frame people of color, women of all racial identities, Nonhuman Animals, and other vulnerable social groups as unworthy of full citizenship and in need of domination. The very identities of these groups are framed as incurably flawed. Disadvantaged humans are thus encouraged to exaggerate their religiosity to compensate for the religious narratives that pit them as the embodiment of evil. Therefore, not only is religion imposed on vulnerable groups to justify their oppression, but also religious claimsmaking encourages them to oppress themselves in conforming to inherently exploitative systems as a matter of survival. Just as Nonhuman Animal advocates seek to dismantle the ill-effects of religion with religious tactics, human groups have attempted to overcome their own religiously based suffering by relying on increased religiosity. Vulnerable groups thus come to self-police, a consequence that is an especially potent mechanism of power.

To be clear, an argument for rational thinking in collective action and social movement claimsmaking does not imply that all activists must become agnostic or atheist and begin to advocate that other oppressed groups do the same. One's personal belief system, religion, or spiritual affiliation is one's own personal business. Atheist theory is thus applied as a respectful critique of *institutionalized* religion, an institution that exists as an important hindrance to critical thinking at the societal level and a major barrier to achieving social equality. As educational attainment increases, belief in religion decreases (Lynn et al., 2009). Religion easily flourishes in ignorance, and systemic ignorance makes social change difficult because the need for change and even the *potential* for change can be obscured from the social imagination.

A criticism of religion does not presuppose that there cannot be respect for aspects of religion that serve as important social functions. Forgoing the oppressiveness of religion need not entail the rejection of community and tradition. Secularized alternatives to these social goods abound. Many atheists practice Christmas and Easter, for example. Atheist "churches" are also forming, where nonbelievers can foster togetherness in their community on a regular basis and in a structured manner. Recall that Durkheim also sees virtue in those secular ideologies with the ability to pull societies together for a common purpose. Morality continues to flourish in the absence of religion (Harris, 2010). Some research even demonstrates that atheists are more likely than their religious counterparts to react to feelings of compassion with increased generosity (Saslow et al., 2012).

Unfortunately, atheists are subject to intense discrimination. It is often presumed that atheists, by rejecting religion, refuse to cooperate with mainstream society. This creates an atmosphere of distrust that is quite toxic to nonbelievers (Gervais et al., 2011). It should come as no surprise that a demographic that values critical thinking over unquestioning obedience to authority should come under scrutiny in a society that operates through hierarchy and oppression. Atheists are a threat to existing systems of power. Outspoken atheists are not granted the same "freedom of religion" that the faithful enjoy. It is not illegal to be an atheist in America, but the social stigma that surrounds atheism ensures that most remain silent about their secular identification. If critical thinking is crucial to dismantling social inequality, the distrust and disdain of atheism may act as a considerable impediment to social change. However, it is also possible that the atheist project itself may also be responsible for this stagnation by frequently replicating many of the same irrationalities that characterize a religious state.

Atheism in the anthroparchy

Atheist privilege: Guilty of being human

To be clear, atheism is not synonymous with critical thinking. The secular argument thus presented has implied that religion is largely incongruent with anti-speciesist efforts, but this is not to suggest that one's *personal* theism or atheism is necessarily relevant to social movement efforts. Atheists are not automatically any more rational than Christians or Hindus. Neither does scientific training grant immunity from irrationality, as was explored in Chapter 4. Authority and privilege can sometimes trump rationality.

Anthroparchy[8] maintains powerful ideologies of domination, even in free-thinking spaces. The atheist movement, for instance, tends to be very resistant to anti-speciesism. The movement's leading intersectional feminist project, *Skepchick*, often harbors discrediting discourse on veganism and Nonhuman Animal rights. In one essay published with the intention of tackling the disconnect between atheism and veganism, a contributor argues that readers need not feel guilty for eschewing veganism due to life complications that "can get in the way of perfect food of behavior" (James, 2013). The hesitancy to go vegan for reasons related to dietary restrictions, eating disorders, or financial cost is made analogous to avoiding stressful life obligations, like visiting with family. Going vegan and visiting parents are both considered ethically important actions, but *Skepchick* presents them as moral exemptions because they are emotionally draining: "Each of us has a finite amount of time, money, and energy, and we have to decide which arenas to focus those resources in." Social justice activism thus becomes a zero-sum game: "we simply cannot do all of them." Veganism is thought to deplete resources in a way that leaves humans unable to act ethically. This perceived depletion impacts not only finances but also mental well-being and physical health. If skepchicks do not get "adequate protein," for instance, they can become "anxious," "unhappy," "cranky," and generally less capable of engaging in pro-social behavior.

Skepchick's position echoes that of *Vegan Soapbox*, cited in the previous chapter. The anti-intersectionality argument which supposes that the adoption of veganism necessitates a choice between one's personal well-being and the well-being of others conjures a conflict of interest that does not actually exist. Unfortunately, many in the atheist community rely on a litany of unsupported justifications for continued participation in Nonhuman Animal oppression, with human privilege often misconstrued as "need." The *Skepchick* essay in question was authored by a woman who identifies as having an eating disorder, but few secularists are constrained in this way. Indeed, they are an extremely privileged group aside from their atheist status, with the majority identifying as white, male, young, educated, and middle to upper class (Keysar, 2007, pp.34–6). Too frequently, critical thinking appears valuable only until it challenges atheist privilege. If skepticism were appropriately prioritized, there would be an active engagement with the bountiful scientific literature that demonstrates the dangerousness of Nonhuman Animal products for human health and environmental sustainability. The research is also quite clear that humans can easily meet their protein quota from a plant-based, vegan diet. Indeed, too much protein (and animal-derived protein in general) is a problem commonly associated with a non-vegan diet. It is linked to many serious diseases, like heart disease, cancer, osteoporosis, and diabetes (Campbell, 2006, pp.27–41). Considerable research also speaks to the devastation that non-vegan eating poses to at-risk nonhuman communities. Science is on the side of veganism, if only skeptics were willing to acknowledge it.

It is unfortunate that projects like *Skepchick*'s, which attempt to challenge male supremacy in the atheist movement, also dismiss other social justice movements as though they are competing for resources and energy. Veganism is framed as an individual choice rather than as a collective action on behalf of disenfranchised Nonhuman Animals. In making a case for individualism, the anti-vegan atheist position sees egalitarianism as something that each person can strive for if so inclined. Importantly, the same case is not made for misogyny in atheist circles. It is unlikely that feminist atheists would relieve other activists of moral responsibility if treating women with respect was thought to run counter to an individual's available resources. It is also doubtful that the feminist atheist position would claim that men need not concern themselves with women's rights if doing so would be a stressful experience. Almost certainly, feminist atheism would not suggest that treating women equally is detracting atheists from other anti-oppression work. Therefore, a very strange condition of cognitive dissonance appears to be present. On the one hand, there is a growing demand for intersectionality in atheist advocacy efforts, but on the other hand, the same rationalizations of privilege insist that intersectionality efforts are distracting in the context of speciesism.

The ability to decide which issues are important and worth fighting for is, in this case, a matter of privilege. The secular movement is privileged in that it is dominated by moneyed white, Western men. It is therefore predictable that feminist atheists meet with resistance, ridicule, and harassment by atheist men who insist that feminism is unnecessary and divisive. However, feminist atheists are capable of demonstrating extreme privilege themselves. White, Western, middle-class women can make claims that benefit them (women's equality in atheism) and subsequently denounce claims that are a threat to their own privilege. For those not facing significant structural barriers, the consumption of Nonhuman Animal products is complacent with systemic violence enacted on other animals. The ability to decide that veganism is optional is reflective of extreme privilege, as is the framing of non-veganism as an individual choice. *Skepchick*, in this example, points to atheism's failure to engage vegan solidarity as a problem specifically because of the associated feelings of guilt. It is not enough that secular speciesists want to continue to hurt others for their benefit; they also appear to desire immunity to criticism. Freedom from criticism, however, is a direct violation of skeptic values.

The ideological supports for privilege can be overwhelmingly powerful. This response is also common to anti-racist work. It is not uncommon for whites to interpret criticisms of *systemic* white supremacy and its relationship to the perpetuation of violence against the vulnerable as a personal attack. They often respond with excuses and appeals to hurt feelings in such a way as to undermine the relevance of social justice claimsmaking and re-center white privilege. For one, people with privilege are simply not used to having this privilege challenged. For two, privilege allows them to protect what they may understand to be an "innocent" participation in violence. For example, in 2013, Hamilton College hosted a series on internalized racism for students and faculty. In response, the university's daily bulletin published a poem for campus distribution that lamented that discussing race and racism might actually be racist. The authors suggest that racism discourse creates a divide between whites and non-whites and is discriminatory against whites (New Wave Feminism, 2013):

I'm sorry
For something that I didn't do
Lynched somebody
But I don't know who
You blame me for slavery
A hundred years before I was born

Guilty of being white
(*The Daily Bull*, 2013)

In a society where oppression is made invisible by a false consciousness of egalitarianism and where few still openly admit to being prejudiced or bigoted, discussions of systemic inequality are often taken very personally.

It is this same process that may lead atheists to also feel unhappy about being made to feel "guilty of being human." Like some white students of Hamilton College, non-vegan skeptics may fail to see the utility in being criticized for things they believe they have no personal responsibility for. They are drawing on their social privilege to deflect attention from their connection to an oppressive system by highlighting the potentially negative impact that "divisive" criticism is thought to have on social justice activism. Subsequently, topics relating to speciesism and veganism, if not ignored altogether, are often met with intense ridicule or ideologically inspired claimsmaking that lacks supporting evidence. This routine disregard for Nonhuman Animal rights issues is quite telling given the growing body of scientific literature that demonstrates the disastrous impact of Nonhuman Animal agriculture and other forms of speciesism. Identification with the atheist and skeptic movements will not provide an individual immunity from the obfuscating effects of socialization and privilege. Rather, it could actually aggravate these impediments if skeptic activists presume themselves to be especially skilled in critical thinking and thus incapable of irrational thinking.

Atheism and anti-speciesist attitudes

In lieu of these issues, a small subset of skeptical vegans has materialized, as evidenced in the modest growth of science-based abolitionist grassroots groups. Also encouraging, the National Secular Society (2012) advocates against some religious practices deemed especially cruel, such as ritual slaughter. As early as 1921, Henry Salt reports that the Society had begun to advocate for more humane treatment of other animals. Of course, skeptical vegans, who are human after all, sometimes fall short of true objectivity as well. Critical thinking, rationality, and reasoning are skills independent of personal beliefs and ideology. Atheism, though, encourages critical thinking and is more compatible with anti-speciesist attitudes. This compatibility surfaces in the demographic data of Nonhuman Animal rights activists.

Perhaps the most obvious counter-example to this correlation is the long history of plant-based eating and cow worship in Indian culture. While India is a land of many millions of vegetarians, Indian vegetarianism may be better understood as a reflection of social stratification than as an ethical obligation to other animals (Ilaiah, 2009, p.108).

Consuming animal flesh in these cases is considered polluting (Ruby et al., 2013). Vegetarianism is often reserved for the upper castes interested in maintaining status purity and a "last resort" for the poorer populations who have no choice but to consume cheaper plant-based diets.

In the West, where non-vegan diets are the norm, however, there appears to be a correlation between veganism and atheism. A 1984 survey of *Animals Agenda* subscribers finds that 65 per cent of respondents identified as atheist or agnostic (Guither, 1998, p.67). A 1992 study reports that 48 per cent of Nonhuman Animal rights activists identified as atheist or agnostic, compromising the largest demographic among its participants (Galvin and Herzog, 1992, p.144). In a 1997 study of protest attendees and college students, those respondents who reported no religious affiliation demonstrated more support for Nonhuman Animal rights than did religiously affiliated respondents (Peek et al., 1997). A 2007 study finds that those who believe in evolution are more likely to support Nonhuman Animal rights than those of certain religious denominations (DeLeeuw et al., 2007). A 2012 study finds that atheist and agnostic participants offer more support for Nonhuman Animal rights than their religious counterparts do (Gabriel et al., 2012, p.391). The influence of rationality appears to be quite strong in anti-speciesism circles. Many activists become interested in advocating for other animals as a result of rational considerations, while others also buttress their emotional concerns for other animals with rationality and logic (Herzog, 1993, p.107).

Many theorists have attempted to reconcile religious doctrine with justice for other animals, but few published works of the modern Nonhuman Animal rights era have framed a moral obligation to other animals as a strictly secular endeavor absent of religious potentiality. Given the large demographic of atheist and religiously unaffiliated individuals in Nonhuman Animal advocacy and the increased receptiveness to Nonhuman Animal rights claimsmaking by nonbelievers in the general public, this seems a strange oversight. It is possible that societal anti-atheist discrimination could impact how the Nonhuman Animal rights movement attempts to frame itself. Recall that social movements attempt to frame their claimsmaking in a way that is thought to best resonate with their audience. Perhaps an outspoken atheist identity might be seen as a liability if it could potentially redirect atheist discrimination toward the movement. As discussed in earlier chapters, the Nonhuman Animal rights movement has already shouldered a good deal of societal prejudice based on its association with women. While it is impossible to hide the gender demographic, atheism is an invisible identity. It can be successfully minimized and probably is.

Instead, the Nonhuman Animal rights movement attempts to resonate with a largely religious public by relying on claimsmaking based on faith and compassion. This occurs in spite of the fact that religiosity tends to run counter to pro-animal attitudes and despite the tendency for religiously framed claimsmaking to lack resonance to the point of eliciting negative reactions. Francione's (2012c) vegan slogan "Go ahimsic,"[9] for instance, is not likely to be attractive to nonbelievers. Indeed, the most receptive demographic – the nonreligious – is rarely specifically targeted, at least in the United States. For that matter, the atheists and nonbelievers already involved within the movement enjoy little collective identity and representation.[10] The Nonhuman Animal rights movement could be said to act as a microcosm of the anti-atheist marginalization that characterizes larger society.

Atheist exclusion

Atheists remain one of the most discriminated against groups in the United States as well as abroad. According to the International Humanist and Ethical Union, atheists and other nonreligious persons face laws that

> deny atheists' right to exist, curtail their freedom of belief and expression, revoke their right to citizenship, restrict their right to marry, obstruct their access to public education, prohibit them from holding public office, prevent them from working for the state, criminalize their criticism of religion, and execute them for leaving the religion of their parents. (2012, p.9)

Atheists are not trusted by mainstream society: they are considered un-American, immoral, dangerous, arrogant, and evil. In short, they are otherized (Edgell et al., 2006). Due to rampant and largely unacknowledged discrimination, many nonbelievers shirk from openly identifying as atheist. While an outspoken celebrity atheist himself, advocate Sam Harris urges the free-thinking community to move away from brandishing the "Scarlet A" as a means to avoid the ideological barriers that inevitably arise and complicate the movement's efforts for science, reason, and critical thinking. He explains: "I think this whole conversation about the new atheists and militant atheism has been used to keep our criticism of religion at arm's length and has allowed people to reject our arguments without meeting the burden of actually answering them" (2007). To be sure, the Nonhuman Animal rights agenda has met with considerable resistance from exploitative industries and interest groups that reframe the threat to their privilege as a threat to their god, a threat to the nation's interest, and a threat to morality in general:

> To question the wholesale exploitation of animals by concerns like agribusiness or the biomedical industry is considered atheistic, since many believe that the word "dominion," as used in Genesis, means that God has given us the unconditional right to exploit all creatures, for whatever purpose. (Fox, 1983, p.171)

In other words, because speciesism is protected by religious ideology, a challenge to speciesism could be interpreted as a challenge to divine rule. Embracing an atheist ethic could create yet another avenue for the demonization of Nonhuman Animal rights activism.

Because the Nonhuman Animal rights movement is composed largely of female-identified activists, and women are an extremely devalued group across most societies, the movement has sought to distance itself from "effeminate" claimsmaking. That is, emotionality is often avoided, and men are pushed into leadership positions (Groves, 2001, pp.224–6). Just as the movement moved away from femininity, it seems to have moved away from secularism. One of the most detrimental aspects of the Nonhuman Animal rights industrial complex is the need for organizations to moderate their positions to appeal to the conservative foundations that supply many of their grants and to resonate with the largest public demographic to secure the greatest number of donations. This responsibility entails and active denunciation of radical claimsmaking. Though women and atheists constitute large percentages of the movement's demographic, they are routinely silenced or marginalized, perhaps more so for atheists.

So, while atheists seem to have a predisposition for anti-speciesism, the Nonhuman Animal rights movement ignores them as a group, excluding them from outreach efforts, theory, and discourse. The "Scarlet A" of atheism seems to emulate the "Scarlet V" of veganism. For professionalized organizations, atheism – like veganism – is likely seen as too "radical," too "extreme," and too off-putting to funders. If the communities that value and celebrate critical thinking were targeted, the movement could tap into a very powerful and influential demographic. In ostracizing atheists, the movement shuts the door on an important source of people power.

So long as the Nonhuman Animal rights movement frames its outreach according to the elite white, Western, male, theistic, able-bodied, heterosexual framework, it will be very difficult to create a sizable and diverse – and ultimately influential – constituency. The movement will not be able to create the important alliances and coalitions needed to address the complexities of oppression and the enormity of social inequality. It could be suggested that in order to dismantle this inequality, social change actors should focus on mobilizing powerful elites. But such an approach disregards the power of the critical mass, and it does so in a manner that is rather paternalistic. Appealing to elites also wrongly presumes that the privileged are the most receptive to change. Instead of advocating for radical structural change, the movement simply falls back into the discourse of oppression.

Atheism Plus

This chapter has argued that anti-speciesism efforts are most appropriately kept secular. Religious rhetoric has sometimes been used in the service of liberation, but more often than not, it is used to oppress. Furthermore, without grounding in the objective, observable world, claims for equality are lost in the fluidity of competing claims. The atheist demographic has demonstrated considerable receptivity to anti-speciesism, and it comprises a large percentage of the movement base. Yet, likely because the Nonhuman Animal rights movement has remained silent on intersections with atheism, the atheist community and secular movement have been particularly adverse to anti-speciesism and veganism. There may be a disdain for unquestionable authority and a celebration of critical thinking in atheist activism, but this does not mean that an interest in anti-speciesism will sprout up independently of vegan outreach. Atheism and skepticism are not impervious to the limitations of social conventions.

As explored in Chapter 4, rationality has traditionally been a masculine endeavor that legitimates patriarchy and both excludes and marginalizes women and other oppressed groups. This unchecked privilege is evidenced in the growing discord over inclusiveness and minority representation that has polarized the atheist community.[11] The constraints experienced by atheism as a collectivity is undoubtedly related to this vulnerability. Fundamentally, atheism itself is nothing more than the nonbelief in religion or deity: "atheism is not a thing. It is not a philosophy, just as non-racism is not one. It is not a worldview, and yet it is regularly construed as one and attacked as such" (Harris, 2007).

While some atheist advocates like Harris abandon self-identifying as atheist in favor of emphasizing strong argument and rigorous skepticism, others have attempted to advance atheism as a project that seeks to put critical thinking, skepticism, and free thought in the service of dismantling social inequality. Known as Atheism Plus,[12] this new wave, "welcomes all sexes, races, ages, and abilities and encourages an appreciation of human richness" (Myers, 2012, p.46). Non-belief, in this case, does not negate concern for social justice. This connection is particularly salient because atheists do not believe in an afterlife, thus lending greater weight to the importance of pro-social behavior before death:

> If we have any morality at all – and the evidence strongly suggests that we do, that human beings have some common moral principles wired into our brains through millions of years of evolution as a social species – then seeing terrible harm done to others through no fault of their own should make us cringe and demand our immediate and passionate attention. (Christina, 2012, p.40)

By specifically identifying as a *social justice* movement, Atheism Plus may be better suited to more inclusive notions of equality despite its anthropocentric shortcomings. The speciesist reaction to Nonhuman Animal issues in the *Skepchick* project (a major player in the Atheism Plus movement), however, demonstrates that atheism, too, has its own ideological barriers to overcome. True inclusivity must recognize Nonhuman Animals as a distinct social group, a group that experiences extreme inequality as a result of religious *and* secular institutions of oppression.

7
Conclusion

This book has argued a case for rational advocacy on behalf of Nonhuman Animals. The foundation for this approach is a basic requirement for substantiation. Advocates and organizations will benefit from grounding their theory and tactics in evidence and conducting efficacy research according to the scientific method. More than this, a rational approach will be cognizant of how social systems interfere with social movement decision-making. This approach recognizes the tendency for organizations to rationalize to the point of irrationality, having been pressured to professionalize under the constraints of the non-profit industrial complex. A rational approach also recognizes the importance of intersectionality. It is not rational to exclude persons of color, women, atheists, and other marginalized groups from claimsmaking and outreach. Building coalitions outside of the movement is absolutely essential for social movement success (Davis, 1990, pp.3–15; Jason, 2013, p.77; Szymanski, 2003, pp.212–16).

Rationalized advocacy must be engaged with sensitivity. A rational approach should recognize the tendency for rationality to favor masculinity at the expense of the feminine, meaning that advocates should take care to apply rationality within an anti-oppression framework. In addition to its patriarchal bias, the tendency for rationality to be misused in the service of other forms of privilege, such as whiteness and able-bodiedness, should also be acknowledged. Claims to rationality, in other words, may represent only another ideological barrier to critical thinking. This chapter will synthesize these points in the formulation of new theory of vegan abolitionism, one that works in the service of oppressed communities and resists aggravating oppression for others in the process.

Minding the evidence

For a movement with so few resources, the Nonhuman Animal rights movement has been rather enterprising in its ability to establish hundreds of grassroots and professionalized organizations, spearhead new tactics and creative outreach, and network both regionally and internationally to rally a rich variety of resources. Nonetheless, positive change for other animals has been slow coming in spite of this tremendous growth from so little. It seems that many activists and organizations are floundering in the dark, unsure of how to put their desire for social change into effective action. With the stakes so high and the suffering so great, many are rushing forward with any and every tactic available without stopping to seriously evaluate what works, what does not work, and what improvements might be made. Aggravating this, frustrated activists might belittle those who pause to read, discuss theory, and research, demanding of them, "What are you doing to help animals that are suffering *right now*?" Recall the organizational leaders cited in Chapter 1 who bemoan the "in-fighting" over strategy that is thought to distract from activism. It is unstructured frustration of this kind that impedes social change. This reaction stigmatizes reason and discourse, and it facilitates tactics that have not been shown to work.

This mentality is not just a reflection of genuine desperation to help other animals. It might also indicate an attempt to protect problematic movement structures that generally benefit persons with privilege and *not* Nonhuman Animals. Challenges to welfare reform, violence, sexism, racism, religiosity or other counterproductive aspects of the movement can elicit movement policing that charges critics with wasting time and allowing Nonhuman Animals to suffer. This is a rhetoric of censorship designed to protect the status quo. In her ethnographic study of women in the Nonhuman Animal rights movement, Emily Gaarder warns, "A movement culture that excessively and uncritically embraces 'movement unity' fails to challenge overt or unconscious acts of male dominance and white privilege" (2011, p.115). Many movement participants are made uncomfortable by disruptions to traditional advocacy pathways,[1] problematic as they might be. Movement monitoring and counter-claimsmaking divert attention from critical structural problems in the movement that are sometimes *intentionally* dysfunctional.

Abolitionist advocates may understandably feel considerable exasperation, thoroughly confused as to why organizations cooperate with institutional exploiters to improve their brand image and profitability, why they recruit so many young, thin white women to leaflet in the nude, or why they protect white boundaries around vegan outreach and knowingly exclude marginalized populations. The problem runs deeper than ignorance: organizations are in some ways benefiting from this unequal, irrational system. Welfarist, violent, sexist, racist, and religious advocacy may be dysfunctional in its inability to liberate Nonhuman Animals (and the humans whose suffering is entangled with that of other animals), but it is quite functional for achieving success within the non-profit industrial complex. It could be that no amount of evidence that dispels the utility of problematic pathways will ultimately be of any worth. This is because professionalized organizations are not exactly in the business of liberating other animals. More precisely, they are in the business of non-profit growth. Subsequently, Nonhuman Animals' interests are sidelined for bureaucratic purposes, while their suffering is tokenized for fundraising efforts. Growth within the capitalist system is difficult to reconcile with efforts for social restructuring and the abolition of exploitation.

Oftentimes, these organizations and their spokespersons superficially draw on scientific literature and conduct perfunctory evaluations to improve efficacy. Unfortunately, their allegiance to the conservative foundations that control grant disbursement means that the research will be framed in a way that exacts particular results, and any research conducted by outsiders will be interpreted in a way that suits the organization's mission. Non-profit status acts as a powerful bias that corrupts evidence and alienates radical theory. Admittedly, there will always be differing interpretations of data, but so long as an activist or organization knows that whatever they extrapolate must be presented in a manner that does not put off their funders, it cannot reasonably be expected that they interpret the data honestly or accurately. Professionalization creates a conflict of interest.

For those smaller, less formalized organizations that enjoy the luxury of answering to only their constituency, the data can be applied to outreach with true efficacy in mind, not grant proposals. Yet, grassroots activists, too, are tempted down this problematic pathway of non-profit growth. This is because larger organizations have become the shining example of success for the many smaller collectives that look up to them. Their hegemonic presence in the movement dictates advocacy norms that become cemented in the movement culture as natural, common sense, or most appropriate and effective. Chapter 4 discussed, for instance, the standardization of naked protest "for the animals." Having successfully associated nudity and pornography with female-appropriate Nonhuman Animal rights activism, PETA unwittingly encourages smaller groups across the country to sexually objectify young, white female-identified volunteers in its campaigning efforts as well. Other groups may presume that this tactic works based on PETA's bureaucratic success despite evidence that would suggest that it is unhelpful for achieving abolition.

Localized grassroots groups may also prioritize growth with the expectation of eventually incorporating as a non-profit. Again, the presumption is that this model is the best approach because the larger organizations have normalized this pathway as the natural progression for activists. It is worth considering, however, that activists have been mobilizing with some success for quite some time before the rise of professionalization in the 1970s and 1980s. The non-profit way has not always been the only way. For that matter, many marginalized groups do not have access to the non-profit model, but they have nonetheless continued to make important transformations in their communities without the resources available to privileged demographics and larger groups.

The misleading "common sense" of advocacy also adulterates effective social change repertoires regarding the tolerance of violent methods. As a popular tactic for many centuries, violence has always been central or at least peripheral in social movement strategies. Whether or not violence works is highly contextual, but recall previously discussed research that establishes that social change that results from nonviolent mobilization is the most successful and lasting (Chenoweth and Stephan, 2011). Nonviolence should not be confused with inaction. Nonviolent resistance *is* resistance. Nonviolent tactics *are* tactics. Nonviolence is a strategy, not surrender.[2] Violence in advocacy on behalf of other animals is particularly problematic because it often extends beyond threats of physical harm, arson, and emotional terror and because it can actually normalize oppressive structures. As discussed in Chapter 3, this tactic aggravates the marginalization of women and people of color who are imperiled by the consequences of violent mobilization. Furthermore, violence and militarization are traditionally associated with patriarchal control and capitalist exploitation. Strategically and theoretically, violence is incongruent with a vegan abolitionist goal.

The Nonhuman Animal rights movement also relies heavily on health claims when promoting veganism, though the utility in this strategy is contested. Concerns with a vegan diet's ability to meet nutritional needs means that some discussion of health will always be necessary, but focusing too much on this area may not be very helpful. Research indicates that most people go vegetarian or vegan for ethical reasons

(Cron and Pobocik, 2013; Haverstock and Forgays, 2012, p.1033; Hussar and Harris, 2010, pp.633–5), and those who transition to veganism in solidarity with Nonhuman Animal rights are more likely to remain committed to the change (Menzies and Sheeshka, 2012, p.167). Framing veganism as a political act against structures of oppression will be more effective than framing veganism as just another part of a healthy lifestyle. When understood as a diet, veganism becomes individualized as a strategy for personal improvement, not collective action toward social equality. Furthermore, ethical vegans also recognize that speciesism is infinitely more complex than individual food choices. The health argument excludes concerns about Nonhuman Animals used in non-food items, entertainment, sports, and science. Health arguments also tend to ostracize fat body types. When vegan activists promote veganism as a means of shedding pounds and getting fit, especially when young, thin white women are used as mascots for healthy veganism, the implied meaning is that body types that deviate from this ideal are undesirable and devalued (Harper, 2010b, p.175).

One consideration is that Nonhuman Animal rights claims may not resonate with all demographics equally. For communities ravaged by illness and disease, health is a more immediate and pressing concern. Importantly, promoting veganism "for health" is distinct from promoting veganism as a resistance to structural discrimination. For instance, white-identified vegans might devalue Harper's approach to veganism because it prioritizes human experiences with colonization, slavery, and environmental racism. She relegates other animals into one of several vulnerable groups facing oppression. Nonhuman Animals are no longer *the* group of concern, which challenges the anti-speciesism framework that the white-centric movement is accustomed to. Of course, non-vegan abolitionist activists often harbor the same criticisms for vegan abolitionists, as people of color, women, and other vulnerable humans are not the first objects of concern in the Nonhuman Animal rights movement. Therefore, it may be wiser to promote veganism, not as a means to improve health but as a means to dismantle oppression. This approach satisfies the fundamental interest of all liberal social justice movements. It may also reduce recidivism rates. Veganism as an ethical commitment to collective social justice action is anchoring.

Similarly to health and diet claimsmaking, a framework of spirituality has also been cultivated in the Nonhuman Animal rights movement despite considerable evidence that contradicts the utility of doing so. It was argued that religious claimsmaking makes persuasion difficult, as religious beliefs are bound to oppressive social structures and can be extremely subjective. It was also suggested that claimsmaking of this kind detracts attention from the vulnerable group in question. For example, white abolitionist Angelina Grimké (1836) spoke out against slavery, not specifically as an injustice to those held in bondage, but as a sin sure to damn the souls of white "masters" and their families. Today, I suspect that many would find such a position disconcerting. From a modern perspective, African Americans deserve freedom for *themselves*, not for white salvation. In a similar manner, framing Nonhuman Animal rights as a matter of spiritual obligation and human acquittal strips other animals of their right to be liberated for themselves.

Advocates should be hesitant to ground demands for equality in fluctuating or self-centered ideologies, inconstant religious doctrine, and personal gains. This is not to say that ideologies, religiosity, and personal benefits have not been influential in achieving social change, but these approaches should not become *foundational* to social justice claimsmaking. Rather, for any oppressed group, advocates should demand that the rights of those sentients be taken seriously regardless of any shifting subjectivities or social trends, and that demand should be rationally constructed. Women, African Americans, Nonhuman Animals, and other persons deserve rights because there are no defensibly rational reasons for excluding them from the moral community.

While not specifically included in the discussions of institutionalized religion of Chapter 6, the movement's association with the "New Age" discourse has also fostered a tolerance for unsubstantiated claims. Veganism is sometimes seen as a means of communing with the hidden worlds in nature (Leadbeater, 2007, p.3), aligning energies to tap into the "vibrations" of food (Virtue and Prelitz, 2001, pp.25–46) or achieving spiritual transcendence (Adams, 2000b). Veganism and anti-speciesism rhetoric is even used to validate anti-vaccination activism (Bell and Lind, no date). To each their own, but this trend may be lending to negative stereotypes about veganism.

By way of an example, Supreme Master Ching Hai's Loving Hut enterprise has launched well over a hundred vegan restaurants across the world (using a sliding price scale to accommodate people of all income levels) along with a litany of other social justice commitments (Tuttle, 2011). Ching Hai (of Supreme Master Ching Hai International) has *thousands* of "followers" who fund these efforts. Supposedly, only initiated members who are trained by Ching Hai's disciples in her teachings and meditation techniques can operate a Loving Hut franchise. Having journeyed to the "higher regions of the cosmos,"[3] Ching Hai claims powers of clairvoyance and has predictions for pending apocalypse that she incorporates into her organization's ethos. Supreme Master Television is aired in some restaurants, and it is also streamed on the organization's website. Ching Hai herself is shrouded in mystery and makes few public appearances. *VegNews* refers to her organization as the "fastest growing cult in the world" (Young, 2010, p.46). It is questionable how this type of veganism might appeal to a general audience, especially in an increasingly secular world with a media culture that is quick to sensationalize cults.

Vegan claimsmaking must be grounded in objective, observable reality if advocates hope to create lasting and meaningful change in the interests of other animals. An anti-speciesist argument that relies on the good "vibrations" of vegan food will not hold much weight. Additionally, prioritizing personal interests over those of other animals turns a social justice movement into a self-improvement movement. Just as advocates would not mobilize to end sexual violence against women by emphasizing men's potential for spiritual purity and enlightenment (though some religious sects may), they should not promote veganism by emphasizing the potential for human spiritual transcendence. This tactic diverts attention from the interests of the oppressed groups (women and other animals in these examples) to that of the oppressors (men and humans). There is no challenge to the hierarchy that supports and nurtures oppression. Aiding the vulnerable becomes a self-centered act of paternalistic pity that can be exchanged for spiritual favor. Spirituality and religiosity are also highly fluid, fluctuating with economic trends and changes in power. Grounding social justice claims in rationality, scientific evidence, and objective reality is the best hope for infiltrating the moral consciousness of society in a lasting way. Rationality is certainly not impervious to ideological biases, but a rational approach will be more difficult to dismiss or corrupt.

An intersectional approach

While social change workers should be wary of including approaches in the abolitionist repertoire that lack evidence in support of their utility, a rational abolitionist approach should also be sensitive to the needs of the oppressed, regardless of gender, race, nationality, religion (or lack of religion), sexual orientation, size, ability, age, and species. This is a practical matter as much as it is a moral one. There are over a million and a half non-profit organizations in the United States alone (National Center for Charitable Statistics, 2010). This makes for a *lot* of competition for the good will of the American public. Social psychological research demonstrates that a superabundance of need can reduce prosocial behavior. The theory of decision paralysis suggests that when there are too many decisions to make or too many choices available, people can become overwhelmed and may make no decision at all (Heath and Heath, 2010, p.50). Counter to common sense, *less* choice is actually better than *more* choice (Schwartz, 2004). What is more, the availability of alternatives means that the decisions that *are* made tend to be less satisfying because individuals tend to look back on "what could have been" if they had chosen differently. This information is particularly damning for multi-issue advocacy. Professionalized Nonhuman Animal rights groups offer far too much choice. At any given time, a non-profit organization might be offering as many as ten *or more* campaigns for the public to support. For the average person with only a moderate interest or limited time and resources, this huge variety of issues can become overwhelming and could easily trigger decision paralysis.

This strategy of compartmentalization is probably utilized to muster as much money as possible. Professionalized groups cast a wide net with a huge variety of options for far-reaching appeal. Under the non-profit business model, groups want more "customers," and they want repeat "customers" who make many "purchases." They hope that horse carriage campaigns will attract horse lovers, that seal-clubbing campaigns will attract "wildlife" lovers, and so on. There is something for everyone, and every campaign is likely to appeal to everyone at least a little. Social psychology warns that too many choices could mean that no choices are made at all, but organizations bank on the hope that their audience will choose many. The decision-making process is further complicated when these organizations offer veganism (if it is mentioned at all) as only one of many choices that can be made to help other animals. Most groups actively promote reductionism. Interested participants can go vegetarian or semi-vegetarian, switch from factory-farmed products to "humanely produced" products, or skip "meat" on Mondays. Decisions, decisions.

As an alternative, activists could single out veganism as the most important choice with the farthest reaching impact. Instead of signing a petition to end horse carriages, donating 20 dollars to help abused lab monkeys, writing 30 letters to 30 different companies that test on animals, or going vegetarian one day a week, one could become *vegan* and immediately cease support for most exploitative industries. Veganism explicitly rejects *all* use, not just those that are singled out as especially important (or enticing) by large non-profits hustling for donations. Looking back regretfully on "what could have been" is much less likely with the vegan option. All the bases are covered.

Of the 1.5 million charities in the United States, only a small fraction is concerned with Nonhuman Animals (about 2 per cent). Of that fraction, an even *smaller* portion is relegated to advancing the interests of animals who are not dogs and cats (Cooney, 2011, p.21). Vegan messages, then, face a lot of competition. The hearts and minds of the public are already heavily saturated with human causes, environmental campaigns, and dog and cat issues. *This is a critical reason why highlighting the intersected nature of abolitionism is so important.* Throughout this text, is has been argued that all oppressions are linked. Advocating against the violence that impacts Nonhuman Animals should include some attention to the violence that impacts vulnerable human groups as well. One of the greatest strengths of the vegan project is its comprehensiveness. Veganism is a political act that rejects oppression. Veganism rejects the murder of Nonhuman Animals for their flesh, milk, eggs, and hair, but it rejects their use in labor, entertainment, and experimentation as well. Specifically, it prioritizes the interests of other animals, but it also positively impacts others in the process. Because human and nonhuman oppressions are so intimately linked, veganism also happens to reject the objectification of women, the discrimination against people of color, and the marginalization of other at-risk groups, such as atheists. Veganism not only saves the lives of cows destined for the slaughterhouse but it also saves the lives of illiterate and impoverished migrants who are exploited, injured, and killed there, too. This comprehensiveness extends to the rejection of environmental havoc that disproportionately harms free-living animals and persons living in impoverished regions of the Global South. It rejects the debilitating diet-related illnesses that harm individuals and destroy communities. Instead of barraging the public with an endless list of singular issues that require attention – Save the Whales! Save the Earth! Food Not Bombs! – it is infinitely more efficient to simply promote the most all-encompassing option: ethical veganism.

While single-issue campaigning has been discussed primarily in the context of Nonhuman Animal advocacy, this formula is also problematic when advocates single out Nonhuman Animals at the expense of oppressed humans. Vegan advocates must extend abolitionist theory to include the interests of all nonhumans, women, people of color, disabled persons, elderly persons, children, homosexual persons, transgender persons, intersex persons, and others. That is, *all* persons, regardless of demographic affiliation, are included in a rational abolitionist ethic. The tree analogy presented in Chapter 3 positions oppression as the root cause of human *and* nonhuman suffering. Speciesism, sexism, racism, ableism, and other "isms" are all interconnected as branches in this tree of oppression.

Abolitionist theory should not cease to be relevant beyond the imagination of Nonhuman Animal liberation, just as it did not cease to be relevant when human slavery was abolished in the 19th century. Abolitionism seeks emancipation. Consequently, abolitionism cannot ignore continued enslavement and oppression wherever it may exist, whomever it may concern. A rational approach to achieving Nonhuman Animal rights is one that seeks to achieve human rights as well. It is irrational to assume that Nonhuman Animals can be liberated while millions of humans continue to languish. Humans are privileged to have been born with special moral consideration in an anthropocentric society, yet millions are routinely denied basic rights. How can advocates liberate Nonhuman Animals if so many humans remain enslaved? How can they argue to end Nonhuman Animal suffering while ignoring or dismissing the suffering of humans? If the interests of vulnerable humans are so easily dismissed, how can there be any hope for those of other species? All oppressions are linked. Advocates must get their own house in order before they can invite others in. A single-issue approach to social justice does nothing to address root problems. The strategy for liberation must be intersectional.

The inter-species connection makes it quite clear that there is little rational justification for the continued use of Nonhuman Animals. Even low levels of Nonhuman Animal products in the human diet create substantial health risks leading to a vast array of chronic, life-threatening illnesses (Campbell, 2006, pp.242–4). Producing other animals for human consumption is also intensely detrimental to the environment (Nibert, 2003, p.14). The switch to "humane" and "sustainable" systems cannot escape the wholly inefficient use of water, grain, and energy needed to produce these nonessential products. The human species cannot flourish if it should continue to depend on Nonhuman Animals in this fashion. The violence inherent to Nonhuman Animal exploitation is also directly linked to violence against humans. So long as it is thought acceptable to inflict harm and suffering on those sentient beings who have been dubbed "lesser" and are conceptualized as "resources," it will always be seen as acceptable to do the same to vulnerable humans who are similarly classified. For instance, so long as some men think it is acceptable to enter the forest homes of deers, turkeys, and other free-living Nonhuman Animals and shoot, pierce, and bludgeon them to death for fun, male-bonding, relaxation, or "necessity," there will always be men who find it acceptable to force themselves on women and rape, beat, and kill them for fun, male-bonding, relaxation, or "necessity." The logic of oppression allows for violence against the vulnerable, regardless of species. There will always be justification for human violence in a world that has justified violence against other animals.

The other side of this coin, then, is the realization that acceptable violence against humans can translate into acceptable violence against other animals. If vegan advocates insist that impoverished people need to "stop complaining" about the systematic exploitation that they endure, how can it be expected that outsiders will not claim the same of Nonhuman Animal rights advocacy? If vegan advocates dismiss "whiny" women, why is it surprising that omnivores disregard "whiny" vegans? If white-identified advocates take a flippant attitude in regard to violence against people of color, what right do they have to take offense when non-vegans accuse vegans of being overly sentimental, obnoxious, or too angry about the plight of Nonhuman Animals? Advocacy on behalf of other animals must adopt a comprehensive strategy against oppression. It should be one that does not recreate a hierarchy of need ("the animals come first"). It should also avoid trivializing the interests of any sentient being who has the misfortune of existing outside the favored in-group.

Capitalist complications

An intersectional approach must also recognize the role of capitalism in facilitating these entangled oppressions. In his critique of Francione's abolitionist approach, Elise notes a general failure to seriously address economic influences: "In addition to abolishing the property status of animals, the other most effective means of achieving animal liberation is abolition of private property itself. This means the abolition of capitalism" (2013, p.41). Nibert (2002, p.242; 2013, p.270) and Torres (2006, p.123) are also relatively skeptical that a capitalist framework can be manipulated by Nonhuman Animal rights activists to relieve or otherwise benefit the vulnerable. Capitalism is *inherently* exploitative, competitive, divisive, and unstable. Capitalism protects elite control over the state and allows industries to proliferate oppressive ideologies that hinder liberation efforts. The extensive suffering associated with a capitalist economy can also stifle the political imagination. Those who are overworked, undernourished, and highly stressed may be too busy and too burdened to mobilize.

Commodifying veganism as an economic motivator for Nonhuman Animal liberation theoretically utilizes capitalist mechanisms to promote ethically sound products to the effect of lessening the demand for products of suffering. But "voting with your dollar" is a strategy that is ultimately limited in its ability to dismantle the oppressive structure itself (Wrenn, 2011, p.18). In the neoliberal state, it is easier for a movement to seek recognition as a political identity bound by a right to consume, but such an agenda can overshadow concerns with serious social justice issues (Chasen, 2000, p.24). There are negative consequences for meaningful social change if social movement success is equated with the market's recognition of a vegan consumer identity. This is because the ability to consume is misconstrued with the acquisition of rights or social progress. In the case of the Nonhuman Animal rights movement, the neoliberal co-optation of social change is even more insidious when the interests of vegan humans as individual consumers obscure the interests of nonhumans. The movement's constituency is often unclear: vegans or Nonhuman Animals? Are the campaigns to increase vegan options in stores and restaurants primarily concerned with dismantling speciesism or with improving vegans' "right" to consume in the market? Whether or not this form of participation is a genuine act of economic boycott is questionable.

Nor is this type of political action universally accessible in societies with expansive wealth disparities. Those who do have access are more likely to represent interests of privilege. Furthermore, the notion of consumer sovereignty is overly simplistic and perhaps naïve in its assumption that powerful industries can be swayed by customers and not the reverse (Lerner, 1972). The "free market" is hardly free at all. It is heavily shaped by government grants, loans, subsidies, bailouts, embargoes, and influence on international governing bodies. These are all actions that work to benefit particular political and economic interests. This is bad news for anti-speciesism efforts because state and industry alliances rig the market for Nonhuman Animal products in their favor (Simon, 2013).

As only one example of many, the dairy industry plans to expand its market by promoting its product through globalization, fast food partnerships, and state and school programs. Over one hundred million dollars in grants will be supplied to farmers and universities to lend evidence to the necessity of dairy using funds provided by government checkoff programs (AgWeb, 2013). Case in point, Colorado State University has been the recipient of millions of dollars in grant money from a foundation established by Carnation Milk Products, Co. to fund cancer research

(Cornelius, 2014). Because the consumption of animal protein has been identified as a *cause* of cancer (Campbell, 2006, pp.43–67), corporate-funded research of this kind should be cause for concern.

The collective power and institutional support enjoyed by Nonhuman Animal industries is astronomical. Therefore, the problem cannot be resolved by simply voting with the vegan dollar (for those with the resources to "vote" at all). Francione (2013) insists, "The abolitionist approach sees the problem of animal exploitation primarily as one of demand and not supply," but the concept of "supply and demand" does not accurately apply. This is not merely a tussle between vegan and non-vegan purchasing in a free market. As with gasoline, tobacco products, pornography, fashion, and many pharmaceutical products, Nonhuman Animal flesh, milk, eggs, and labor are pushed by heavily networked industries with billions of dollars invested in creating a demand where there was none before. These industries also wield their incredible power to fiercely combat potential restrictions on their operations and to prevent the availability of alternatives to their products. Consumers are not creating these demands; it is the industries – with state support – that are in the driver's seat. In a society with high levels of poverty, large groups of people have little financial power to create the necessary demand for more ethical and healthful products. Many have little choice but to rely on whatever is most affordable and accessible.

Capitalism exploits the vulnerable to extract resources, labor, and production cheaply, but it doubly victimizes by selling unethically sourced and often dangerous products back to those who have been so oppressed by the system that they have little ability to object. With this in mind, abolitionist veganism must stand for more than vegan purchasing power:

> With veganism as part of the commodity system, capitalism will give us cookbooks, diet books, pleather, faux fur, "cheese," mock meat, and t-shirts and bumper stickers that declare our veganism to passerby. [...] they are *human* indulgences available only to those who have the financial means to buy them. Meanwhile, if all goes as planned, meat consumption will continue to rise. (Socha, 2013b, p.59)

Abolitionist veganism entails contentious action against a capitalist state. Due to the enormous constraints on consumer power, buying vegan products should be only one part of the strategy and should not take precedence. Social change workers should prioritize collective action over individual purchasing power. Dissociated individuals ticking off items on their grocery list in Whole Foods can make a dent, but it will be a *conscious group of vegans strategizing together to create a more equitable society* that will be the most effective weapon. Social change requires an engaged *movement*. It needs a "we."

The vegan consumption strategy is also suspect because it is extremely difficult to produce "cruelty-free" foodstuffs in the capitalist system. As documented by the Food Empowerment Project (2014a, p.8), many chocolates considered suitable for vegans actually contain cocoa produced by child slaves in West Africa. Farm workers in the United States fair little better, systematically subject to a number of hurtful capitalist pressures (Food Empowerment Project, 2014b, pp.4–5; Harper, 2013b). For instance, around 70 per cent of agriculture employees are undocumented (Serrano, 2012), and many more have only a temporary work visa. This means that most of the people who grow, harvest, and process fruits, nuts, and vegetables are hideously underpaid, ineligible for benefits, unable to organize, and they are vulnerable to harassment, violence, and deportation. If the number of vegans in the United States were to double tomorrow, millions of Nonhuman Animals would be spared, but this human suffering would persist. Explicitly vegan companies built on social justice values also run into trouble. The Loving Hut restaurant chain, for example, has been investigated for the use of undocumented "volunteer" employees (Malatesta, 2010). Readers caught *VegNews Magazine* using stock photographs of actual Nonhuman Animal flesh to illustrate its vegan recipes, apparently with the intention of reducing costs to remain competitive (Rudolf, 2011). One *VegNews* founder also stands accused of inappropriately using company funds and harassing the other (female-identified) founder to obtain sole ownership (Beck, 2013). Another problem is that small vegan companies that were founded with strong ethical values (such as Tom's of Maine, Gardein, and WhiteWave) are routinely bought up by huge conglomerates that prioritize profit and growth over social justice. Capitalism creates a competitive, high pressure situation where ethical values are difficult to maintain.

Veganism that is centered within epistemologies of anti-oppression will be more difficult to weaken and more difficult to co-opt with capitalist interests. When put in the service of dismantling oppression, intersectional veganism is protected as a *collective* political action. Collective, critical veganism will entail a reimagining of those social structures that facilitate slavery, environmental racism, dangerous working conditions, gendered violence, and corporate elite rule. Because capitalism thrives on these exploitations and because these exploitations are carefully constructed as normal, natural, and necessary, an intersectional approach to veganism poses a direct challenge to the economic system as it is currently understood. That is, veganism has the power to dissolve the speciesist foundations of the economy, but it can also dissolve the racist, sexist, disablist, classist, ageist, anti-atheist, and heterosexist foundations as well. Without these exploitative foundations on which it thrives, capitalism is not likely to endure.

Organizing under neoliberalism

"Voting with your dollar" in support of non-profits is similarly problematic. Large non-profits have successfully convinced the public that demonstrating support for social change involves signing checks, becoming a paying "member," and gifting estates. Again, this model of social activism necessarily excludes large demographics of people who simply cannot afford to participate in this way. For that matter, it also bequeaths the business of social change to a small group of elites in control of the organization's decision making and grant writing. The focus on donations illustrates the impact of neoliberal co-optation. Major structural changes and tactics that might actually work toward a goal of liberation are counterintuitive to bureaucratic growth. Superficial modifications to the status quo maintain the illusion of organizational effectiveness without upsetting the structures that support non-profits and ensure their continued relevancy. Social inequality has become big business in more ways than one.[4] Industry elites benefit from the immense profits extorted from oppressed groups by directly exploiting them in the economic sector. Elites then streamline this exploitation by controlling the non-profit sector.

Therefore, a vegan challenge to capitalist hegemony will also necessitate an examination of formal organizations and collectives. As demonstrated in Chapter 2, advocacy on behalf of other animals has been normalized as professional mobilization. Many advocates assume that social change mobilization requires the adoption of a capitalist model. Groups professionalize to legitimize their status, secure a safe space within the state, and access elite funding. They also become highly competitive, often forgoing meaningful cooperation as they fight for access to grants and donations. Groups will hire highly educated and privileged individuals (who tend to be white, male, and from middle to upper classes) to network with other elites and negotiate funding. The real work of social change is outsourced to unpaid interns and volunteers. Professionalized organizations ensure that their elite employees earn adequate salaries; meanwhile, women and young people (two highly vulnerable and easily exploited groups) are persuaded to work for free "for the cause." This is not to suggest that all activists should expect a paycheck. To the contrary, as Torres insists, "You cannot buy the revolution" (2006, p.97).[5]

The neoliberal infiltration of collective action has transformed radical social change efforts into corporatized non-profit enterprises that equate effective activism with limited reforms and successful fundraising. Immediately, there is a neutralization effect, as organizations must adopt a state-sanctioned model, reduce their political involvement, and make operations transparent to surveillance. The race, gender, class, culture, and ability requirements for meeting standards of professionalism also mean that persons of privilege (generally white, Western, middle-class, able-bodied men with advanced degrees) will disproportionately occupy positions of power in the movement, another devastating blow to radical mobilization.

The focus on fundraising is indicative of neoliberal influence, and neoliberalism is an ideology of oppression. Market participation and the accumulation of wealth is valued as a foundational right and the epitome of a democratic and just society despite major discrepancies in ability and opportunity for vulnerable groups. Neoliberalism takes social inequality as a given in the so-called free market, fully expecting that elites will require protection from those who are resentful of being disadvantaged (Chasen, 2000, p.7). Complacency with the neoliberal system will not dismantle inequality, because equality requires much more than an economic potential for success in the marketplace. Success in the marketplace requires competition, and competition always necessitates inequality: some will win, but others will lose. Those with structural privileges will always stand a better chance of winning, and they use this success to continuously modify the system in order to protect and improve their future chances of winning. The neoliberal system is thus fundamentally opposed to and incongruent with a vision of fairness and equal opportunity. Social movements that try to "play the game" and enter the system with an intention of disrupting elite power and structures of inequality will not be successful.

The non-profit struggle to survive, succeed, and accumulate wealth and power in the capitalist system denatures advocacy. Advocacy becomes business, and business interests are rarely in alignment with those of oppressed groups. The social change needed for Nonhuman Animal liberation will entail a radical restructuring of political, economic, and social institutions. This work will require the contributions of thousands, if not millions. Few can expect a paycheck: "Fighting for freedom has always been, and remains, unpaid work, regardless of what any capitalist system might tell us" (Burrowes et al., 2007, p.233). Advocates might also question the utility in granting large paychecks to the hundreds of careerists from privileged backgrounds who, well-intentioned as they may be, profit from the public interest in Nonhuman Animal suffering. Some grant writers and other executives are paid salaries that are well above the national average. These persons are hired to maximize fundraising, and that fundraising is then funneled into circumscribed work that is designed to improve the image of the organization. Much less fundraising is invested in tactics geared toward structural change. Is this a wise investment of resources? If radical grassroots mobilization is to be excluded from elite coffers because of its genuine commitment to social change, perhaps this separation will be advantageous in the freedom and integrity that it allows. For all its benefits, the non-profit model often entails a disastrous compromise for many social movements. When organizations must rely on funding to survive, the interests of the funders can take precedence over the interests of the constituency.

This is not to say that radical collectives should completely abstain from fundraising. The concern is specifically with the strings that are so often attached. Many grassroots organizations marginalized from mainstream funding sources rely instead on their communities for financial support (Guilloud and Cordery, 2007, pp.107–10). Activists can raise money through bake sales, merchandise sales, event tickets, raffles, and online crowdsourcing. Recall that the abolitionist approach to dismantling oppression is based on education. Fortunately, education need not be an expensive endeavor. Anyone can positively influence their communities, if not through leafleting, teaching, screenings, or sharing food, then by simply being vegan. As explained in Chapter 3, veganism spreads through networks. Familiarity with veganism encourages veganism.

The rationalist argument presented thus far is largely suspicious of non-profitization, but it does not necessarily follow that non-profits are useless to the movement. Some grassroots operations have been able to elicit the help of larger non-profits without compromising their goals. In this relationship, the non-profit is not given the power to dictate the movement but is instead made *accountable* to the movement (Rojas, 2007, p.207). Others have opted to incorporate as non-profits only strategically, capitalizing on political and economic trends that favor their interests. When the demands of professionalization begin to compromise the organization's goals, they can simply abandon their 501(c)(3) status and revert to their original formulation (Tang, 2007, p.224).

Reflecting on many decades of professionalized advocacy, Stallwood (1996, p.202) suggests that a unifying professional association for groups and advocates might prove helpful for sharing resources, mediating conflict, and promoting best-practice advocacy standards. However, increased professionalization and additional levels of hierarchy are likely to be detrimental for an already overly professionalized movement. Grassroots efforts are already under immense pressure to conform. A national or international association would only further marginalize them, posing a great cost to movement diversity and innovation. Nor is such an association likely, given that it would require that large welfarist organizations surrender some degree of identity. Recall that the non-profit industrial complex necessitates competition for survival because grants and other resources are often scarce and difficult to access.

Elise (2013, p.35) has suggested that abolitionist activists consider an organization model that is collectively controlled and democratic in both decision making and strategy building. The Abolitionist Vegan Society and the International Vegan Association (formerly the Boston Vegan Association) have explored non-profit status, maintaining their radical goals for total liberation as well as a strong community presence with workshops, reading groups, and lectures. Both organizations also support a wider network of Nonhuman Animal rights activists by printing and mailing vegan literature to other abolitionists across the country and by making advocacy materials freely available online.

Kheel (1985: 4) also suggests a move away from the hierarchal model, which she views as patriarchal, controlling, and oppressive. A feminist approach to collective action on behalf of other animals might emphasize collective decision making with no tolerance for celebrity or hero worship. Instead, all participants would be treated as equally valuable. In the pursuit of a safe and nurturing space for women to advocate free from patriarchal control, she also suggests the possibility of women-only organizations. A division among activists based on gender identification may be an unfortunate route, but it would be preferable and even necessary until the male-led movement takes seriously its issues with sexism and violence against women.

Creating a community of accountability

Whatever the structure, maintaining a grassroots model will require considerable ingenuity because activists struggle not only with the difficult work of creating social change, but also with the countermobilization efforts of the larger non-profits that routinely defame them, usurp resources, and otherwise dominate the field. Activists will need to be accountable to one another, their community, and their constituents. This includes both nonhuman *and* human animals who stand to benefit from veganism and anti-oppression work. Accountability must be a grounding principle to abolitionist work.

As discussed in Chapters 4, 5, and 6, a considerable amount of violence occurs within the Nonhuman Animal rights community. Unfortunately, there is often little recourse for activists who are victims of violence. Many victims who speak out are ignored, blamed, or not believed. Sometimes the harassment intensifies in response. Victims can be silenced or forced to withdraw from the movement to protect their mental and physical well-being. This is an extension of the oppression that advocates seek to dismantle, but it is also a *political* problem (Chen et al., 2011, xvi). A considerable amount of victim-blaming surfaces in retaliation against criticisms of sexism, racism, ableism, sizeism, anti-atheism, and classism in the ranks. Victimization tends to be cumulative when violent behaviors are reported but then go without validation. Victims are doubly oppressed by their community when their reasonable requests for empathy and safety are dismissed as "drama," "political correctness," or "attention seeking." Those who dismiss the presence of violence and the requests for accountability are invariably themselves persons with privilege who, for lack of direct experience, have not had to seriously consider the reality of ongoing human discrimination. Instead, victims are ignored or bullied into silence "for the cause." That is, converting new vegans and saving Nonhuman Animals are deemed more important than challenging the suffering of humans. Many people understandably rationalize that Nonhuman Animals are suffering more and thus deserve the movement's undivided attention. This justification, however, ignores the intersectionality of oppression and becomes counterintuitive. Neither does it excuse participation in or complacency with discriminatory or hurtful behavior.

There is also a concern that diverting attention to violence within the movement may make the movement appear unprofessional to the public. But what really puts the movement in an unattractive light is its inability to appropriately handle human oppression. Victims and survivors cannot be responsible for tarnishing the image of Nonhuman Animal rights advocacy; only the perpetrators and apologists can be. The "veganism-or-bust" approach that prioritizes vegan advocacy over the well-being of activists fails to recognize that a movement rife with unchecked violence is not an attractive one. Because intra-movement violence is draining and distracting, it is a considerable weakness that should be addressed. If the movement cannot be considered a safe space for activists to work, activists cannot expect to be very successful. Nor can there be a reasonable expectation of dismantling the violence and oppression that the movement mobilizes against. Advocates cannot undermine societal violence if the movement exists as a microcosm of that violence.

A community of accountability requires that activists be accountable not only to others but also to themselves. Those who advocate, care-give, or otherwise provide assistance on a routine basis are highly susceptible to burn-out given the heavy and persistent burden of traumatic knowledge. Indeed, many are susceptible to secondary traumatic stress, particularly those who are especially empathetic (Figley, 1995, p.1). When advocates become overloaded with the suffering of others, they risk shutting down. For example, urban areas (where the needy are so often encountered) demonstrate lower levels of helping behavior (Levine et al., 1994). Known as the "urban unhelpfulness effect," the more densely populated an area, the less helpful its population will be (Yousif and Korte, 1995). But unhelpfulness can surface anywhere that need is thought too great. This compassion fatigue can impact activism in two ways. First, an already overburdened public may simply be too overwhelmed by other issues to pay adequate attention to the needs of other animals. Second, vegan advocates can themselves become exhausted and drop out.

To sustain the movement, advocates must sustain themselves. The struggle for a vegan world is a draining endeavor. The danger of giving up altogether is entirely real. The Compassion Fatigue Awareness Project (2013) suggests exercising, eating healthy, enjoying social activities, journaling, and getting adequate sleep. It also encourages self-management (the wisdom of knowing when to say "no"), surrounding oneself with supportive and positive people, getting organized, and balancing life in general. For social movement participants in particular, it could also be necessary to manage online activity. Internet forums, Facebook, and other social networking tools can be immensely helpful in creating community and keeping activists up to date, but they can also be vicious time sinks that aggravate stress and crush self-esteem. The internet's anonymity can often bring out the worst in people, and debates can linger for days. It is usually a good idea to put a cap on how much time and effort is expended on internet engagement. Another consideration is the need to carefully protect personal identity. Online harassment is a serious issue for anyone on the internet, but it is especially serious for social justice activists in general and women in particular.[6] Learning to choose battles and committing to putting oneself first can sometimes can be a difficult task, especially when so many are suffering, dying, and desperately in need of help. However, a happy activist is a more effective activist. For those with the privilege of doing so, self-care is worth prioritizing because it is an investment for the social justice collective as well as for the activists themselves.

A new definition of abolitionism

Abolitionist Nonhuman Animal rights is, in many ways, an appropriation of the centuries-old human abolitionist project (Wrenn, 2013c, p.178). For human rights mobilizers, abolitionism has come to involve more than the abolition of slavery in the conventional sense. Activists recognize that slavery perpetuates in a white supremacist society in less visible, socially "appropriate" forms. For example, prisons disproportionately incarcerate people of color, robbing them of their freedom and disrupting both families and communities. Prison abolitionists such as Angela Davis (2005) seek to emancipate people of color from a very discriminatory criminal justice system. Likewise, vegan abolitionists should recognize that abolitionism will entail more than the abolishment of Nonhuman Animal slavery; it must include anti-discriminatory work as well, which is why vegan outreach is so critical. Liberation from bondage is only the first step. For Nonhuman Animal liberation to succeed, a transformation in the cultural psyche must take place. So long as ideological barriers remain intact, discrimination will continue to manifest. Just as human slavery perpetuates in a society that has abolished chattel slavery but maintains racist, sexist, and classist ideologies, nonhuman slavery will persist in a society that does not value Nonhuman Animals as persons worthy of moral consideration. In an oppressive social structure, legislative reforms will be relatively meaningless without social support to maintain them. Abolition involves the dismantling of physical *and* ideological structures of oppression.

It is inappropriate for organizations to self-identify as abolitionist if they are working to strengthen institutional exploitation through reforms that are known to increase the industry's public image, efficiency, and productivity. It is also inappropriate for organizations to self-identify as abolitionist if they accommodate speciesism by promoting "Meatless Mondays," vegetarianism, and other forms of reductionism, especially if they are simultaneously ignoring or denigrating veganism. To abolish means to *end*. To abolish speciesism means to *end* the institutions that oppress other animals. Efforts to improve business for exploitative industries and positions that suggest that some non-vegan consumption is acceptable are not abolitionist. Ending the practice of tail docking, replacing battery cages with "cage-free" sheds, and prosecuting employees who inflict slightly more suffering onto their "products" than is considered standard in the industry might create marginal improvements for the horrific lives of Nonhuman Animals, but no amount of reform will eliminate the system. Indeed, the unending series of marginal reforms actually perpetuate the system. The state is content because non-profits are handling the loose ends and not making a nuisance of themselves with radical ideas. The industries are content because the insignificant reforms that they adopt improve the public's perception of their product's quality. The non-profits are content because they have a constant supply of easily won victories to decorate their grant proposals. But Nonhuman Animals are anything but content, as they continue to fill dinner plates, aquarium tanks, kill "shelters," laboratories, and department store clothing racks in ever growing numbers. Nor are marginalized humans contented, as they continue to endure the exploitative labor conditions, diet-related diseases, environmental pollution, and natural disasters linked to speciesist industrial practices. This is a capitalist complex that is of great benefit to society's elites but of huge consequence to vulnerable human and nonhuman populations.

That said, abolitionism should mean more than working to end the violence against other animals; it must also entail working to end violence against *all* sentient beings. Abolitionism is a strategy originally designed in the framework of human slavery, so to apply it to only Nonhuman Animals is to tokenize the meaning. Oppression is not specific to one group; it applies to any person – human or nonhuman – who suffers under a theistic, patriarchal, white, capitalist supremacy. Nonhuman Animal oppression is deeply entangled with the oppression of women, people of color, elderly persons, children, mentally and physically disabled persons, homosexuals, transgender persons, and other vulnerable groups. The abolitionist Nonhuman Animal rights movement will not succeed so long as it perpetuates or ignores sexism, racism, ageism, ableism, heterosexism, anti-atheism, or any other form of violence.

The definition of abolitionism thus presented is both critical and intersectional. Abolitionism must be inclusive of all who are marginalized, and it must be recognizant of systems of oppression. Speciesism is only one of many institutions that should be challenged. Capitalism, patriarchy, white supremacy, religion, and the other institutions that they control and influence should also be examined. Such a radical approach will likely necessitate a grassroots model, as professionalization often plays into the hands of oppressive institutions. It will also require a rejection of popular but ineffectual individualistic solutions. This means that veganism ought to involve more than what one individually consumes and how one individually behaves. Veganism is *collective* action in the service of social justice. As a collective, advocates will need to value accountability for their tactics, their theory, and their behavior toward one another. Indeed, the rational approach to Nonhuman Animal rights is fundamentally concerned with accountability. The movement must be accountable for its claimsmaking and strategies, but advocates must also be accountable to themselves and to their comrades. Above all, advocates must be accountable to their constituents: oppressed animals of all species.

Notes

1 Rationality and Nonhuman Animal Rights

1. Where relevant, problematic, reifying language and mass terms have been modified.
2. See Francione and Garner's 2010 publication *The Animal Rights: Abolition or Regulation?* for a nuanced discussion.
3. For a relevant exploration of "pinkwashing," see Chapter 5 of Alexandra Chasin's (2013) *Selling Out: The Gay and Lesbian Movement Goes to Market*.
4. Tom Regan's work (2004b, 2004c) has also been hugely influential in the development of vegan-based, liberation-focused mobilization on behalf of other animals. He also uses the language of abolition and has been critical of welfare reform and violent tactics. The primary distinction between Regan and Francione in regard to movement politics is that Regan continues to see value in legal reform and single-issue campaigning (2004b, p.196–7), which Francione largely rejects.
5. As of this writing, this publication is available only in e-book formatting that lacks page numbering. See Part Three: Responses: The Prize and the Plow, specifically Chapter 15, "'Abolitionism:' The Agitation-Only Approach to Animal Rights."
6. For some time in 2012, Francione's website featured an upturned hand (the symbol of ahimsa) encapsulating a circle representing the Samasara (the symbol of reincarnation). This image was partnered with one of his quotes: "Veganism is about nonviolence: nonviolence to other sentient beings; to yourself; to the earth."
7. Feminist Marti Kheel (1985) suggests this structure is specifically related to patriarchal co-optation of the Nonhuman Animal rights movement:

    The dominance of men within the animal rights movement is regrettable not only because they have taken over women's leadership positions, but also because of the overwhelming acceptance of male values within the movement. Thus, most organizations are run in a traditionally male, hierarchical fashion. A small, elite group makes up all the major decisions which the rank and file obediently carry out. "Stars" or "heros" [sic] are periodically produced who then become official spokespersons for the movement. [...] The "heros" [sic] are instructed to speak to, and presumably enlighten, the rank and file. (p.4)

8. One example is found within Cooney's presentation at the 2012 Animal Rights Conference. This presentation draws on scientific research to insist that welfare reforms lead to a reduction in Nonhuman Animal consumption, a "fact" as he calls it (Farm Sanctuary, 2012). However, *Daily Livestock Report* (2011) associates the rising cost of Nonhuman Animal products (which is thought to be responsible for a decline in US "meat" consumption) with increased US exports

to feed "meat" demand in modernizing countries and the increased cost of ethanol production. The industry also believes the aging baby boomer population is responsible for the decline, as they eat smaller portion sizes (especially women, who outnumber men in old age) (CME, 2011). The industry seems more concerned with globalization, fuel costs, and aging consumers than with welfare campaigning. Other research that is discussed in Chapter 1 and Chapter 2 also contradicts Cooney's interpretation.

9. From the 2013 ACE mission statement:
   Given our current recommended charities, it may seem that we are a vegan advocacy organization; however, this is not the case. Based on our current findings and available research, advocating for farm animals seems to be the most effective way to help the largest number of animals and prevent the largest amount of suffering. Therefore, we currently recommend farm-animal advocacy groups. To that end, we wouldn't state that we specifically promote veganism, even though that is one way for an individual to help prevent suffering.
10. From the 2013 ACE mission statement: "As an organization, we are open to considering both direct (such as leafleting) and indirect (such as research on animal sentience) methods of alleviating suffering." I take "methods of alleviating suffering" to mean welfare reform given the organization's focus on factory farming and its failure to hold veganism as the baseline in advocacy efforts.
11. While many organizations prioritize cats and dogs, farmed animals, or popular species such as horses and whales, Cooney (2013b, no pagination) takes the utilitarian approach and thus suggests that vegan advocates prioritize chickens over all others as they compromise the largest number of animals killed for humans. As discussed in Chapter 2 and Chapter 3, selective approaches tend to lend themselves better to fundraising than to liberation.
12. See *A Primer on Animal Rights: Leading Experts Write about Animal Cruelty and Exploitation* (Stallwood, 2002) as another example of non-profit conservative interests equated with effective advocacy.
13. The Cassuto and Francione references provided speak directly to the problems with legal mobilization. Hall (2010, p.102) tends to favor legal mobilization but is especially critical of direct action advocacy (2006). More recently, Stallwood's position is closer to that of Hall.
14. In 2013 PETA announced its "youngest pin up": a 16-year-old female musician. The ad states that, "Vegans go all the way." A staff writer explains, "PETA normally waits until people turn 18 before asking them to star in a 'provocative' campaign, but not this time" (Kretzer, 2013).
15. Travis Elise (2013) discusses Francione's inability to engage criticism in his examination of the abolitionist faction:
    Francione's [sic] brushes off his own critics in [...] broad strokes. While his views on welfare reform may be accurate and his views on building a solid political base through vegan education may be the correct path for the movement, as a movement leader, Francione's ability to persuade others in the movement is compromised by his problematic and, some might argue, authoritarian personality. (p.40)
16. Note that the term "faith" is used to denote a confidence and trust in something without supporting evidence; this is not restricted to religious notions.

17. To clarify, this critique is meant to apply to specifically Nonhuman Animal liberation work and only partially to vegan outreach efforts. Veganism is in many ways as vital to human rights as it is to nonhuman rights. It is also recognized that attacking "self-interest" is problematic given the intersectional nature of oppression. Many disadvantaged human groups who participate in anti-speciesist efforts are subsequently acting in their own self-interest as well. This position is elaborated in Chapter 5.
18. I wish to acknowledge my colleague Sarah K. Woodcock, founder of The Abolitionist Vegan Society, who often employs this phrase. Woodcock argues that veganism is best located within an intersectional framework; however, veganism should remain distinct as an ethical position that directly and exclusively represents Nonhuman Animals.

2 Irrationalities in Welfarist Organizational Pathways

1. Free-riding refers to the tendency for individuals to avoid incurring the costs of participation by allowing others to incur those costs while nonetheless enjoying the benefits should the social good be achieved. In other words, free riders can enjoy the benefits of social movement efforts without having to participate. This is a "rational" choice with an irrational outcome, as social change will be slower or weaker when most choose to opt out and leave a smaller number to shoulder the work.
2. See Francione's (1996) *Rain without Thunder: The Ideology of the Animal Rights Movement*, specifically Chapter 4, "The Results of New Welfarism: The 'Animal Confusion' Movement" (pp.78–109) for further explanation and specific examples.
3. According to its 2012 IRS 990 form (pp.9–10), the HSUS paid out $2.7 million dollars for the salaries of just nineteen employees. Of this, $347,675 went to President and CEO Wayne Pacelle.
4. The combined assets of all "animal-related" public charities in the United States is 12.5 billion dollars; however, this accounts for only 0.5 per cent of the non-profit assets (National Center for Charitable Statistics, 2010).
5. Farm Sanctuary (2005), for example, notes that name and mailing information required of anyone who signs up for updates and outreach support will be shared with other entities with "similar interests and goals." Likewise, PETA (n.d.c) states that this same information is made available to "reputable advocacy and nonprofit organizations and commercial companies." There are opt-out options, but this requires an email or a phone call.
6. The economic logic of growth is an ideology that has been criticized as a major impediment to interventions in environmental destruction. Rather than entertain the serious structural adjustments needed to curb climate change, social institutions more often adhere to capitalist solutions of increased technological advancement and consumption.
7. The financial disincentive to engage deep social change efforts in outreach material is exemplified in an explanation provided by Vegan Outreach (2015) following the reintroduction of its *Guide to Cruelty-Free Eating*:
   > One big change from the old Guide is that the booklet is now the same size as all of our other booklets – 16 pages. This has reduced the cost of

printing, shipping, and overhead. In the past, due to the increased cost, we asked people not to leaflet with the Guide, but now if people feel that a crowd is particularly educated and would benefit most from a Guide, it won't be any more expensive than one of our other booklets.
8. In practice, this has not been the case. Many abolitionists rally behind the leadership of Francione, who is actively involved in overseeing the abolitionist movement.

3 Rational Advocacy and the Logic of Persuasion

1. See Nick Cooney's (2011) *Change of Heart* and Melanie Joy's (2008) *Strategic Action for Animals*.
2. This concept was developed by bell hooks (2004, p.29), who means it as "interlocking political systems." Patricia Hill Collins (2000, p.18) refers to this notion as a "matrix of domination."
3. Philosopher and psychologist William James (1988 [1902–1910], p.519) makes a similar argument for relieving individual responsibility in regard to morality, suggesting that humans should "take a moral holiday" and leave the world and its issues in the hands of a higher power.
4. This study was actually conducted as a means to explain how ordinary people abetted Nazi atrocities in the early 20th century.
5. From *Walden* (1854, p.98).
6. Flinn and Cudahy's original analogy was published on Gentle World's website: http://gentleworld.org/are-anti-cruelty-campaigns-really-effective. It is detailed here with permission. Sociologists tend to disagree with the authors regarding the source of oppression, and the analogy thus presented reflects this distinction. It is suggested that ideologies of oppression are products of the prevailing economic mode of production, not the reverse. This modified analogy thus presented was constructed with the assistance of Lucas Hayes.
7. This bad analogy was pointed out by Dan Cudahy in *Unpopular Vegan Essays* on October 27, 2008: http://uvearchives.wordpress.com/2008/10/27/picking-the-low-hanging-fruit-what-is-wrong-with-single-issue-campaigns/. It is discussed here with his permission.
8. Braunsberger's study utilizes a 30-second video clip, emphasizing that a longer video may not be necessary to elicit attitude change. Nabi was able to increase the number of participants who paid attention and watched the entire film clip because the research was conducted in an experimental setting. That is, participants were less likely to stop watching or leave the room. Professionalized advocacy organizations mimic this by training pay-per-view volunteers to monitor participants.
9. By 2013, the phrasing has changed in such a way as to appear more conducive to Nonhuman Animal rights. Instead of "decreased consumption," they now frame it as "working toward a vegan diet."
10. Mercy for Animals' *Farm to Fridge*.
11. Cooney (2011, pp.116–17) is an advocator of "professional" appearance, though this is likely a reflection of his commitment to the non-profit model. It is worth considering that advocates from disadvantaged backgrounds will

not have access to the cultural, class, racial, able-bodiedness, and, in some cases, gender requirements for this professional access.
12. The average food stamp household receives about $281 per month for groceries (USDA Food and Nutrition Service, 2012, p.15). It costs an average of $134 to feed a child on a low-income budget in the United States each month (Bauer, Rettig, and Son, 2009). Wiig and Smith (2008, p.1728) and Flynn et al. (2013, p.74) report that low-income families funnel as much as 50 per cent of their food budget into "meat" products. Abstaining from Nonhuman Animal flesh could free up as much as $140 dollars a month, enough to feed an extra child.
13. Participants in the study were first-year psychology students having just read the book and second-year students who had been assigned the book a year prior. Of note, while attitude change was only temporary, the second year students did demonstrate more knowledge and concern about those problems that Pollan has highlighted about the US food system.
14. These are all examples of actual tactics that have been employed in the Nonhuman Animal rights movement.
15. A notable exception is the role of slave "rebellions" (a pejorative for what were really social movements) in hastening the abolition of slavery in Great Britain (Matthews, 2006). These uprisings coincided with a strong abolitionist sentiment in Britain and economic forces that made distant slave colonies less desirable and less lucrative to maintain (Jennings, 1997).

4 Reconciling Gender and Rationality

1. The terms "women" and "men" generally refer to gender and are meant to be inclusive of transgender and intersex persons. It is acknowledged that this binary language unfortunately excludes many other genders, gender-neutral individuals, and non-conforming individuals, though some non-conforming persons may experience similar issues discussed in this chapter.
2. Native American women experience rape or sexual assault at double the rate of any other racial group (Perry, 2004, p.5). In addition, 77 per cent of Hispanic Texans report having personally experienced domestic violence or know someone close to them who has (Texas Council on Family Violence, 2002). In one survey, over 80 per cent of Asian American women report experiencing at least one form of intimate partner violence (McDonnell and Abdulla, 2001). African American women, however, experience more domestic violence and deadly violence than any other racial group (Rennison and Welchans, 2000). Homosexuals and transgender persons are also disproportionately victimized. For instance, one study finds that same-sex cohabitants are far more likely to experience violence at the hands of their partner than were opposite-sex cohabitants (Tjaden and Thoennes, 2000: 29). Another study on sexual violence in the gay and lesbian community finds that 52 per cent of participants reported at least one instance of sexual assault (Waldner-Haugrud and Gratch, 1997). Disabled women experience abuse at rates twice that of non-disabled women (Sobsey, 1994). Research also indicates that at least 50–60 per cent of female welfare recipients have experienced physical abuse by an intimate partner (almost three times that

of the general population) (Tolman and Raphael, 2000). Of homeless women, 82 per cent have experienced domestic violence (Lyon, 1997).
3. Patricia Hill Collins (2004, pp.26–7) gives the example of Sarah Baartman, the "Hottentots Venus," an African woman who was toured around early 19th-century Europe. Baartman was sexualized, animalized, and displayed as a "freak" due to her accentuated (by Western standards) body parts. After her death, she was dissected and her body continued on as public property in a Parisian museum. The name "Hottentots Venus" is a play on words meant to contrast the "vulgarity" of African sexuality and African female form with that of the idealized white female form in European Renaissance imagery.
4. From LUSH's blog:
We felt it was important, strong, well and thoroughly considered that the test subject was a woman. This is important within the context of Lush's wider Fighting Animal Testing campaign, which challenges consumers of cosmetics to feel, to think and to demand that the cosmetics industry is animal cruelty free. It is also important in the context Jacqui's [the actress] performance practice: a public art intervention about the nature of power and abuse. It would have been disingenuous at best to have pretended that a male subject could represent such systemic abuse. (Omond, 2012)
5. This is a popular pornography genre that features women in subservient positions choking on large penises. The women's makeup often runs as their eyes tear up, and they often vomit. The man usually directs her to maintain eye contact with her as she gags. Their degradation, humiliation, and suffering is sexualized (Jensen, 2007, pp.73–4).
6. In societies where women's social worth is based on their sexual availability to men and their desirousness, women are often pitted against each other in competition for male attention. It is to the benefit of patriarchy that women are kept as competitive individuals rather than as a cooperative collective capable of dismantling unequal social structures (Armstrong and Rudúlph, 2013, pp.184–96).
7. To name a just a few of the higher-profile women in Nonhuman Animal rights advocacy: founder of United Poultry Concerns Karen Davis; founder of PETA Ingrid Newkirk; founder of *VegNews* Colleen Holland; founder of The Abolitionist Vegan Society Sarah K. Woodcock; founders of Our Hen House Jasmin Singer and Mariann Sullivan; founder of The Vegan Society Elsie Shrigley; artist Sue Coe; theorists Carol Adams, Josephine Donovan, Lee Hall, Breeze Harper, pattrice jones, Melanie Joy, and Barbara Noske; and chef activists Isa Chandra Moskowitz and Colleen Patrick-Goudreau.
8. One psychological study found that 85 per cent of heterosexual women are, in fact, satisfied with their male (and presumably omnivorous) partner's penis size (Lever et al., 2006).
9. Some examples include the discovery of DNA structure, which is popularly attributed to Francis Crick and James Watson to the exclusion of Rosalind Franklin, the disproving of the Parity Law in physics by Dr. Chien-Shiung Wu and two male colleagues (they received a Nobel Prize, whereas she did not) (Rossiter, 1993, p.329), and "double consciousness" (competing racial and national identities faced by African Americans), which is attributed to W.E.B. DuBois, though Anna Julia Cooper and Sojourner Truth had theorized this notion ten and 50 years prior, respectively (Simien, 2006, pp.2–3).

10. According to this reference, approximately 2.5 per cent of Americans identify as vegan, meaning that they consume no Nonhuman Animal products.
11. The prioritization of scientifically grounded notions of sentience as a basis for moral inclusion and the devaluation of experiential ways of knowing Nonhuman Animal worth is one gendered dichotomy that Luke provides. As I explain in Chapter 6, it is important to respect the fact that "objective" knowledge is packed in privilege and institutionalized power itself, but grounding social justice claimsmaking in the subjective can leave the position quite vulnerable.
12. Vance examines various narratives of human/nonhuman relationships which reflect the human and male privilege behind the construction and dissemination of knowledge. For example, the "progress" narrative of patriarchal Western culture understands humans as having an imperative to subdue nature, and that nature (which includes women and other animals) must be tamed and controlled.
13. For an in-depth discussion of animal-friendly feminist science, see Lynda Birke's (1994) *Feminism, Animals and Science: The Naming of the Shrew*.

5 Problematizing Post-Race Ideology

1. This declaration is hosted on Change.org, available at https://www.change.org/p/the-animal-rights-movement-the-non-humans-first-declaration-individual-signatories, as well as the group's Facebook page, available at https://www.facebook.com/notes/non-humans-first-declaration-supporters-page/the-non-humans-first-declaration/219797418177536.
2. Ongoing political turmoil and ethnic conflict in the Israeli state complicates this claimsmaking. Some have suggested that heavy vegan mobilization in the area is an attempt to obscure human rights violations against Palestinians and bolster an image of Israeli morality (Jadali, 2014).
3. Women, too, have been largely excluded from the historical narrative of veganism, though women were heavily involved in the political construction of veganism and Nonhuman Animal advocacy (Ferguson, 1998; Leneman, 1997), including the formation of vegan societies in the United Kingdom (The Vegan Society, no date) and the United States (American Vegan Society, no date).
4. *All* Nonhuman Animal use is exploitative and cruel. That many organizations single out particular practices as especially cruel is problematic in itself because this framework normalizes routine (but equally oppressive) practices.
5. Recognizing that it overlaps with human rights language, the term "abolitionist" refers to vegan activists unless otherwise indicated.
6. This information was obtained from personal correspondence with the organization's founder, Sarah K. Woodcock, who identifies as a woman of color.
7. Food insecurity involves more than hunger and lack of access to healthy foods. Research shows a correlation with decreased academic performance, weight gain, and stunted social skills among schoolchildren (Jyoti et al., 2005).

8. As of this writing, Animals Asia focuses on dog and cat welfare, the bear bile industry, zoos, and safari parks (Animals Asia, 2013).
9. Out of the 19 members of management pictured and named on its website in 2014, only six appeared to be persons of color. Animal Asia's offices are located in Hong Kong, Australia and New Zealand, China, Germany, Italy, the United Kingdom, the United States, and Vietnam.
10. This proposal was a response to research suggesting that Plan B contraceptives lose effectiveness among people of size. Veganism, it suggests, is correlated with a lower body weight, which is thought to improve the effectiveness of Plan B.
11. Despite popular belief, most waste results from industry; only 2.5 per cent is municipal garbage (Leonard, 2010, p.186).
12. Reactions to the story covered by Free From Harm took place in the online comments section, which has since been closed.

6 The Case for Secular Activism

1. Live export entails the shipment of thousands of cows and sheeps to Muslim countries where they are killed and butchered while fully conscious for religious purposes. Many die in the stressful transport before they even reach their destination.
2. During ritual, chickens are swung by their wings (which are painfully bent backwards) around the practitioner's head three times before being killed. Chickens are caged under stressful, unhealthy conditions prior to the ritual, meaning that many die before they are even used. In 2013, for example, the *New York Daily News* reports that thousands of hens died of heat exhaustion in crates as they awaited their slaughter for the late summer ritual (Warerkar and Yaniv, 2013). Many times, unused chickens are simply abandoned in their crates to die.
3. One caveat: those ascribing to religions that are distrustful of science and those who believe god is in nature are more receptive to Nonhuman Animal rights than are other religious respondents.
4. Grimké's essay attempts to reinterpret Biblical passages to denounce the legitimacy of slavery. The work is not completely based in appeals to religion; she also draws on the language of democracy and natural rights. While hugely popular in the North and widely distributed by the American Anti-Slavery Society, it was burned in her native South Carolina, and Grimké was threatened with mob violence and imprisonment should she ever return (Lerner, 2004, p.100).
5. Stowe also draws heavily on nationalism in this work (Riss, 1994, p.115).
6. Symbolic capital refers to a sociological concept developed by Pierre Bourdieu (2005). Groups that possess the power to construct the symbols and meanings that are both legitimated and prestigious tend to be those groups with considerable social power. This power reproduces itself to maintain social stratification and to protect the privileged position of the powerful. Importantly, social facts and social objects that are subsequently understood to be "legitimate," "prestigious," or otherwise meaningful are *subjectively* bound (Bourdieu, 2010 [1984]). For instance, the consumption of Nonhuman

Animal products has historically been associated with affluence, while vegan diets are seen as the last resort of the impoverished. Omnivorous/non-vegan consumption – a sort of consumption primarily afforded to the world's privileged – is legitimized as both preferable and normal. "Meat," "fur," "leather," and other Nonhuman Animal products become symbols of social power.
7. Stowe wrote *Uncle Tom's Cabin* immediately following the Compromise of 1850, which reaffirmed Southern political power. Under this compromise, the Utah and New Mexico territories could someday become slave states and the Fugitive Slave Act was strengthened.
8. Cudworth defines anthroparchy as, "a social system, a complex and relatively stable set of hierarchical relationships in which 'nature' is dominated through formations of social organization which privilege the human" (2011, p.67).
9. Exact quote: "Go vegan. Or, as I say, 'Go ahimsic.'"
10. It is worth considering that improving atheist inclusivity might aggravate the Nonhuman Animal rights movement's white-centrism, as the atheist community is also plagued by this problem. Appeals to atheism must therefore be embedded within a framework of intersectionality and should not be done at the expense of other disadvantaged groups.
11. This divide can be traced to the infamous 2011 "Elevatorgate" incident following *Skepchick* founder Rebecca Watson's experience with sexual harassment at a skepticism conference. Her video commentary on the incident prompted prominent atheist advocate Richard Dawkins to publicly trivialize the offense and ridicule her outspokenness (Watson, 2011).
12. Also referred to as "Atheism+" or "A+."

7 Conclusion

1. Harper's *Sistah Vegan Blog* documents many of these negative reactions to critical race theory.
2. For instance, student civil rights activists of the 1960s actually underwent extensive training in order to successfully implement nonviolent civil resistance.
3. See "Master's Journey to the Higher Regions of the Cosmos." *Teleconference with Supreme Master Ching Hai & Supreme Master TV Staff*. June 16, 2013. Hosted at http://suprememastertv.com/.
4. Similar processes have been documented in the gay rights movement. See Alexandra Chasin's (2000) *Selling Out: The Gay and Lesbian Movement Goes to Market*.
5. INCITE! Women of Color Against Violence mirror this sentiment in *The Revolution Will Not Be Funded* (2007).
6. As it was originally developed by men and continues to reflect male interests, the internet is a notoriously misogynistic space. Research has shown that women are many times more likely than men to be the recipients of stalking, harassment, and other forms of abuse (Hess, 2014; Morahan-Martin, 2004).

Bibliography

Adams, C. 2000a. *The Sexual Politics of Meat: A Feminist Vegetarian Critical Theory.* New York, NY: Continuum.
———. 2000b. *The Inner Art of Vegetarianism: Spiritual Practices for Body and Soul.* New York, NY: Lantern Books.
Adams, C. and V. Messina. 2004. *Help! My Child Stopped Eating Meat!: An A-Z Guide to Surviving a Conflict of Diets.* New York, NY: The Continuum Publishing Company.
AgWeb. 2013. "Dairy Producers Have 'Collective Power' to Grow Sales Through Their Checkoff Program." *Farm Journal.* Retrieved from: http://www.agweb.com/mobile/newsdetail.aspx?ArticleId=346268
Ahn, C. 2007. "Democratizing American Philanthropy." pp.63–76, in *The Revolution Will Not Be Funded: Beyond the Non-Profit Industrial Complex*, edited by INCITE! Women of Color Against Violence. Cambridge, MA: South End Press.
American Vegan Society. [no date]. *History.* Retrieved from: http://www.americanvegan.org/history.htm
Anderson, W. 2012. *This is Hope: Green Vegans and the New Human Ecology.* Hants, UK: Earth Books.
Animal Charity Evaluators. 2013. *Position Statement.* Retrieved from: http://www.effectiveanimalactivism.org/position-statement
Animals Asia. 2012. "Dogs, Cats and Livestock." *Friends....Or Food? Why Dogs and Cats Deserve Better.* Retrieved from: https://www.animalsasia.org/intl/assets/pdf/AnimalsAsia_deserve-better_Jan12_resized.pdf
———. 2013. *Animals Asia Review 2013: 15 Years of Changing Lives.* Retrieved from: http://www.animalsasia.net/upload/AAR2013/flipbook_EN/
Animals Australia. 2013. "Live Export: The Facts." *Ban Live Export.* Retrieved from: http://www.banliveexport.com/facts/
Arendt, H. 2006. *Eichmann in Jerusalem: A Report on the Banality of Evil.* London, UK: Penguin Books, LTD.
Ariely, D. 2008. *Predictably Irrational: The Hidden Forces that Shape Our Decisions.* New York, NY: Harper-Collins Publishers.
Arluke, A. 2002. "A Sociology of Sociological Animal Studies." *Society & Animals* 10 (4): 369–74.
Armstrong, E. 2002. *Forging Gay Identities: Organizing in San Francisco, 1950–1994.* Chicago, IL: University of Chicago Press.
Armstrong, J. and H. Rudúlph. 2013. *Sexy Feminism: A Girl's Guide to Love, Success, and Style.* New York, NY: Houghton Mifflin Harcourt Publishing Company.
Asia for Animals Coalition. 2014. "Mass Animal Sacrifice at Nepal's Gadhimai Festival." *Call for Action.* Retrieved from: http://asiaforanimals.com/call-for-action/farm-animals/item/137-mass-animal-sacrifice-at-nepal-s-gadhimai-festival
Azoulay, E., F. Pochard, S. Chevret, M. Jourdain, C. Bornstain, A. Wernet, I. Cattaneo, D. Annane, F. Brun, P. Bollaert, J. Zahar, D. Goldgran-Toledano, C. Adrie, L. Joly, J. Tayoro, T. Desmettre, E. Pigne, A. Parrot, O. Sanchez, C. Poisson,

J. Le Gall, B. Schlemmer, and F. Lemaire. 2002. "Impact of a Family Information Leaflet on Effectiveness of Information Provided to Family Members of Intensive Care Unit Patients: A Multicenter, Prospective, Randomized, Controlled Trial." *American Journal of Respiratory and Critical Care Medicine* 165 (4): 438–42.
Bafna, D. 2013. "The Law of Karma." *ARF Newsletter March 2013*. Bangalore, India: Animal Rights Fund.
Bailenson, J. and N. Yee. 2005. "Digital Chameleons: Automatic Assimilation of Nonverbal Gestures in Immersive Virtual Environments." *Psychological Science* 16: 814–9.
Bailey, C. 2007. "We Are What We Eat: Feminist Vegetarianism and the Reproduction of Racial Identity." *Hypatia* 22 (2): 39–59.
Bales, K., Z. Trodd, and A. Williamson. 2009. *Modern Slavery: The Secret World of 27 Million People*. Oxford, UK: Oneworld Publications.
Ball, M. [no date]. "Anger, Humor, and Advocacy." *Vegan Outreach*. Retrieved from: www.veganoutreach.org/advocacy/satya.html
———. 2008. *A Meaningful Life: Making a Real Difference in Today's World*. Vegan Outreach. Retrieved from: http://www.veganoutreach.org/advocacy/AMLDec08.pdf
———. 2011. "Matt Ball Interview." *Animal Rights Zone Guest Interviews*. ARZone. Retrieved from: http://arzonetranscripts.wordpress.com/2011/02/12/matt-ball-interview/
———. 2012. "Politics, Personal Conduct, and the Vegan Police: The Vegan Outreach Perspective." *Your Daily Dose of Vegan Outreach!* Retrieved from: http://whyveganoutreach.blogspot.com/2012/11/looking-forward-recently-published-in.html
Barnett, L. 2010. "Just How Responsible is PETA for a Decline in Fur Sales?" *Los Angeles Times*. Retrieved from: http://latimesblogs.latimes.com/unleashed/2010/03/just-how-responsible-is-peta-for-a-decline-in-fur-sales.html
Bauer, J., K. Rettig, and S. Son. 2009. "The Cost of Raising Children." *University of Minnesota Extension*. Retrieved from: http://www.extension.umn.edu/family/personal-finance/spending-and-saving/cost-of-raising-children/
Baur, G. 2013. "#GivingTuesday Campaign." *Farm Sanctuary*. Mailing list email received December 3, 2013.
Bazerman, M. and A. Tenbrunsel. 2011. *Blind Spots: Why We Fail to Do What's Right and What to Do about It*. Princeton, NJ: Princeton University Press.
Beal, F. 1970. "Double Jeopardy: To Be Black and Female." pp.109–22, in *The Black Woman: An Anthology*, edited by T. Bambara. New York, NY: Washington Square Press.
Beaman, A., P. Barnes, B. Klentz, B. McQuirk. 1978. "Increasing Helping Rates Through Information Dissemination: Teaching Pays." *Personality and Social Psychology Bulletin* 4: 406–11.
Beardsworth, A. and T. Keil. 1992. "The Vegetarian Option: Varieties, Conversions, Motives and Careers." *The Sociological Review* 40 (2): 254–93.
———. 1997. *Sociology on the Menu: An Invitation to the Study of Food and Society*. London, UK: Routledge.
Beck, L. 2013. "Domestic Drama Sends Owners of Vegan Magazine to Court." *The Huffington Post*, March 5. Retrieved from: http://www.huffingtonpost.com/laura-beck/domestic-drama-sends-owne_b_2812125.html

Beers, D. 2006. *For the Prevention of Cruelty: The History and Legacy of Animal Rights Activism in the United States.* Athens, OH: Ohio University Press.
Bell, S. and B. Lind. [no date]. "An Introduction to PRISM." *People for Reason and Science in Medicine.* Retrieved from: http://www.peopleforreason.org/intro.html
Bender, C., W. Cadge, P. Levitt, and D. Smilde. 2013. *Religion on the Edge: De-Centering and Re-Centering the Sociology of Religion.* New York, NY: Oxford University Press.
Bergh, H. 1874. "The Protestant Episcopal Convention and Mr. Bergh." *The New York Times*, November 4.
Bergman, L. 2013. *Frontline: Rape in the Fields.* DVD. Public Broadcasting Station.
Bernstein, M. 1997. "Celebration and Suppression: The Strategic Uses of Identity by the Lesbian and Gay Movement." *American Journal of Sociology* 103 (3): 531–65.
Best, S. 2004. "It's War! The Escalating Battle between Activists and the Corporate-State Complex." pp.300–37, in *Terrorists or Freedom Fighters? Reflections on the Liberation of Animals*, edited by S. Best and A. Nocella II. New York, NY: Lantern Books.
———. 2012. "The Paralysis of Pacifism." Lecture presented at the conference of *The Paralysis of Pacifism: In Defense of Militant Direct Action and "Violence" for Animal Liberation*, September 6, Aprilia, Italy.
Best, S. and A. Nocella II. 2004. *Terrorists or Freedom Fighters? Reflections on the Liberation of Animals.* New York, NY: Lantern Books.
Birke, L. 1994. *Feminism, Animals and Science: The Naming of the Shrew.* Bristol, PA: Open University Press.
Bloom, P. 2013. *Just Babies: The Origins of Good and Evil.* New York, NY: Crown Publishing Group.
Bockman, J. [no date]. "Leafleting Information." *Justice for Animals.* Retrieved from: http://justiceforanimals.net/content/leafleting-information/
———. 2013. "Letter from EAA's New Executive Director – Jon Bockman." *Effective Animal Activism.* Retrieved from: http://www.effectiveanimalactivism.org/letter-eaas-new-executive-director-jon-bockman
Bone, J. 2010. "Irrational Capitalism: The Social Map, Neoliberalism and the Demodernization of the West." *Critical Sociology* 36 (5): 717–40.
Bongiorno, R., P. Bain, and N. Haslam. 2013. "When Sex Doesn't Sell: Using Sexualized Images of Women Reduces Support for Ethical Campaigns." *PLoS One* 8 (12): e83311.
Bourdieu, P. 2005. *Language and Symbolic Power.* Cambridge, UK: Polity Press.
———. 2010 [1984]. *Distinction: A Social Critique of the Judgment of Taste.* Abingdon, UK: Routledge.
Braunsberger, K. 2014. "The Impact of Animal Welfare Advertising on Opposition to the Canadian Seal Hunt and Willingness to Boycott the Canadian Seafood Industry." *Anthrozoös* 27 (1): 111–25.
Broadway, M. 2000. "Planning for Change in Small Towns or Trying to Avoid the Slaughterhouse Blues." *Journal of Rural Studies* 16: 37–46.
Bromley, D. and D. Cutchin. 1999. "The Social Construction of Subversive Evil: The Contemporary Anticult and Anti-Satanism Movements." pp.195–220, in *Waves of Protest: Social Movements since the Sixties*, edited by J. Freeman and V. Johnson. Lanham, MD: Rowman & Littlefield Publishers, Inc.

Bruce, S. 2011. *Secularization: In Defence of an Unfashionable Theory*. New York, NY: Oxford University Press.
Bruinius, H. 2006. *Better for All the World: The Secret History of Forced Sterilization and America's Quest for Racial Purity*. New York, NY: Random House, Inc.
Bryan, J. and M. Test. 1967. "Models and Helping: Naturalistic Studies in Aiding Behavior." *Journal of Personality and Social Psychology* 6: 400–7.
Bryman, A. 1999. "The Disneyization of Society." *Sociological Review* 47: 25–47.
Burrowes, N., M. Cousins, P. Rojas, and I. Ude. 2007. "On Our Own Terms." pp.227–34, in *The Revolution Will Not Be Funded: Beyond the Non-Profit Industrial Complex*, edited by INCITE! Women of Color Against Violence. Cambridge, MA: South End Press.
Burt, C. and K. Strongman. 2004. "Use of Images in Charity Advertising: Improving Donations and Compliance Rates." *International Journal of Organisational Behavior*. 8 (8): 571–80.
Bushman, B. 2007. "That Was a Great Commercial, But What Were They Selling? Effects of Violence and Sex on Memory for Products in Television Commercials." *Journal of Applied Social Psychology* 37: 1784–96.
Cacioppo, J., R. Petty, and K. Morris. 1983. "Effects of Need for Cognition on Message Evaluation, Recall, and Persuasion." *Journal of Personality and Social Psychology* 45: 805–18.
Cacioppo, J., R. Petty, J. Feinstein, and W. Jarvis. 1996. "Dispositional Differences in Cognitive Motivation: The Life and Times of Individuals Varying in Need for Cognition." *Psychological Bulletin* 119 (2): 197–253.
Calvert, S. 2008. "'Ours is the Food that Eden Knew': Themes in the Theology and Practice of Modern Christian Vegetarians." pp.123–34, in *Eating and Believing: Interdisciplinary Perspectives on Vegetarianism and Theology*, edited by D. Grummet and R. Muers. London, UK: T&T Clark.
Campbell, T. 2006. *The China Study: The Most Comprehensive Study of Nutrition Ever Conducted and the Startling Implications for Diet, Weight Loss, and Long-term Health*. Dallas, TX: BenBella Books.
Capps, A. 2013. "Help Stop the Practice of 'Live Sushi,' and Make the Connection." *Free From Harm*. Retrieved from: http://freefromharm.org/videos/farm-animal-investigations/help-stop-the-practice-of-live-sushi/
Carman, J. and W. Tuttle. 2008. "Help Us Generate a Universal Energy Field of Compassion: It Takes Less than a Minute Each Day." *Circle of Compassion*. Retrieved from: http://www.circleofcompassion.org/index.html
Carolan, M. 2011. *The Real Cost of Cheap Food*. New York, NY: Routledge.
Carter, B. and N. Charles. 2011. *Human and Other Animals: Critical Perspectives*. New York, NY: Palgrave MacMillan.
Cassuto, D. 2014. "Meat Animals, Humane Standards and Other Legal Fictions." *Law, Culture and the Humanities* 10 (2): 225–36.
Chaiken, S. 1979. "Communicator Physical Attractiveness and Persuasion." *Journal of Personality and Social Psychology* 37 (8): 1387–97.
———. 1980. "Heuristic versus Systematic Information Processing and the Use of Source Versus Message Cues in Persuasion." *Journal of Personality and Social Psychology* 39 (5): 752–66.

Chaiken, S. and A. Eagly 1983. "Communication Modality as a Determinant of Persuasion: The Role of Communicator Salience." *Journal of Personality and Social Psychology* 45 (2): 241–56.
Chasen, A. 2000. *Selling Out: The Gay and Lesbian Movement Goes to Market.* New York, NY: Palgrave Macmillan.
Chen, C., J. Dulani, L. Piepzna-Samarasinha, and A. Smith. 2011. *The Revolution Starts at Home: Confronting Intimate Violence within Activist Communities.* Brooklyn, NY: South End Press.
Chenoweth, E. and M. Stephan. 2011. *Why Civil Resistance Works: The Strategic Logic of Nonviolent Conflict.* New York, NY: Columbia University Press.
Cherry, E. 2006. "Veganism as a Cultural Movement: A Relational Approach." *Social Movement Studies* 5 (2): 155–70.
Childers, M. and H. Herzog, Jr. 2009. "Motivations for Meat Consumption among Ex-Vegetarians." *Meeting of the International Society for Anthrozoology.* Kansas City, MO.
Choudry, A. and D. Kapoor. 2013. *NGOization: Complicity, Contradictions and Prospects.* New York, NY: Zed Books Ltd.
Christian Vegetarian Association. [no date]. *Our Mission.* Retrieved from: http://www.all-creatures.org/cva/mission.htm
Christiano, K., Swatos Jr., W., and P. Kivisto. 2008. *Sociology of Religion: Contemporary Developments.* Lanham, MD: Rowman & Littlefield Publishers.
Christina, G. 2012. "Why Atheism Demands Social Justice." *Free Inquiry* 32 (3): 40–1.
Chung, B., C. Corbett, B. Boulet, J. Cummings, K. Paxton, S. McDaniel, S. Mercier, C. Franklin, E. Mercier, L. Jones, B. Collins, P. Koegel, N. Duan, K. Wells, and D. Glik. 2006. "Talking Wellness: A Description of a Community-Academic Partnered Project to Engage an African-American Community Around Depression Through the Use of Poetry, Film, and Photography." *Ethnicity & Disease* 16 (Winter): 67–78.
Cialdini, R., L. Demaine, D. Barrett, B. Sagarin, and K. Rhoads. 2003. "The Poison Parasite Defense: A Strategy for Sapping a Stronger Opponent's Persuasive Strength." Unpublished manuscript, Arizona State University. Retrieved from: http://osil.psy.ua.edu:16080/~Rosanna/Soc_Inf/week12/Poison%20Parasite.pdf
Clement, S. 2013. "How Americans See Global Warming – in 8 Charts." *The Washington Post.* Retrieved from: http://www.washingtonpost.com/blogs/the-fix/wp/2013/04/22/how-americans-see-global-warming-in-8-charts/
CME. 2011. "Will Meat Consumption Drop with Aging Baby Boomers?" *PorkNetwork.* Retrieved from: http://www.porknetwork.com/pork-news/CME-Will-meat-consumption-drop-with-aging-baby-boomers-136067003.html
Cocciolo, A. 2013. "Public Libraries and PBS Partnering to Enhance Civic Engagement: A Study of a Nationwide Initiative." *Public Library Quarterly* 32 (1): 1–20.
Cohen, E. 2013. "'Buddhist Compassion' and 'Animal Abuse' in Thailand's Tiger Temple." *Society & Animals* 21 (3): 266–83.
Cohen, J. 2003. "Human Population: The Next Half Century." *Science* 302 (5648): 1172–5.
Cole, M. and K. Morgan. 2011a. "Veganphobia: Derogatory Discourses of Veganism and the Reproduction of Speciesism in UK National Newspapers." *The British Journal of Sociology* 62 (1): 134–53.

———. 2011b. "Veganism Contra Speciesism: Beyond Debate." *The Brock Review* 12 (1): 144–63.
Cole, M. and K. Stewart. 2014. *Our Children and Other Animals: The Cultural Construction of Human-Animal Relations in Childhood*. Burlington, VT: Ashgate.
Collins, G. 2015. "Ringling Circus Camels, One Hump or Two, are Singular Attractions." *The New York Times*. Retrieved from: http://www.nytimes.com/2015/02/19/arts/ringling-circus-camels-one-hump-or-two-are-singular-attractions.html
Collins, P. 1998. *Fighting Words: Black Women and the Search for Justice*. Minneapolis, MN: University of Minnesota Press.
———. 2000. *Black Feminist Thought: Knowledge, Consciousness, and the Politics of Empowerment*. New York, NY: Routledge.
———. 2004. *Black Sexual Politics: African Americans, Gender, and the New Racism*. New York, NY: Routledge.
———. 2013. *On Intellectual Activism*. Philadelphia, PA: Temple University Press.
Compassion Fatigue Awareness Project. 2013. *Your Continuing Journey*. Retrieved from: http://www.compassionfatigue.org/pages/nextsteps.html
Cook, D. 1962. "The Hawthorne Effect in Educational Research." *The Phi Delta Kappan* 44 (3): 116–22.
Cooney, N. 2011. *Change of Heart: What Psychology Can Teach Us About Spreading Social Change*. Brooklyn, NY: Lantern Books.
———. 2013a. "Career Advice for High-Impact Activism." *Effective Animal Activism*. Retrieved from: http://www.effectiveanimalactivism.org/career-advice-high-impact-activism
———. 2013b. "Nick Cooney." In *Uncaged: Top Activists Share Their Wisdom on Effective Farm Animal Advocacy*, edited by B. Davidow. Ebook. Self-published.
———. 2013c. "The Powerful Impact of College Leafleting (Part 1)." *Compassionate Communities Campaign*, Farm Sanctuary. Retrieved from: http://ccc.farmsanctuary.org/the-powerful-impact-of-college-leafleting-part-1/
———. 2014. *Veganomics: The Surprising Science on What Motivates Vegetarians, from the Breakfast Table to the Bedroom*. New York, NY: Lantern Books.
Cornelius, C. 2014. "Carnation Heirs Donate $10 Million to the Flint Animal Cancer Center." *Today @ Colorado State*, January 31.
Cron, J. and R. Pobocik. 2013. "Intentions to Continue Vegetarian Dietary Patterns: An Application of the Theory of Planned Behavior." *Journal of the Academy of Nutrition and Dietetics* 113 (9): A90.
Cross, J. 2013. "Three Myths of Behavior Change – What You Think You Know That You Don't." *TEDxTalks*. Retrieved from: http://www.youtube.com/watch?v=l5d8GW6GdR0
Cudworth, E. 2011. *Social Lives with Other Animals: Tales of Sex, Death and Love*. New York, NY: Palgrave Macmillan.
Daily Livestock Report. 2011. "USDA's December Forecasts Indicate another Sharp Drop in U.S. Domestic Meat and Poultry Consumption is Coming in 2012." *Daily Livestock Report* 9 (243). Chicago, IL: CME Group.
Darley, J. and C. Batson. 1973. "From Jerusalem to Jericho: A Study of Situational and Dispositional Variables in Helping Behavior." *Journal of Personality and Social Psychology* 27: 100–8.
Dasgupta, A. 2006. "Fur Trade has Sights Set on Global Growth." *Business Edge* 2 (9).

Dauvergne, P. and J. Lister. 2013. *Eco-Business: A Big-Brand Takeover of Sustainability*. Cambridge, MA: MIT Press.

Davidow, B. 2013. *Uncaged: Top Activists Share Their Wisdom on Effective Farm Animal Advocacy*, edited by Ben Davidow. Ebook. Self-published.

Davis, A. 1983. *Women, Race, & Class*. New York, NY: First Vintage Books.

———. 1990. *Women, Culture & Politics*. New York, NY: Vintage Books.

———. 2003. "Racism, Birth Control and Reproductive Rights." pp.353–67, in *Feminist Postcolonial Theory—A Reader*, edited by R. Lewis and S. Mills. New York, NY: Routledge.

———. 2005. *Abolition Democracy: Beyond Empire, Prisons, and Torture*. New York, NY: Seven Stories Press.

Davis, J. 2013. "Blood Sport and the Moral Politics of American Empire and Nation Building." *American Quarterly* 65 (3): 549–74.

Davis, K. 2005. *The Holocaust and the Henmaid's Tale: A Case for Comparing Atrocities*. New York, NY: Lantern Books.

Deckers, J. 2013. "Obesity, Public Health, and the Consumption of Animal Products: Ethical Concerns and Political Solutions." *Journal of Bioethical Inquiry* 10 (1): 29–38.

Deckha, M. 2013. "Welfarist and Imperial: The Contributions of Anticruelty Laws to Civilizational Discourse." *American Quarterly* 65 (3): 515–48.

DeCoux, E. 2009. "Speaking for the Modern Prometheus: The Significance of Animal Suffering to the Abolition Movement." *Animal Law* 16 (1): 9–64.

DeLeeuw, J., L. Galen, C. Aebersold, and V. Stanton. 2007. "Support for Animal Rights as a Function of Belief in Evolution, Religious Fundamentalism, and Religious Denomination." *Society & Animals* 15: 353–63.

Dhont, K. and G. Hodson. 2014. "Why Do Right-Wing Adherents Engage in More Animal Exploitation and Meat Consumption?" *Personality and Individual Difference* 64: 12–17.

Dickerson, M. 2004. *I-Tal Foodways: Nourishing Rastafarian Bodies* (Master's thesis). Louisiana State University, Baton Rouge, LA.

Diekmann, A. and P. Preisendorfer. 1998. "Environmental Behavior: Discrepancies between Aspirations and Reality." *Rationality and Society* 10 (1): 79–102.

DiMaggio, P. and W. Powell. 1983. "The Iron Cage Revisited: Institutional Isomorphism and Collective Rationality in Organizational Fields." *American Sociological Review* 48 (2): 147–60.

Dines, G. 2010. *Pornland: How Porn Has Hijacked Our Sexuality*. Boston, MA: Beacon Press.

———. 2012. "Neo-Liberalism and the Defanging of Feminism." *Stop Porn Culture*. Retrieved from: http://www.youtube.com/watch?v=kDcTt0emXhE

Dunayer, J. 1995. "Sexist Words, Speciesist Roots." pp.11–31, in *Women and Animals: Feminist Theoretical Explorations*, edited by C. Adams and J. Donovan. Durham, NC: Duke University Press.

Duncan, G. and R. Murnane. 2011. *Whither Opportunity? Rising Inequality, Schools, and Children's Life Chances*. New York, NY: Russell Sage Foundation.

Durkheim, E. 2012 [1915]. *The Elementary Forms of the Religious Life*. Mineola, NY: Dover Publications, Inc.

Dworkin, A. 1981. *Pornography: Men Possessing Women*. New York, NY: PLUME.

Earl, J. and A. Schussman. 2003. "The New Site of Activism: On-Line Organizations, Movement Entrepreneurs, and the Changing Location of Social Movement

Decision Making." *Research in Social Movements, Conflicts and Change* 24: 155–87.
Ecklund, E., A. Lincoln, and C. Tansey. 2012. "Gender Segregation in Elite Academic Science." *Gender and Society* 26 (5): 693–717.
Edgell, P. 2012. "A Cultural Sociology of Religion: New Directions." *Annual Review of Sociology* 38: 247–65.
Edgell, P., J. Gerteis, and D. Hartmann. 2006. "Atheists as 'Other': Moral Boundaries and Cultural Membership in American Society." *American Sociological Review* 71 (2): 211–34.
Edwards, K. 1990. "The Interplay of Affect and Cognition in Attitude Formation and Change." *Journal of Personality and Social Psychology* 59 (2): 202–16.
Effective Animal Activism. 2013. *FAQ*. Retrieved from: http://www.effectiveanimalactivism.org/faq
Eldersveld, S. and R. Dodge. 1954. "Personal Contact or Mail Propaganda? An Experiment in Voting Turnout and Attitude Change." In *Public Opinion and Propaganda*, edited by D. Katz, D. Cartwright, S. Eldersveld, and A. Lee. New York, NY: Dryden Press.
Elise, T. 2013. "Anti-Capitalism and Abolitionism." pp.22–43, in *Confronting Animal Exploitation: Grassroots Essays on Liberation and Veganism*, edited by Kim Socha and Sarahjane Blum. Jefferson, NC: McFarland & Company, Inc., Publishers.
Ellingson, S. 1995. "Understanding the Dialectic of Discourse and Collective Action: Public Debate and Rioting in Antebellum Cincinnati." *American Journal of Sociology* 101 (1): 100–44.
Elsheikh, E. and N. Barhoum. 2013. *Structural Racialization and Food Insecurity in the United States*. Atlanta, GA: US Human Rights Network.
Emswiller, T., K. Deaux, and J. Willits. 1971. "Similarity, Sex, and Requests for Small Favors." *Journal of Applied Social Psychology* 1 (3): 284–91.
Erickson, E. 2013. "Farmers Know Their Animals Best." *AgWeek*, February 25. Retrieved from: http://www.agweek.com/event/article/id/20572/
Fabrigar, L. and R. Petty. 1999. "The Role of the Affective and Cognitive Bases of Attitudes in Susceptibility to Affectively and Cognitively Based Persuasion." *Journal of Personality and Social Psychology* 25 (3): 363–81.
Fanon, F. 2008. *Black Skin, White Masks*. New York, NY: Grove Press.
Farm Animal Rights Movement. 2011. "Bay Area 'Back to School' Pay Per View Reaches 725 Students." *Action Reports Campaign News & Commentary*. Bethesda, MD: FARM. Retrieved from: http://www.blog.farmusa.org/bay-area-back-to-school-pay-per-view-reaches-725-students/
———. 2013. "Opening Minds, Changing Diets!" *The FARM Report*: 5.
Farm Sanctuary. 2005. *Privacy Policy*. Retrieved from: http://www.farmsanctuary.org/privacy-policy/
———. 2012. "Welfare Reform and Vegan Advocacy: The Facts." *Compassionate Communities Campaign*. Retrieved from: http://ccc.farmsanctuary.org/welfare-reform-and-vegan-advocacy-the-facts/
———. 2013. *2013: A Path Forward for Farm Animals*. Retrieved from: http://www.farmsanctuary.org/wp-content/uploads/2012/03/2013-Annual-Report.pdf
Farquhar, J., N. Maccoby, P. Wood, J. Alexander, H. Breitrose, B. Brown, W. Haskell, A. McAlister, A. Meyer, J. Nash, and M. Stern. 1977. "Community Education for Cardiovascular Health." *Lancet*: 1192–5, June 4.

Ferguson, M. 1998. *Animal Advocacy and Englishwomen, 1790–1900*. Ann Arbor, MI: University of Michigan Press.

Festinger, L. 1957. *A Theory of Cognitive Dissonance*. Stanford, CA: Stanford University Press.

Figley, C. 1995. "Compassion Fatigue: Toward a New Understanding of the Costs of Caring." pp.3–28, in *Compassion Fatigue: Coping with Secondary Traumatic Stress Disorder in Those Who Treat the Traumatized*, edited by C. Figley. New York, NY: Routledge.

Fine, A. 2006. *Momentum: Igniting Social Change in the Connected Age*. San Francisco, CA: John Wiley & Sons, Inc.

Fischer, P. and T. Greitemeyer. 2010. "A New Look at Selective-Exposure Effects: An Integrative Model." *Current Directions in Psychological Science* 19 (6): 384–9.

Fitzgerald, K. and D. Rodgers. 2000. "Radical Social Movement Organizations: A Theoretical Model." *Sociological Quarterly* 41 (4): 573–92.

Flinn, A. and D. Cudahy. 2011. "Making a Killing with Animal Welfare Reform." *Care2*. Retrieved from: http://www.care2.com/causes/making-a-killing-with-animal-welfare-reform.html

Flynn, M., S. Reinert, and A. Schiff. 2013. "A Six-Week Cooking Program of Plant-Based Recipes Improves Food Security, Body Weight, and Food Purchases for Food Pantry Clients." *Journal of Hunger & Environmental Nutrition* 8 (1): 73–84.

Fonza, A. 2013. "Black Women, Atheist Activism, and Human Rights: Why We Just Cannot Seem to Keep It to Ourselves!" *Cross Currents* June: 185–97.

Food Empowerment Project. 2014a. "Web Highlight: The Dark Side of Chocolate." *Food Chain Newsletter* 7.

———. 2014b. "Produce Workers: The High Cost of Putting Food on Our Plates." *Food Chain Newsletter* 6.

Foucault, M. 1977. *Discipline & Punish: The Birth of the Prison*. New York, NY: Random House, Inc.

Fox, M. 1983. "The Question of Atheism and Communism in the Animal Welfare/Rights Movement." *International Journal for the Study of Animal Problems* 4 (3): 171–3.

———. 2000. "The Case against Animal Experimentation: Comments on Dunayer's 'In the Name of Science'." *Organization Environment* 13: 463–7.

Francione, G. 1995. *Animals, Property, and the Law*. Philadelphia, PA: Temple University Press.

———. 1996. *Rain without Thunder: The Ideology of the Animal Rights Movement*. Philadelphia, PA: Temple University Press.

———. 2008. *Animals as Persons: Essays on the Abolition of Animal Exploitation*. New York, NY: Columbia University Press.

———. 2009a. "Ahimsa and Veganism." *Jain Digest* Winter: 9–10.

———. 2009b. "We're All Michael Vick." *Philadelphia Daily News*, Opinion, August 14.

———. 2010. "Veganism: Morality, Health, and the Environment." *Animal Rights: The Abolitionist Approach*. Retrieved from: http://www.abolitionistapproach.com/veganism-morality-health-and-the-environment

———. 2012a. "A Facebook Exchange." *The Abolitionist Approach*. Retrieved from: http://www.abolitionistapproach.com/a-facebook-exchange/

———. 2012b. "Moral Concern, Moral Impulse, and Logical Argument in Animal Rights Advocacy." *The Abolitionist Approach*. Retrieved from: http://

www.abolitionistapproach.com/moral-concern-moral-impulse-and-logical-argument-in-animal-rights-advocacy/
———. 2012c. "Anuj Shah Interviews Professor Francione on Veganism, Jainism, and Related Topics." *Vegan World Radio*, April 12.
———. 2013. "Abolitionist Animal Rights/Abolitionist Veganism: In a Nut-shell." *Animal Rights: The Abolitionist Approach*. Retrieved from: http://www.abolitionistapproach.com/abolitionist-animal-rights-abolitionist-veganism-in-a-nutshell
Francione, G. and R. Garner. 2010. *The Animal Rights Debate: Abolition or Regulation?* New York, NY: Columbia University Press.
Francis, R. 2010. *Fruitlands: The Alcott Family and Their Search for Utopia*. New Haven, CT: Yale University Press.
Franklin, A., M. Emmison, D. Haraway, and M. Travers. 2007. "Beasts and Boundaries: An Introduction to Animals in Sociology, Science, and Society." *Qualitative Sociology Review* 3 (1): 23–41.
Freeman, C. 2009. "This Little Piggy Went to Press: The American News Media's Construction of Animals in Agriculture." *The Communication Review* 12 (1): 78–103.
———. 2012. "Fishing for Animal Rights in The Cove: A Holistic Approach to Animal Advocacy Documentaries." *Journal for Critical Animal Studies* 10 (1): 104–18.
Freire, P. 2006. *Pedagogy of the Oppressed*. New York, NY: The Continuum International Publishing Group Inc.
Friedrich, B. ~2010. "Personal Purity vs. Effective Advocacy." *Go Veg*. Retrieved from: http://www.abolitionistapproach.com/media/links/p3136/claims.pdf
Gaard, G. 2013. "Toward a Feminist Postcolonial Milk Studies." *American Quarterly* 65 (3): 595–618.
Gaarder, E. 2011. *Women and the Animal Rights Movement*. New Brunswick, NJ: Rutgers University Press.
Gabriel, K., B. Rutledge, and C. Barkley. 2012. "Attitudes on Animal Research Predict Acceptance of Genetic Modification Technologies by University Undergraduates." *Society & Animals* 20: 381–400.
Galvin, S. and H. Herzog, Jr. 1992. "Ethical Ideology, Animal Rights Activism, and Attitudes toward the Treatment of Animals." *Ethics and Behavior* 2 (3): 141–9.
Gawthorne, S. 2008. "The Women Risking Their Lives to Stop Animal Cruelty." *CLEO* April: 72–4.
Gaylor, A. 1997. *Women without Superstition: No Gods – No Masters*. Madison, WI: Freedom from Religion Foundation.
Gervais, W., A. Shariff, and A. Norenzayan. 2011. "Do You Believe in Atheists? Distrust is Central to Anti-Atheist Prejudice." *Journal of Personality and Social Psychology* 101 (6): 1189–206.
Gilheany, J. 2010. *Familiar Strangers: The Church and the Vegetarian Movement in Britain (1809–2009)*. Cardiff, UK: Ascendant Press.
Gilmore, R. 2007. "In the Shadow of the Shadow State." pp.41–52, in *The Revolution Will Not Be Funded: Beyond the Non-Profit Industrial Complex*, edited by INCITE! Women of Color Against Violence. Cambridge, MA: South End Press.
Glaholt, H. 2012. "Vivisection as War: The 'Moral Diseases' of Animal Experimentation and Slavery in British Victorian Quaker Pacifist Ethics." *Society & Animals* 20 (2): 154–72.

Glasser, C. 2011. "Tied Oppressions: An Analysis of How Sexist Imagery Reinforces Speciesist Sentiment." *The Brock Review* 12 (1): 51–68.
Glick, M. 2013. "Animal Instincts: Race, Criminality, and the Reversal of the 'Human'." *American Quarterly* 65 (3): 639–59.
Gorham, C. 2013. *The Ebony Exodus Project: Why Some Black Women Are Walking Out On Religion—and Others Should Too.* Durham, NC: Pitchstone Publishing.
Gouldner, A. 1960. "The Norm of Reciprocity: A Preliminary Statement." *American Sociological Review* 25: 161–78.
Graça, J., M. Calheiros, and A. Oliveria. 2014. "Moral Disengagement in Harmful but Cherished Food Practices? An Exploration into the Case of Meat." *Journal for Agricultural and Environmental Ethics* 27: 749–65.
Green, J. 1999. "The Spirit Willing: Collective Identity and the Development of the Christian Right." pp.153–68, in *Waves of Protest: Social Movements since the Sixties*, edited by J. Freeman and V. Johnson. Lanham, MD: Rowman & Littlefield Publishers, Inc.
Greenwald, C. 2013. "The Best Kind of Activism." *Our Hen House*. Retrieved from: http://www.ourhenhouse.org/2013/11/the-best-kind-of-activism/
Gruen, L. 1993. "Ecofeminism and the Politics of Reality." pp.60–90, in *Ecofeminism: Women, Animals, Nature*, edited by Greta Gaard. Philadelphia, PA: Temple University Press.
Grimké, A. 1836. *Appeal to Christian Women of the South*. New York, NY: American Anti-Slavery Society.
Grimshaw, K., R. Miller, M. Palma, and C. Kerth. 2014. "Consumer Perception of Beef, Pork, Lamb, Chicken, and Fish." *Meat Science* 96 (1): 443–4.
Grinberg, T. 2013. "Women Forcefully Milked in the Street (269Life Animal Rights Performance)." *YouTube*. Retrieved from: https://www.youtube.com/watch?v=3R6bqSzAsc8
Gross, P. and N. Levitt. 1994. *Higher Superstition: The Academic Left and Its Quarrels with Science*. Baltimore, MD: The Johns Hopkins University Press.
Groves, J. 2001. "Animal Rights and the Politics of Emotion: Folk Constructions of Emotion in the Animal Rights Movement." pp.212–31, in *Passionate Politics: Emotions and Social Movements*, edited by J. Goodwin, J. Jasper, and F. Poletta. Chicago, IL: The University of Chicago Press.
Guilloud, S. and W. Cordery. 2007. "Fundraising Is Not a Dirty Word: Community-Based Economic Strategies for the Long Haul." pp.107–12, in *The Revolution Will Not Be Funded: Beyond the Non-Profit Industrial Complex*, edited by INCITE! Women of Color Against Violence. Cambridge, MA: South End Press.
Guither, H. 1998. *Animal Rights: History and Scope of a Radical Social Movement*. Carbondale, IL: Southern Illinois University Press.
Gutbrod, H. 2013. "Who Views Vegetarians & Vegans Positively? New Poll Results." *Humane Thinking*. Human Research Council. Retrieved from: http://www.humanespot.org/content/who-views-vegetarians-vegans-positively-new-poll-results
Hall, L. 2006. *Capers in the Churchyard: Animal Rights Advocacy in the Age of Terror*. Darien, CT: Nectar Bat Press.
———. 2010. *On Their Own Terms: Bringing Animal-Rights Philosophy Down to Earth*. Darien, CT: Nectar Bat Press.

Hammonds, E. and R. Herzig. 2008. *The Nature of Difference: Sciences of Race in the United States from Jefferson to Genomics.* Cambridge, MA: Massachusetts Institute of Technology.

Harper, B. 2010a. "Race as a 'Feeble Matter' in Veganism: Interrogating Whiteness, Geopolitical Privilege, and Consumption Philosophy of 'Cruelty-Free' Products." *Journal for Critical Animal Studies* 8 (3): 5–27.

———. 2010b. *Sistah Vegan: Black Female Vegans Speak on Food, Identity, Health, and Society.* Brooklyn, NY: Lantern Books.

———. 2013a. "Living in Post Apartheid South Africa Inflicts Such Great Wounds on a Person of Color, Especially One Coming From a Country Where the Settlers Have All But Left." *Sistah Vegan Project*, June 11. Retrieved from: http://sistahvegan.com/2013/06/11/living-in-post-apartheid-south-africa-inflicts-such-great-wounds-on-a-person-of-color-especially-one-coming-from-a-country-where-the-settlers-have-all-but-left/

———. 2013b. *Vegan Consciousness and the Commodity Chain: On the Neoliberal, Afrocentric, and Decolonial Politics of "Cruelty-Free."* Dissertation. Davis, CA: University of California Davis.

———. 2014. *On Ferguson, Thug Kitchen & Trayvon Martin: Intersections of [Post] Race-Consciousness, Food Justice and Hip-Hop Veganism.* October 22. Middlebury, VT: Middlebury College.

Harper, B. and L. Ornelas. 2013. "Animal Liberation, Tokenizing 'Intersectionality', and Resistance Ecology." *Resistance Ecology Conference.* Portland State University. Portland, Oregon. June 1.

Harris, F. 2001. "Religious Resources in an Oppositional Civic Culture." pp.38–64, in *Oppositional Consciousness: The Subjective Roots of Social Protest*, edited by J. Mansbridge and A. Morris. Chicago, IL: The University of Chicago Press.

Harris, P. 2013. "Cosmetic Marginalization: Status, Access and Vegan Beauty Lessons from our Foremothers." *Sistah Vegan Conference.* Web. September 14.

Harris, P. J. 2003. "Gatekeeping and Remaking: The Politics of Respectability in African American Women's History and Black Feminism." *Journal of Women's History* 15 (1): 212–20.

Harris, S. 2007. "Sam Harris on the 'Dangers' of 'Atheism." *Atheist Alliance International Conference.* The Richard Dawkins Foundation. Washington, DC Retrieved from: http://www.youtube.com/watch?v=3KG5s_-Khvg

———. 2010. *The Moral Landscape: How Science Can Determine Human Values.* New York, NY: Free Press.

Hart, W. M., D. Albarracin, A. Eagly, I. Brechan, M. Lindberg, and L. Merrill. 2009. "Feeling Validated Versus Being Correct: A Meta-Analysis of Selective Exposure to Information." *Psychological Bulletin* 135 (4): 555–88.

Hartmann, B. 1995. *Reproductive Rights and Wrongs: The Global Politics of Population Control.* Cambridge, MA: South End Press.

Hastie, D. 2008. "Banner Day for Whaling Protest at Japan's Consulate." *Herald Sun*, January 4.

Haverstock, K. and D. Forgays. 2012. "To Eat or Not to Eat. A Comparison of Current and Former Animal Product Limiters." *Appetite* 58 (3): 1030–6.

Hawthorne, M. 2008. *Striking at the Roots: A Practical Guide to Animal Activism.* Hants, UK: O-Books.

Heath, C. and D. Heath. 2010. *Switch: How to Change Things When Change is Hard*. New York, NY: Broadway Books.

Heldman, C. and M. Cahill. 2007. "The Beast of Beauty Culture: An Analysis of the Political Effects of Self-Objectification." *Western Political Science Association Conference*. Las Vegas, NV, March 8–10.

Hemsley, G. and A. Doob. 1978. "The Effect of Looking Behavior on Perceptions of a Communicator's Credibility." *Journal of Applied Social Psychology* 8 (2): 136–44.

Herbert, J., L. Clemow, L. Pbert, I. Ockene, and J. Ockene. 1995. "Social Desirability Bias in Dietary Self-Report May Compromise Validity of Dietary Intake Measures." *International Journal of Epidemiology* 24 (2): 389–98.

Herzog, H. 1993. "'The Movement is My Life': The Psychology of Animal Rights Activism." *Journal of Social Issues* 49 (1): 103–19.

Hess, A. 2014. "Why Women Aren't Welcome on the Internet." *Pacific Standard* 11 (January/February). Retrieved from: http://www.psmag.com/health-and-behavior/women-arent-welcome-internet-72170

Higginbotham, E. 1993. *Righteous Discontent: The Women's Movement in the Black Baptist Church, 1880–1920*. Cambridge, MA: Harvard University Press.

Higgs, K. 2014. *Collision Course: Endless Growth on a Finite Planet*. Cambridge, MA: MIT Press.

Hix, L. 2013 "Should You Feel Guilty about Wearing Vintage Fur?" *Collector's Weekly*. Retrieved from: http://www.collectorsweekly.com/articles/should-you-feel-guilty-about-wearing-vintage-fur/

Hobden, K. and J. Olson. 1994. "From Jest to Antipathy: Disparagement Humor as a Source of Dissonance-Motivated Attitude Change." *Basic and Applied Social Psychology* 15 (3): 239–49.

Hochschild, A. 2012. *The Managed Heart: Commercialization of Human Feeling*. Berkeley, CA: University of California Press.

Hoek, A., P. Luning, P. Weijzen, W. Engels, F. Kok, and C. de Graaf. 2011. "Replacement of Meat by Meat Substitutes. A Survey on Person- and Product-Related Factors in Consumer Acceptance." *Appetite* 56 (3): 662–73.

Hoen, T. and J. Lankhaar. 1999. "Controlled Atmosphere Stunning of Poultry." *Poultry Science* 78 (2): 287–9.

Hohl, K., B. Bradford, and E. Stanko. 2010. "Influencing Trust and Confidence in the London Metropolitan Police: Results from an Experimental Testing the Effect of Leaflet Drops on Public Opinion." *The British Journal of Criminology* 50 (3): 491–513.

hooks, b. 1994. *Outlaw Culture: Resisting Representations*. New York, NY: Routledge.

———. 2004. *The Will to Change: Men, Masculinity, and Love*. New York, NY: Atria Books.

———. 2015. *Ain't I a Woman: Black Women and Feminism*. New York, NY: Routledge.

Hoorens, V. 1993. "Self-Enhancement and Superiority Biases in Social Comparison." *European Review of Social Psychology* 4 (1): 113–39.

Hormes, J., P. Rozin, M. Green, and K. Fincher. 2013. "Reading a Book Can Change Your Mind, But Only Some Changes Last for a Year: Food Attitude Changes in Readers of *The Omnivore's Dilemma*." *Frontiers in Psychology* 4 (778).

Huffington Post. 2012. "PETA Boyfriend Went Vegan Ad: Campaign Pairs Up Violence and Veganism." *Huffpost Living Canada*. Retrieved from: http://www.huffingtonpost.ca/2012/02/15/peta-boyfriend-went-vegan-ad_n_1280061.html

Human Rights Watch. 2004. *Blood, Sweat, and Fear: Workers' Rights in U.S. Meat and Poultry Plants*. Retrieved from: http://www.hrw.org/sites/default/files/reports/usa0105.pdf

Humane Research Council. 2011. *Readability of Vegan Outreach Literature*. Olympia, WA: Humane Research Council. Retrieved from: http://www.humanespot.org/content/readability-vegan-outreach-literature

———. 2012. *Video Comparison Study: Youth Response to Four Vegetarian/Vegan Outreach Videos*. Olympia, WA: Human Research Council. Retrieved from: http://www.humanespot.org/system/files/Citation2126_VideoComparisonStudy.pdf

Humane Society of the United States. 2012. "The US Humane Society Doesn't Like Animals? That's a Crock." *Huffington Post*. Retrieved from: http://www.huffingtonpost.ca/the-humane-society-of-the-united-states/human-society-of-the-united-states_b_2005792.html

Hussar, K. and P. Harris. 2010. "Children Who Choose Not to Eat Meat: A Study of Early Moral Decision-Making." *Social Development* 19 (3): 627–41.

Hutchinson, S. 2011. *Moral Combat: Black Atheists, Gender Politics, and the Value Wars*. Infidel Books.

———. 2013a. *Godless Americana: Race and Religious Rebels*. Infidel Books.

———. 2013b. "Why Did So Many Black Women Die? Jonestown at 35." *Religion Dispatches*. Los Angeles, CA: University of Southern California. Retrieved from: http://www.religiondispatches.org/archive/culture/7402/why_did_so_many_black_women_die_jonestown_at_35/

Hutchinson, W. 2013. "Woman 'Force-Fed' at Fortnum & Mason Showing Foie Gras Cruelty, London." *Demotix*, August 7. Retrieved from: http://www.demotix.com/news/2368621/woman-force-fed-fortnum-mason-showing-foie-gras-cruelty-london

Ilaiah, K. 2009. *Post-Hindu India; A Discourse in Dalit-Bahujan, Socio-Spiritual and Scientific Revolution*. London, UK: SAGE Publications Ltd.

INCITE! Women of Color Against Violence. 2007. *The Revolution Will Not Be Funded: Beyond the Non-Profit Industrial Complex*. Cambridge, MA: South End Press.

International Humanist and Ethical Union. 2012. *Freedom of Thought 2012: A Global Report on Discrimination against Humanists, Atheists and the Nonreligious*. Retrieved from: http://www.iheu.org/files/IHEU%20Freedom%20of%20Thought%202012.pdf

Irvine, L. 2013. *My Dog Always Eats First: Homeless People and Their Animals*. Lynne Rienner Pub.

Islamic Concern. [no date]. *Halal Living*. Retrieved from: http://www.islamicconcern.com

Jabs, J., C. Devine, and J. Sobal. 1998. "Maintaining Vegetarian Diets: Personal Factors, Social Networks, and Environmental Resources." *Canadian Journal of Dietetic Practice and Research* 59 (4): 183–9.

Jadali, S. 2014. "Vegan Killers: Israeli Vegan-Washing and the Manipulation of Morality." *Turkey Agenda*. Retrieved from: http://www.turkeyagenda.com/

vegan-killers-israeli-vegan-washing-and-the-manipulation-of-morality-1656.html

James, O. 2013. "You Meat Eating Murderer! Non Vegan Guilt." *Skepchick*, September 23. Retrieved from: http://skepchick.org/2013/09/you-meat-eating-murderer-non-vegan-guilt

James, W. 1907. *Pragmatism: A New Name for Some Old Ways of Thinking.* Minneapolis, MN: Filiquarian Publishing, LLC.

———. 1988. *William James: Writings 1902–1910: The Varieties of Religious Experience/Pragmatism/A Pluralistic Universe/The Meaning of Truth/Some Problems of Philosophy/Essays.* New York, NY: Penguin Books.

James, W. S. 1948. "Veganism and Science—And a Warning." *The Vegan* 4 (1): 6–7.

Jamieson, J., M. Reiss, D. Allen, L. Asher, M. Parker, C. Wathes, and S. Abeyesinghe. 2013. "Adolescents Care but Don't Feel Responsible for Farm Animal Welfare." *Society & Animals*. In press.

Janis, I., D. Kaye, and P. Kirschner. 1965. "Facilitating Effects of Eating While Reading on Responsiveness to Persuasive Communications." *Journal of Personality and Social Psychology* 1 (2): 181–6.

Jason, L. 2013. *Principles of Social Change.* New York, NY: Oxford University Press.

Jasper, J. and D. Nelkin. 1992. *The Animal Rights Crusade: The Growth of a Moral Protest.* New York, NY: Free Press.

Jasper, J. and J. Poulsen. 1993. "Fighting Back: Vulnerabilities, Blunders, and Countermobilization by the Targets in Three Animal Rights Campaigns." *Sociological Forum* 8 (4): 639–57.

———. 1995. "Recruiting Strangers and Friends: Moral Shocks and Social Networks in Animal Rights and Anti-Nuclear Protests." *Social Problems* 42 (4): 493–512.

Jennings, J. 1997. *The Business of Abolishing the British Slave Trade, 1783–1807.* New York, NY: Routledge.

Jensen, R. 2007. *Getting Off: Pornography and the End of Masculinity.* Cambridge, MA: South End Press.

Jewish Vegetarians of North America. [no date]. *History of Jewish Vegetarians of North America.* Retrieved from: http://jewishveg.com/schwartz/history.html

Joy, M. 2008. *Strategic Action for Animals: A Handbook on Strategic Movement Building, Organizing, and Activism for Animal Liberation.* Brooklyn, NY: Lantern Books.

———. 2010. *Why We Love Dogs, Eat Pigs, and Wear Cows: An Introduction to Carnism.* Newburyport, MA: Conari Press.

———. 2012. "Our Voices, Our Movement: How Vegans Can Move Beyond the 'Welfare-Abolition Debate.'" *One Green Planet.* Retrieved from: http://www.onegreenplanet.org/animalsandnature/our-voices-our-movement-how-vegans-can-move-beyond-the-welfare-abolition-debate/

Jyoti, D., E. Frongillo, and S. Jones. 2005. "Food Insecurity Affects School Children's Academic Performance, Weight Gain, and Social Skills." *The Journal of Nutrition* 135 (12): 2831–9.

Kahan, D., H. Jenkins-Smith, and D. Braman. 2010. "Cultural Cognition of Scientific Consensus." *Journal of Risk Research* 14: 147–74.

Kandel, W. 2009. *Recent Trends in Rural-Based Meat Processing.* Economic Research Service, US Department of Agriculture. Retrieved from: http://migrationfiles.ucdavis.edu/uploads/cf/files/2009-may/kandel.pdf

Kandiyoti, D. 1988. "Bargaining with Patriarchy." *Gender & Society* 2 (3): 274–90.
Keating, J. and T. Brock. 1974. "Acceptance of Persuasion and the Inhibition of Counterargumentation under Various Distraction Tasks." *Journal of Experimental Social Psychology* 10 (4): 301–9.
Kemmerer, L. and A. Nocella, II. 2011. *Call to Compassion: Religious Perspectives on Animal Advocacy*. Brooklyn, NY: Lantern Books.
Keralis, S. 2012. "Feeling Animal: Pet-Making and Mastery in the Slave's Friend." *American Periodicals* 22 (2): 121–38.
Keysar, A. 2007. "Who Are America's Atheists and Agnostics?" pp.33–40, in *Secularism & Secularity: Contemporary International Perspectives*, edited by B. Kosmin and A. Keysar. Hartford, CT: Institute for the Study of Secularism in Society and Culture, Trinity College.
Kheel, M. 1985. "Speaking the Unspeakable: Sexism in the Animal Rights Movement." *Feminists for Animal Rights Newsletter* 2 (1): 1–7.
———. 2006. "Direct Action and the Heroic Ideal: An Ecofeminist Critique." pp.306–18, in *Igniting a Revolution: Voices in Defense of the Earth*, edited by A. Nocella II and S. Best. Oakland, CA: AK Press.
Kim, C. 2011. "Moral Extensionism or Racist Exploitation? The Use of Holocaust and Slavery Analogies in the Animal Liberation Movement." *New Political Science* 33 (3): 311–33.
Kim, C., D. Losen, and D. Hewitt. 2010. *The School-to-Prison Pipeline: Structuring Legal Reform*. New York, NY: New York University Press.
King, T. and E. Osayande. 2007. "The Filth on Philanthropy: Progressive Philanthropy's Agenda to Misdirect Social Justice Movements." pp.79–89, in *The Revolution Will Not Be Funded: Beyond the Non-Profit Industrial Complex*, edited by INCITE! Women of Color Against Violence. Cambridge, MA: South End Press.
Knudsen, L. 2006. *Reproductive Rights in a Global Context: South Africa, Uganda, Peru, Denmark, United States, Vietnam, Jordan*. Nashville, TN: Vanderbilt University Press.
Kretzer, M. 2013. "PETA's Youngest Pinup Encourages Teens to 'Go All the Way' for Animals." *PETA Blog*. Retrieved from: http://www.peta.org/blog/petas-youngest-pinup-encourages-teens-go-way-animals/
———. 2014. "Progress! China Allows Some Cosmetics to Be Marketed Without Animal Tests." *PETA Blog*. Retrieved from: http://www.peta.org/blog/progress-china-allows-cosmetics-marketed-without-animal-tests/
Krosnick, J. and D. Alwin. 1989. "Aging and Susceptibility to Attitude Change." *Journal of Personality and Social Psychology* 57 (3): 416–25.
Kurth, H. 2012. "Vegan Activist Talks Animal Rights, Activism." *Northern Star*, February 5. DeKalb, IL: Northern Illinois University.
Kurzban, R. 2010. *Why Everyone (Else) Is A Hypocrite: Evolution and the Modular Mind*. Princeton, NJ: Princeton University Press.
Latané, B. and J. Darley. 1968. "Group Inhibition of Bystander Intervention in Emergencies." *Journal of Personality and Social Psychology* 10 (3): 215–21.
———. 1970. *The Unresponsive Bystander. Why Doesn't He Help?* New York, NY: Appleton-Century-Crofts.
LaVeck, J. and J. Stein. 2012. "Meatopia on the March: HSUS President Seeks to Join Tyson Board." *HumaneMyth*. Retrieved from: http://www.humanemyth.org/meatopiaonthemarch.htm

Lea, E. 2001. *Moving from Meat: Vegetarianism, Beliefs and Information Sources.* Department of Public Health. Dissertation. Adelaide, Australia: The University of Adelaide.

Leadbetter, C. 2007. *Vegetarianism and Occultism.* New York, NY: Cosimo, Inc.

Leitch, M. 2013. "Killing Them Softly: Marketing a Movement, Marketing Meat." pp.191–203, in *Confronting Animal Exploitation: Grassroots Essays on Liberation and Veganism,* edited by K. Socha and S. Blum. Jefferson, NC: McFarland & Company, Inc., Publishers.

Leneman, L. 1997. "The Awakened Instinct: Vegetarianism and the Women's Suffrage Movement in Britain." *Women's History Review* 6 (2): 271–87.

Lepic, E. 2012. "PETA Gave une Femme en Pleine Rue pour Dénoncer la Fabrication du Foie Gras." *Le Tribunal Du Net,* December 5. Retrieved from: http://www.letribunaldunet.fr/actualites/peta-gave-une-femme-en-pleine-rue-pour-denoncer-la-fabrication-du-foie-gras.html

Leonard, A. 2010. *The Story of Stuff: How Our Obsession with Stuff is Trashing the Planet, Our Communities, and Our Health—and a Vision for Change.* New York, NY: Free Press.

Lerner, A. 1972. "The Economics and Politics of Consumer Sovereignty." *The American Economic Review* 62 (1/2): 258–66.

Lerner, G. 2004. *The Grimké Sisters from South Carolina: Pioneers for Women's Rights and Abolition.* Chapel Hill, NC: University of North Carolina Press.

Lerner, M. 1980. *The Belief in a Just World: A Fundamental Delusion.* New York, NY: Plenum.

Lever, J., D. Frederick, and L. Peplau. 2006. "Does Size Matter? Men's and Women's Views on Penis Size across the Lifespan." *Psychology of Men & Masculinity* 7 (3): 129–43.

Levine, J., T. Martinez, G. Brase, and K. Sorenson. 1994. "Helping in 36 U.S. Cities." *Journal of Personality and Social Psychology* 67: 69–82.

Levine, S. 2003. "Documentary Film and HIV/AIDS: New Directions for Applied Visual Anthropology in Southern Africa." *Visual Anthropology Review* 19 (1–2): 57–72.

Levy, A. 2005. *Female Chauvinist Pigs: Women and the Rise of Raunch Culture.* New York, NY: Free Press.

Lindsey, L. 2011. *Gender Roles: A Sociological Perspective.* Boston, MA: Pearson.

Lovitz, D. 2010. *Muzzling a Movement: The Effects of Anti-Terrorism Laws, Money & Politics on Animal Activism.* Brooklyn, NY: Lantern Books.

Luke, B. 1995. "Taming Ourselves or Going Feral? Toward a Nonpatriarchal Metaethic of Animal Liberation." pp.290–319, in *Animals and Women: Feminist Theoretical Explorations,* edited by C. Adams and J. Donovan. Durham, NC: Duke University Press.

———. 2007. *Brutal: Manhood and the Exploitation of Animals.* Champaign, IL: University of Illinois Press.

Lundblad, M. 2012. "Archaeology of a Humane Society: Animality, Savagery, Blackness." pp.75–102, in *Species Matters: Humane Advocacy and Cultural Theory,* edited by M. DeKoven and M. Lundblad. New York, NY: Columbia University Press.

Lupkin, S. 2013. "PETA's 'Plan V' for Contraception Misses Mark." *ABC News,* December 4. Retrieved from: http://abcnews.go.com/Health/petas-plan-contraception-misses-mark/story?id=21087355

Lynch, J. 2002. "Theodicy and Animals." *Between the Species* 2 (August): 1–10.
Lynch, R. 2012. "Humane Society CEO Seeks Seat on Board of Meat Company Tyson." *Los Angeles Times*, October 2. Retrieved from: http://articles.latimes.com/2012/oct/02/nation/la-na-nn-humane-society-tyson-20121002
Lynn, R., J. Harvey, and H. Nyborg. 2009. "Average Intelligence Predicts Atheism Rates Across 137 Nations." *Intelligence* 37 (1): 11–15.
Lyon, E. 1997. *Poverty, Welfare and Battered Women: What Does the Research Tell Us?* Harrisburg, PA: The National Resource Center on Domestic Violence.
MacKinnon, C. and A. Dworkin. 1997. *In Harm's Way: The Pornography Civil Rights Hearings*. Cambridge, MA: Harvard University Press.
MacKinnon, C. 1989. *Toward a Feminist Theory of the State*. Cambridge, MA: Harvard University Press.
Magistad, M. 2013. "Vegan Lunch: Going Meatless in Beijing." *Public Radio International*, June 27.
Mahanta, S. 2014. "Big Beef." *Washington Monthly* January/February. Retrieved from: http://www.washingtonmonthly.com/magazine/january_february_2014/features/big_beef048356.php
Malatesta, J. 2010. "Roquebrune Search within the Movement Ching Hai." *Nice-Matin*, August 26..
Marcus, E. 2011. *A Vegan History: 1944–2010*. Summertown, TN: Book Publishing Company.
Marsh, C. 2005. *The Beloved Community: How Faith Shapes Social Justice, from the Civil Rights Movement to Today*. New York, NY: Basic Books.
Mason, M. 2011. "Necessary but Not Sufficient: Revolutionary Ideology and Antislavery Action in the Early Republic." pp.11–31, in *Contesting Slavery: The Politics of Bondage and Freedom in the New American Nation*, edited by J. Hammond and M. Mason. Charlottesville, VA: University of Virginia Press.
Masri, A. 2009. *Animal Welfare in Islam*. Leicestershire, UK: The Islamic Foundation.
Matthews, G. 2006. *Caribbean Slave Revolts and the British Abolitionist Movement*. Baton Rouge, LA: Louisiana State University Press.
Matthies, C. 2013. "What's the Biggest Threat to Homeless Animals Today?" *The PETA Files*, November 11. Retrieved from: http://www.peta.org/b/thepetafiles/archive/2013/11/11/no-kill-betrayal.aspx
Maurer, D. 2002. *Vegetarianism: Movement or Moment?* Philadelphia, PA: Temple University Press.
McCarthy, J. and M. Zald. 1973. *The Trend of Social Movements in America: Professionalization and Resource Mobilization*. Morristown, NJ: General Learning Press.
McCarthy, J., D. Britt, and M. Wolfson. 1991. "The Institutional Channeling of Social Movements by the State in the United States." *Research in Social Movements, Conflicts and Change* 13: 45–76.
McCord, L. 1853. "Art. III.—Uncle Tom's Cabin." *Southern Quarterly Review* January: 81–120.
McDonald, B. 2000. "'Once You Know Something, You Can't Not Know It.' An Empirical Look at Becoming Vegan." *Society & Animals* 8 (1): 1–23.
McDonnell, K. and S. Abdulla. 2001. *Project AWARE: Asian Women Advocating Respect and Empowerment*. Washington, DC: Asian/Pacific Islander Domestic Violence Resource Project.

McKenzie, L. 2012. "Abolitionism and Discrimination." *Linda McKenzie's Blog.* Retrieved from: http://lindaamckenzie.blogspot.com/2012/11/abolitionism-and-discrimination.html

McKivigan, J. 1999. *Abolitionism and American Religion.* New York, NY: Garland Publishing, Inc.

McMichael, P. 2008. *Development and Social Change: A Global Perspective.* 4th ed. Los Angeles, CA: Pine Forge Press.

McWilliams, J. 2012. "Vegan Feud." *Slate.* Retrieved from: http://www.slate.com/articles/life/food/2012/09/hsus_vs_abolitionists_vs_the_meat_industry_why_the_infighting_should_stop_.html

———. 2013a. "The Data of Experience." *Eating Plants.* Retrieved from: http://james-mcwilliams.com/?p=4138

———. 2013b. "Radical Activism and the Future of Animal Rights." *Pacific Standard*, July 3. Retrieved from: http://www.psmag.com/culture/radical-activism-and-the-future-of-animal-rights-61789/

Meinberg, T. [no date]. "About." *Vegan Pinup.* Retrieved from: http://veganpinup.com/about/

Menzies, K. and J. Sheeshka. 2012. "The Process of Exiting Vegetarianism: An Exploratory Study." *Canadian Journal of Dietetic Practice and Research* 73 (4): 163–8.

Midgley, M. 2003. *The Myths We Live By.* New York, NY: Routledge.

Mika, M. 2006. "Framing the Issue: Religion, Secular Ethics and the Case of Animal Rights Mobilization." *Social Forces* 85 (2): 915–41.

Milgrim, S. 1974. *Obedience to Authority: An Experimental View.* New York, NY: Harper & Row, Publishers, Inc.

Miller, N., G. Maruyama, R. Beaber, and K. Valone. 1976. "Speed of Speech and Persuasion." *Journal of Personality and Social Psychology* 34 (4): 615–24.

Miller, P., J. Kozu, and A. Davis. 2001. "Social Influence, Empathy, and Prosocial Behavior in Cross-Cultural Perspectives." pp.54–66, in *The Practice of Social Influence in Multiple Cultures*, edited by W. Wosinka, R. Cialdini, D. Barrett, and J. Reykowski. Mahwah, NJ: Erlbaum. Mahwah, NJ: Lawrence Erlbaum Associates, Publishers.

Millington, K. 2012. "Vegetarian Roots: The Extraordinary Tale of William Cowherd." *BBC News Magazine.* Retrieved from: http://www.bbc.co.uk/news/magazine-20666581

Mitchel, S. 2004. *Frances Power Cobbe: Victorian Feminist, Journalist, Reformer.* Charlottesville, VA: University of Virginia Press.

Mirk, S. 2015. "Liberal Problems." *Popaganda* [Podcast]. Retrieved from: https://soundcloud.com/bitch-media/wtf-peta

Monteiro, C. 2012. "The Effects of Graphic Images on Attitudes towards Animal Rights." *FARM*, October 17. Retrieved from: http://www.blog.farmusa.org/the-effects-of-graphic-images-on-attitudes-towards-animal-rights/

Morahan-Martin, J. 2004. "Women and the Internet: Promise and Perils." *CyberPsychology & Behavior* 3 (5): 683–91.

Myers, P. 2012. "Atheism's Third Wave." *Free Inquiry* 32 (5): 46–7.

Nabi, R. 2009. "The Effect of Disgust-Eliciting Visuals on Attitudes toward Animal Experimentation." *Communication Quarterly* 46 (4): 472–84.

National Center for Charitable Statistics. 2010. *Number of Nonprofit Organizations in the United States, 1999–2009.* Retrieved from: http://nccsdataweb.urban.org/PubApps/profile1.php?state=US

National Science Foundation, Division of Science Resources Statistics. 2015. *Women, Minorities, and Persons with Disabilities in Science and Engineering: 2015.* Special Report NSF 15–311. Arlington, VA. Retrieved from: http://www.nsf.gov/statistics/2015/nsf15311/digest/nsf15311-digest.pdf

National Secular Society. 2012. *Religious Slaughter of Animals.* Retrieved from: http://www.secularism.org.uk/uploads/ritual-slaughter-of-animals-briefing.pdf

Nearing, H. and S. Nearing. 1973. *Living the Good Life: How to Live Sanely in a Troubled World.* New York, NY: Schocken Books.

New Wave Feminism. 2013. "A Hamilton College Cultural Education." *New Wave Feminism*, September 23. Tumblr post. Retrieved from: http://newwavefeminism.tumblr.com/post/62121216024/a-hamilton-college-cultural-education

Newsom, J. 1999. *Another Side to Caregiving: Negative Reactions to Being Helped.* Institute on Aging. Portland State University.

Nibert, D. 2002. *Animal Rights, Human Rights: Entanglements of Oppression and Liberation.* New York, NY: Rowman and Littlefield.

———. 2003. "Humans and Other Animals: Sociology's Moral and Intellectual Challenge." *International Journal of Sociology and Social Policy* 23 (3): 5–25.

———. 2013. *Animal Oppression and Human Violence: Domesecration, Capitalism, and Global Conflict.* New York, NY: Columbia University Press.

Nichols, S., W. Waters, M. Woolaway, M. Hamilton-Smith. 1988. "Evaluation of the Effectiveness of a Nutritional Health Education Leaflet in Changing Public Knowledge and Attitudes about Eating and Health." *Journal of Human Nutrition and Dietetics* 1 (4): 233–38.

Norris, J. 1997. "Why Leaflet?" *Vegan Outreach.* Retrieved from: http://www.veganoutreach.org/articles/whyleaf.html

———. 2009. *Does Veganism Spread Itself?* [Presentation]. Retrieved from: http://whyveganoutreach.blogspot.com/2011/12/friday-video-jack-from-2009.html

Noske, B. 1989. *Humans and Other Animals: Beyond the Boundaries of Anthropology.* Winchester, MA: Pluto Press.

Obenchain, T. 2012. *The Victorian Vivisection Debate: Frances Power Cobbe, Experimental Science and the "Claims of Brutes."* Jefferson, NC: McFarland & Company, Inc., Publishers.

Oliver, P. and G. Marwell. 1992. "Mobilizing Technologies for Collective Action." pp.251–72, in *Frontiers of Social Movement Theory*, edited by A. Morris and C. Mueller. New Haven, CT: Yale University Press.

Omond, T. 2012. "Power, Oppression and Abuse: Performing Animal Tests." *Fighting Animal Testing.* Retrieved from: http://www.fightinganimaltesting.com/our-blog/power-oppression-and-abuse-performing-animal-tests-2/

Osterhouse, R. and T. Brock. 1970. "Distraction Increases Yielding to Propaganda by Inhibiting Counterarguing." *Journal of Personality and Social Psychology* 15: 344–58.

Pacelle, W. 2012. "It's Time to Unite for the Animals." *A Humane Nation.* The Humane Society of the United States. Retrieved from: http://hsus.typepad.com/wayne/2012/09/its-time-to-unite-for-animals.html

Parker, C., C. Brunswick, and J. Kotey. 2013. "The Happy Hen on Your Supermarket Shelf: What Choice Does Industrial Strength Free-Range Represent for Consumers?" *Journal of Bioethical Inquiry* 10 (2): 165–86.

Patterson, C. 2002. *Eternal Treblinka: Our Treatment of Animals and the Holocaust.* New York, NY: Lantern Books.

Peace Advocacy Network. [no date]. *PAN Horse-Drawn Carriage Handout.* Retrieved from: http://www.peaceadvocacynetwork.org/litresources/PAN_HDC.pdf

Peek, C., M. Konty, and T. Frazier. 1997. "Religion and Ideological Support for Social Movements: The Case of Animal Rights." *Journal for the Scientific Study of Religion* 36 (3): 429–39.

Peggs, K. 2012. *Animals and Sociology.* New York, NY: Palgrave Macmillan.

———. 2013. "The 'Animal-Advocacy Agenda': Exploring Sociology for Non-Human Animals." *The Sociological Review* 61 (3): 591–606.

Pelaez, V. 2013. "The Prison Industry in the United States: Big Business or a New Form of Slavery." *Centre for the Research on Globalization.* Retrieved from: http://www.globalresearch.ca/the-prison-industry-in-the-united-states-big-business-or-a-new-form-of-slavery/

People for the Ethical Treatment of Animals. [no date a]. *Veggie Love Casting Session.* Retrieved from: http://features.peta.org/casting-session/default.aspx

———. [no date b]. "Why Does PETA Sometimes Use Nudity in Its Campaigns?" *FAQ.* Retrieved from: http://www.peta.org/about/faq/Why-does-PETA-sometimes-use-nudity-in-its-campaigns.aspx

———. [no date c]. *Privacy Policy.* Retrieved from: http://www.peta.org/about/learn-about-peta/privacy.aspx

———. 2009. *Controlled-Atmosphere Killing vs. Electric Immobilization: A Comparative Analysis of Poultry-Slaughter Systems from Animal Welfare, Worker Safety, and Economic Perspectives.* Norfolk, VA: PETA.

———. 2010. "'No-Kill' Shelters: Hoarding a Secret." *Animal Times,* Winter: 12–13.

———. 2012. "PETA Offers Pro-Vegan Banner to Joel Osteen's Megachurch." *News Releases.* Retrieved from: http://www.peta.org/mediacenter/news-releases/PETA-Offers-Pro-Vegan-Banner-to-Joel-Osteen-s-Megachurch.aspx

———. 2013. "Keep Pregnant Women Out for the Sake of Their Sons' Sex Organs, PETA Tells Buffalo Wing Festival." *News Releases.* Retrieved from: http://www.peta.org/mediacenter/news-releases/Keep-Pregnant-Women-Out-for-the-Sake-of-Their-Sons-Sex-Organs-PETA-Tells-Buffalo-Wing-Festival.aspx

Peraino, A. 2013. "Veganism Saved My Life: Natalie Palmer." *VegNews.* Retrieved from: http://vegnews.com/articles/page.do?pageId=5262&catId=5

Pérez-Peña, R. 2015. "Elephants to Retire from Ringling Brothers Stage." *The New York Times.* Retrieved from: http://www.nytimes.com/2015/03/06/us/ringling-brothers-circus-dropping-elephants-from-act.html

Perry, S. 2004. *A BJS Statistical Profile, 1992–2002: American Indians and Crime.* Washington, DC: US Department of Justice.

Petty, R., C. Haugtvedt, and S. Smith. 1995. "Elaboration as a Determinant of Attitude Strength: Creating Attitudes that are Persistent, Resistant, and Predictive of Behavior." pp.93–130, in *Attitude Strength: Antecedents and Consequences,* edited by R. Petty and J. Krosnick. Hillsdale, NJ: Erlbaum.

Petty, R., J. Barden, and S. Wheeler. 2009. "The Elaboration Likelihood Model of Persuasion: Developing Health Promotions for Sustained Behavioral Change." pp.185–214, in *Emerging Theories in Health Promotion Practice and Research* 2nd ed. edited by R. DiClemente, R. Crosby, and M. Kegler. San Francisco, CA: Jossey-Bass.

Petty, R., J. Cacioppo, and R. Goldman. 1981. "Personal Involvement as a Determinant of Argument-Based Persuasion." *Journal of Personality and Social Psychology* 41 (5): 847–55.

Phelps, N. 2004. *The Great Compassion: Buddhism and Animal Rights.* New York, NY: Lantern Books.

———. 2007. *The Longest Struggle: Animal Advocacy from Pythagoras to PETA.* New York, NY: Lantern Books.

———. 2013. *Changing the Game: Why the Battle for Animal Liberation is So Hard and How We Can Win It.* Brooklyn, NY: Lantern Books.

Pierleoni, A. 2011. "Our Ties with Animals—Sometimes Heartwarming, Other Times Horrific." *The Sacramento Bee.* Retrieved from: http://www.sacbee.com/2011/06/20/3712437/our-ties-with-animals-sometimes.html

Pinker, S. 2011. *The Better Angels of Our Nature.* New York, NY: Viking.

Piven, F. and R. Cloward. 1977. *Poor People's Movements: Why They Succeed, How They Fail.* New York, NY: Pantheon Books.

Pollan, M. 2006. *The Omnivore's Dilemma: A Natural History of Four Meals.* New York, NY: The Penguin Press.

Popper, K. 2002. *The Logic of Scientific Discovery.* 2nd ed. New York, NY: Routledge.

Potter, W. 2011. *Green is the New Red: An Insider's Account of a Social Movement Under Siege.* San Francisco, CA: City Lights Publishers.

Public Policy Polling. 2013. *Americans Pick Ronald McDonald over Burger King for President.* Raleigh, NC: Public Policy Polling. Retrieved from: http://www.publicpolicypolling.com/pdf/2011/PPP_Release_NationalFOOD_022613.pdf

Raines, J. Ed. 2002. *Marx on Religion.* Philadelphia, PA: Temple University Press.

Rashkin, S. 2014. "*Thug Kitchen*: Local Authors of Vegan Cookbook in the Center of Race Debate." *LA Weekly,* October 15. Retrieved from: http://www.laweekly.com/squidink/2014/10/15/thug-kitchen-local-authors-of-vegan-cookbook-in-the-center-of-race-debate

Regan, D. and J. Cheng. 1973. "Distraction and Attitude Change: A Resolution." *Journal of Experimental Social Psychology* 9 (2): 138–47.

Regan, T. [no date]. "How to Prolong Justice." *Tom Regan Rights & Writes.* Retrieved from: http://tomregan.info/essays/how-to-prolong-justice/

———. 1990. "Christianity and Animal Rights: The Challenge and Promise." pp.73–87, in *Liberating Life: Contemporary Approaches in Ecological Theology,* edited by C. Birch, W. Eaken, and J. McDaniel. Maryknoll, NY: Orbis Books.

———. 2004a. "How to Justify Violence." pp.231–6, in *Terrorists or Freedom Fighters? Reflections on the Liberation of Animals,* edited by Steven Best and Anthony Nocella II. New York, NY: Lantern Books.

———. 2004b. *Empty Cages: Facing the Challenge of Animal Rights.* Lanham, MD: Rowman and Littlefield.

———. 2004c. *The Case for Animal Rights.* Berkeley, CA: The University of California Press.

Regner, M., F. Hermann, and L. Ried. 1987. "Effectiveness of a Printed Leaflet for Enabling Patients to Use Digoxin Side-Effect Information." *The Annals of Pharmacotherapy* 21 (2): 200–4.

Rennison, C. and S. Welchans. 2000. *Intimate Partner Violence.* NCJ 178247. Washington, DC: US Department of Justice.

Rich, B. 1998. *Chick Flicks: Theories and Memories of the Feminist Film Movement.* Durham, NC: Duke University Press.
Riss, A. 1994. "Racial Essentialism and Family Values in 'Uncle Tom's Cabin.'" *American Quarterly* 46 (4): 513–44.
Ritzer, G. 2010. *McDonaldization of Society.* 6th Edition. Thousand Oaks, CA: Pine Forge Press.
Rodríguez, D. 2007. "The Political Logic of the Non-Profit Industrial Complex." pp.21–40, in *The Revolution Will Not Be Funded: Beyond the Non-Profit Industrial Complex,* edited by INCITE! Women of Color Against Violence. Cambridge, MA: South End Press.
Rojas, P. 2007. "Are the Cops In Our Heads and Hearts?" pp.197–214, in *The Revolution Will Not Be Funded: Beyond the Non-Profit Industrial Complex,* edited by INCITE! Women of Color Against Violence. Cambridge, MA: South End Press.
Rollin, B. 2006. *Animal Rights & Human Morality.* Amherst, NY: Prometheus Books.
Rossiter, M. 1993. "The Matthew Matilda Effect in Science." *Social Studies of Science* 23 (2): 325–41.
Ruby, M., S. Heine, S. Kamble, T. Cheng, and M. Waddar. 2013. "Compassion and Contamination: Cultural Differences in Vegetarianism." *Appetite* 71: 340–8.
Rudolf, J. 2011. "Vegan Promoter Uses Photos of Meat and Dairy Items, and Fury Follows." *The New York Times,* April 18. Retrieved from: http://www.nytimes.com/2011/04/19/science/earth/19vegan.html
Rushton, J. and A. Campbell. 1977. "Modeling, Vicarious Reinforcement and Extraversion on Blood Donating in Adults: Immediate and Long-Term Effects." *European Journal of Social Psychology* 7 (3): 267–306.
Sabin, L. 2014. "Anti-Dairy Campaign Billboard Poster by PETA Removed from Public for Being Too Sexual." *The Independent,* December 4. Retrieved from: http://www.independent.co.uk/news/uk/home-news/antidairy-campaign-billboard-poster-by-peta-removed-from-public-for-being-too-sexual-9903618.html
Salamano, G., A. Cuccurese, A. Poeta, E. Santella, P. Sechi, V. Cambiotti, and B. Cenci-Goga. 2013. "Acceptability of Electrical Stunning and Post-Cut Stunning Among Muslim Communities: A Possible Dialogue." *Society & Animals* 21 (5): 443–58.
Salt, H. 1921. *Seventy Years among Savages.* London, UK: George Allen & Unwin Ltd.
Salvage, B. 2012. "Welfare Advancements Benefit Chickens, Industry." *MeatPoultry.com.* Retrieved from: http://www.meatpoultry.com/Writers/Bryan%20Salvage/Welfare%20advancements%20benefit%20chickens%20industry.aspx?cck=1
Sandberg, L. 2007. "Horse Slaughter Ban Has Gruesome Results." *Houston Chronicle.* Retrieved from: http://www.chron.com/news/houston-texas/article/Horse-slaughter-ban-has-gruesome-results-1817383.php
Sarkeesian, A. 2015. "How to Be a Feminist." *All about Women.* Retrieved from: https://www.youtube.com/watch?v=uOmIIAact4s
Saslow, L., R. Willer, M. Feinberg, P. Piff, K. Clark, D. Keltner, and S. Saturn. 2013. "My Brother's Keeper? Compassion Predicts Generosity More Among Less Religious Individuals." *Social Psychological and Personality Science* 4 (1): 31–8.
Schlosser, E. 2001. *Fast Food Nation: The Dark Side of the American Meal.* Boston, MA: Houghton Mifflin Company.
Schnall, S., J. Roper, and D. Fessler. 2010. "Elevation Leads to Altruistic Behavior." *Psychological Science* 21: 315–20.

Schösler, H., J. de Boer, and J. Boersema. 2012. "Can We Cut Out the Meat of the Dish? Constructing Consumer-Oriented Pathways towards Meat Substitution." *Appetite* 58 (10): 39–47.
Schwartz, B. 2004. *The Paradox of Choice: Why More is Less.* New York, NY: Harper Perennial.
Scully, M. 2002. *Dominion: The Power of Man, the Suffering of Animals, and the Call to Mercy.* New York, NY: St. Martin's Press.
Serrano, A. 2012. "Bitter Harvest: U.S. Farmers Blame Billion-Dollar Losses on Immigration Laws." *TIME.* Retrieved from: http://business.time.com/2012/09/21/bitter-harvest-u-s-farmers-blame-billion-dollar-losses-on-immigration-laws/
Shoemaker, P. and S. Reese. 1996. *Mediating the Message: Theories of Influences on Mass Media Content.* White Plains, NY: Longman Publishers.
Shtulman, A. and J. Valcarcel. 2012. "Scientific Knowledge Suppresses but Does Not Supplant Earlier Intuitions." *Cognition* 124 (2): 209–15.
Sky News. 2013. "China: Animal Campaigners Expose Puppy Trade." *Sky News*, September 12. Retrieved from: http://news.sky.com/story/1140745/china-animal-campaigners-expose-puppy-trade
Silverstone, A. 2012. *The Kind Diet: A Simple Guide to Feeling Great, Losing Weight, and Saving the Planet.* New York, NY: Rodale Books.
Simien, E. 2006. *Black Feminist Voices in Politics.* Albany, NY: State University of New York Press.
Simon, D. 2013. *Meatonomics: How the Rigged Economics of Meat and Dairy Make You Consume Too Much and How to Eat Better, Live Longer, and Spend Smarter.* Newburyport, MA: Conari Press.
Singer, P. and J. Mason. 2006. *The Way We Eat and Why Our Food Choices Matter.* Emmaus, PA: Rodale Books.
Smith, A. 2007. "Introduction." pp.1–18, in *The Revolution Will Not Be Funded: Beyond the Non-Profit Industrial Complex*, edited by INCITE! Women of Color Against Violence. Cambridge, MA: South End Press.
Smith, D. 1990. *The Conceptual Practices of Power: A Feminist Sociology of Knowledge.* Toronto, ON: University of Toronto Press.
Snow, D., E. Rochford, Jr., S. Worden, and R. Benford. 1986. "Frame Alignment Processes, Micromobilization, and Movement Participation." *American Sociological Review* 51 (4): 464–81.
Sobsey, D. 1994. *Violence and Abuse in the Lives of People with Disabilities: The End of Silent Acceptance?* Baltimore, MD: Paul H. Brookes Publishing Co.
Socha, K. 2013a. "The 'Dreaded Comparisons' and Speciesism: Leveling the Hierarchy of Suffering." pp.223–40, in *Confronting Animal Exploitation: Grassroots Essays on Liberation and Veganism*, edited by K. Socha and S. Blum. Jefferson, NC: McFarland & Company, Inc., Publishers.
———. 2013b. "'Just Tell the Truth': A Polemic on the Value of Radical Activism." pp.44–65, in *Confronting Animal Exploitation: Grassroots Essays on Liberation and Veganism*, edited by K. Socha and S. Blum. Jefferson, NC: McFarland & Company, Inc. Publishers.
Socha, K. and S. Blum. 2013. *Confronting Animal Exploitation: Grassroots Essays on Liberation and Veganism.* Jefferson, NC: McFarland & Company, Inc., Publishers.
Somolu, O. 2007. "'Telling Our Own Stories': African Women Blogging for Social Change." *Gender and Development* 15 (3): 477–89.

Southern Literary Messenger. 1852. "Uncle Tom's Cabin." *Southern Literary Messenger* XVIII, December: 721–31.
Spiegel, M. 1996. *The Dreaded Comparison: Human and Animal Slavery*. London, UK: Heretic Books.
Staggenborg, S. 1988. "The Consequences of Professionalization and Formalization in the Pro-Choice Movement." *American Sociological Review* 53 (4): 585–605.
Stallwood, K. 1996. "Utopian Visions and Pragmatic Politics: Challenging the Foundations of Speciesism and Misothery." pp.194–208, in *Animal Rights: The Changing Debate*, edited by R. Garner. New York, NY: New York University Press.
———. 2002. Ed. *A Primer on Animal Rights: Leading Experts Write about Animal Cruelty and Exploitation*. New York, NY: Lantern Books.
———. 2004. "A Personal Overview of Direct Action in the United Kingdom and the United States." pp.81–90, in *Terrorists or Freedom Fighters? Reflections on the Liberation of Animals*, edited by S. Best and A. Nocella II. New York, NY: Lantern Books.
———. 2011. "Animal Rights and Public Policy." *Animals and the Law Conference*, October 24–5. Barcelona, Spain: Universitat Autónoma de Barcelona.
———. 2013. "The Politics of Animal Rights Advocacy." *Relations: Beyond Anthropocentrism* 1 (1): 47–57.
———. 2014. *GROWL. Life Lessons, Hard Truths, and Bold Strategies from an Animal Advocate*. Brooklyn, NY: Lantern Books.
Stewart, J. 1976. *Holy Warriors: The Abolitionists and American Slavery*. New York, NY: Hill and Wang.
Stibbe, A. 2001. "Language, Power, and the Social Construction of Animals." *Society & Animals* 9 (2): 145–61.
Stiglitz, J. 2012. *The Price of Inequality: How Today's Divided Society Endangers Our Future*. New York, NY: W.W. Norton & Company, Inc.
Stowe, H. 1852. *Uncle Tom's Cabin*. Boston, MA: John P. Jewett & Company.
Strohmetz, D., B. Rind, R. Fisher, and M. Lynn. 2002. "Sweetening the Till: The Use of Candy to Increase Restaurant Tipping." *Journal of Applied Social Psychology* 32 (2): 300–9.
Stull, D. and M. Broadway. 1995. "Killing Them Softly: Work in Meat-Packing Plants and What It Does to Workers." pp.61–84, in *Any Way You Cut It: Meat Processing and Small Town America*, edited by D. Stull, M. Broadway, and D. Griffith. Lawrence, KS: University Press of Kansas.
Swanson, M. 2013. "How 'Humane' Labels Harm Chickens: Why Our Focus as Advocates Should be Egg-Free Diets, Not Cage-Free Eggs." pp.204–22, in *Confronting Animal Exploitation: Grassroots Essays on Liberation and Veganism*, edited by K. Socha and S. Blum. Jefferson, NC: McFarland & Company, Inc., Publishers.
Szymanski, D., L. Moffit, and E. Carr. 2011. "Sexual Objectification of Women: Advances to Theory and Research." *The Counseling Psychologist* 39 (1): 6–38.
Szymanksi, A. 2003. *Pathways to Prohibition: Radicals, Moderates, and Social Movement Outcomes*. Durham, NC: Duke University Press.
Tang, E. 2007. "Non-profits and the Autonomous Grassroots." pp.215–25, in *The Revolution Will Not Be Funded: Beyond the Non-Profit Industrial Complex*, edited by INCITE! Women of Color Against Violence. Cambridge, MA: South End Press.

Taylor, B. 2005. "Back to the Land Movements." *Encyclopedia of Religion and Nature*. New York, NY: Continuum.
Taylor, V. and N. Raeburn. 1995. "Identity Politics as High-Risk Activism: Career Consequences for Lesbian, Gay, and Bisexual Sociologists." *Social Problems* 42 (2): 252–73.
Terry, B. 2014. "The Problem with 'Thug' Cuisine." *CNN*, October 10. Retrieved from: http://edition.cnn.com/2014/10/10/living/thug-kitchen-controversy-eatocracy/
Texas Council on Family Violence. 2002. *Facts and Statistics*. Retrieved from: http://www.tcfv.org/resources/facts-and-statistics
The Daily Bull. 2013. No title. *The Daily Bull: Events on the Hill*, September 23. Clinton, NY: Hamilton College.
The Humane League. 2011. *HiddenFaceOfFood.com Facebook Ads Survey – Fall 2011*. Retrieved from: http://www.thehumaneleague.com/extra/FacebookAdsSurveyResults2011.pdf
———. 2014. *What Elements Make a Vegetarian Leaflet More Effective?* Philadelphia, PA: The Humane League.
The Pew Forum on Religion & Public Life. 2008. *U.S. Religious Landscape Survey: Religious Affiliation: Diverse and Dynamic*. Washington, DC: Pew Research Center.
The Vegan Society. [no date]. "History." *About the Society*. Retrieved from: http://www.vegansociety.com/about/history.aspx
Thoreau, H. 1854. *Walden*. Boston, MA: Ticknor and Fields.
Thug Kitchen LLC. 2014. *Thug Kitchen: The Official Cookbook: Eat Like You Give a Fuck*. New York, NY: Rodale Books.
Thunder Hawk, M. 2007. "Native Organizing Before the Non-Profit Industrial Complex." pp.101–6, in *The Revolution Will Not Be Funded: Beyond the Non-Profit Industrial Complex*, edited by INCITE! Women of Color Against Violence. Cambridge, MA: South End Press.
Tjaden, P. and N. Thoennes. 2000. *Extent, Nature, and Consequences of Intimate Partner Violence*. Washington, DC: US Department of Justice.
Tobach, E. and B. Rosoff. 1994. *Challenging Racism & Sexism: Alternatives to Genetic Explanations*. New York, NY: The Feminist Press at The City University of New York.
Tolman, R. and J. Raphael. 2000. "A Review of Research on Welfare and Domestic Violence." *Journal of Social Issues* 56 (4): 655–82.
Tomm, W. 1987. *The Effects of Feminist Approaches on Research Methodologies*. Waterloo, Canada: Wilfrid Laurier University Press.
Topalli, V., T. Brezina, and M. Bernhardt. 2013. "With God on My Side: The Paradoxical Relationship between Religious Belief and Criminality among Hardcore Street Offenders." *Theoretical Criminology* 17 (1): 49–69.
Topping, A. 2010. "Morrissey Reignites Racism Row By Calling Chinese a 'Subspecies.'" *The Guardian*, September 3. Retrieved from: http://www.theguardian.com/music/2010/sep/03/morrissey-china-subspecies-racism
Toronto Vegetarian Association. 2015. *Challenges and Supports for Vegetarians*. Toronto, CA: Toronto Vegetarian Association.
Torres, B. 2006. *Making a Killing: The Political Economy of Animal Rights*. Oakland, CA: AK Press.
Treuhaft, S. and A. Karpyn. 2010. *The Grocery Gap: Who Has Access to Healthy Food and Why It Matters*. Philadelphia, PA: The Food Trust.

Tucker, C. 2014. "The Significance of Sensory Appeal for Reduced Meat Consumption." *Appetite* 81: 168–79.

Tuttle, W. 2005. *The World Peace Diet: Eating for Spiritual Health and Social Harmony.* New York, NY: Lantern Books.

———. 2011. "Loving Hut – Part of Something Bigger." *VegSource.com.* Retrieved from: http://www.vegsource.com/dr-will-tuttle/loving-hut---part-of-something-bigger.html

US Bureau of Labor Statistics. 2013. *Job Openings and Labor Turnover Summary.* Retrieved from: http://www.bls.gov/news.release/jolts.nr0.htm

US Department of Agriculture Food and Nutrition Service. 2012. *Characteristics of Supplemental Nutrition Assistance Program Households: Fiscal Year 2011—Summary.* Retrieved from: http://www.fns.usda.gov/sites/default/files/2011Characteristics.pdf

US Department of Agriculture. 2009. "Access to Affordable and Nutritious Food: Measuring and Understanding Food Deserts and Their Consequences." *ERS Report Summary.* Retrieved from: http://www.ers.usda.gov/media/242654/ap036_reportsummary_1_.pdf

US Government Accountability Office. 2005. *Workplace Safety and Health: Safety in the Meat and Poultry Industry, While Improving, Could Be Further Strengthened.* Retrieved from: http://www.gao.gov/new.items/d0596.pdf

United Poultry Concerns. [no date]. "A Wing & A Prayer: The Kapparot Chicken-Swinging Ritual." *Alliance to End Chickens and Kaporos.* Retrieved from: http://www.endchickensaskaporos.com/

Usborne, S. 2013. "Ingrid Newkirk: 'It's Bizarre to Kill Animals for a Sandwich.'" *The Independent*, November 17. Retrieved from: http://www.independent.co.uk/news/people/profiles/ingrid-newkirk-its-bizarre-to-kill-animals-for-a-sandwich-8944582.html

van Peer, W., F. Hakemulder, and S. Zyngier. 2012. *Scientific Methods for the Humanities.* Amsterdam, NLD: John Benjamins Publishing Company.

Vance, L. 1993. "Ecofeminism and the Politics of Reality." pp.118–45, in *Ecofeminism: Women, Animals, Nature*, edited by Greta Gaard. Philadelphia, PA: Temple University Press.

———. 1995. "Beyond Just-So Stories: Narrative, Animals, and Ethics." pp.163–91, in *Animals and Women: Feminist Theoretical Explorations*, edited by C. Adams and J. Donovan. Durham, NC: Duke University Press.

Vaught, J. 2013. "*Materia Medica*: Technology, Vaccination, and Antivivisection in Jazz Age Philadelphia." *American Quarterly* 65 (3): 575–94.

Vegan Outreach. [no date]. *Advocacy for the Greatest Good.* Retrieved from: http://www.veganoutreach.org/articles/greatestgood.html

———. 2015. *E-News – March 25.* Retrieved from: http://www.veganoutreach.org/enewsletter/20150325.html

Vegetarian Resource Group. 2011. "How Many Adults Are Vegan in the U.S.?" *The Vegetarian Resource Group Blog.* Retrieved from: http://www.vrg.org/blog/2011/12/05/how-many-adults-are-vegan-in-the-u-s/

Vesa, T., P. Marteau, and R. Korpela. 2000. "Lactose Intolerance." *Journal of American College of Nutrition* 19 (2): 165S-175S.

vGirls|vGuys. 2014. "About." *vGirls|vGuys.* Retrieved from: http://www.vgirlsvguys.net/about

Victoria. 2013. "Past Event: VOKRA Float in the Vancouver Pride Parade." *Polarity Pole Dance Performances*. Retrieved from: http://www.polaritypoledance.dx.am/blog_vokra.html
Vigneault, E. 2013. "We Have to Choose. We Have to Focus." *Vegan Soapbox*, March 21. Retrieved from: http://www.vegansoapbox.com/we-have-to-choose-we-have-to-focus/
Virtue, D. and B. Prelitz. 2013. *Eating in the Light: Making the Switch to Vegetarianism on Your Spiritual Path*. Carlsbad, CA: Hay House, Inc.
Waldner-Haugrud, L. and L. Gratch. 1997. "Sexual Coercion in Gay/Lesbian Relationships: Descriptives and Gender Differences." *Violence and Victims* 12 (1): 87–98.
Walker, R., C. Keane, and J. Burke. 2010. "Disparities and Access to Healthy Food in the United States: A Review of Food Deserts Literature." *Health & Place* 16 (5): 876–84.
Wallace, R. 1973. "The Secular Ethic and the Spirit of Patriotism." *Sociological Analysis* 34 (1): 3–11.
Wallerstein, I., R. Collins, M. Mann, G. Derluguian, and C. Calhoun. 2013. *Does Capitalism Have a Future?* New York, NY: Oxford University Press.
Walster, E. and L. Festinger. 1962. "The Effectiveness of 'Overheard' Persuasive Communications." *Journal of Abnormal and Social Psychology* 65 (6): 395–402.
Walter, T. and G. Davie. 1998. "The Religiosity of Women in the Modern West." *The British Journal of Sociology* 49 (4): 640–60.
Ward, C. 1996. *Anarchy in Action*. London, UK: Freedom Press.
Warerkar, T. and O. Yaniv. 2013. "No One Here But Us (Dead) Chickens! Thousands of Birds Die from Heat, Not Jewish Sin Ritual." *New York Daily News*, September 12. Retrieved from: http://www.nydailynews.com/new-york/brooklyn/birds-die-annual-ritual-slaughter-article-1.1454098
Watson, D. 1948. "Should the Vegetarian Movement Be Reformed?" *The Vegetarian* 1 (2): 23–7.
Watson, J. 2005. "China's Big Mac Attack." pp.163–82, in *The Cultural Politics of Food and Eating: A Reader*, edited by J. Watson and M. Caldwell. Malden, MA: Blackwell Publishing.
Watson, P. 2012. "The Laws of Ecology and Human Population Growth." pp.130–7, in *Life on the Brink: Environmentalists Confront Overpopulation*, edited by P. Cafaro and E. Crist. Athens, GA: University of Georgia Press.
Watson, R. 2011. "The Privilege Delusion." *Skepchick*, July 5. Retrieved from: http://skepchick.org/2011/07/the-privilege-delusion/
We Are Fur. 2012. "Global Fur Sales Hit Record High." *News*, August 3. Retrieved from: http://www.wearefur.com/latest/news/global-fur-sales-hit-record-high-0
Webb, S. 1998. *On God and Dogs: A Christian Theology of Compassion for Animals*. New York, NY: Oxford University Press.
Weber, M. 1993 [1922]. *The Sociology of Religion*. Boston, MA: Beacon Press.
———. 2001 [1905]. *The Protestant Ethic and the Spirit of Capitalism*. New York, NY: Routledge.
Whiteman, M., P. Langenberg, K. Kjerulff, R. McCarter, and J. Flaws. 2003. "A Randomized Trial of Incentives to Improve Response Rates to a Mailed Women's Health Questionnaire." *Journal of Women's Health* 12 (8): 821–8.

Wiig, K. and C. Smith. 2008. "The Art of Grocery Shopping on a Food Stamp Budget: Factors Influencing the Food Choices of Low-Income Women as They Try to Make Ends Meet." *Public Health Nutrition* 12 (10): 1726–34.
Wing, S., D. Cole, and G. Grant. 2000. "Environmental Injustice in North Carolina's Hog Industry." *Environmental Health Perspectives* 108 (3): 225–31.
Winograd, N. 2009. *Redemption: The Myth of Pet Overpopulation and the No Kill Revolution in America.* Los Angeles, CA: Almaden Books.
———. 2012. *Friendly Fire.* CreateSpace Independent Publishing Platform.
Wolfson, M. 2011. *Vegucated.* FilmBuff.
Wrenn, C. 2011. "Resisting the Globalization of Speciesism: Vegan Abolitionism as a Site for Consumer-Based Social Change." *Journal of Critical Animal Studies* 9 (3): 9–27.
———. 2013a. "Nonhuman Animal Rights, Alternative Food Systems, and the Non-Profit Industrial Complex." *Phaenex: Journal of Existential and Phenomenological Theory and Culture* 8 (2): 209–42.
———. 2013b. "Resonance of Moral Shocks in Abolitionist Animal Rights Advocacy: Overcoming Contextual Constraints." *Society & Animals* 21 (4): 379–94.
———. 2013c. "Abolition Then and Now: Tactical Comparisons between the Human Rights Movement and the Modern Nonhuman Animal Rights Movement in the United States." *Journal for Agricultural and Environmental Ethics* 27 (2): 177–200.
———. 2013d. "Edible Women: Models Dressed as Food Will Never Be Activism." *Feminspire.* Retrieved from: http://feminspire.com/edible-women-models-dressed-as-food-will-never-be-activism/
———. 2013e. "The New Frontier of Rape Porn in Animal Rights." *Vegan Feminist Network.* Retrieved from: http://veganfeministnetwork.com/the-new-frontier-of-rape-porn-in-animal-rights/
———. 2015. "The Role of Professionalization Regarding Female Exploitation in the Nonhuman Animal Rights Movement." *Journal of Gender Studies* 24 (2): 131–46.
Wrenn, C. and R. Johnson. 2013. "A Critique of Single-Issue Campaigning and the Importance of Comprehensive Abolitionist Vegan Advocacy." *Food, Culture & Society* 16 (4): 651–68.
Wright, D. 2011. "Another PETA Exhibit Compares Animal Cruelty to Slavery." *BET News*, July 21. Retrieved from: http://www.bet.com/news/national/2011/07/21/another-peta-exhibit-compares-animal-cruelty-to-slavery.html
Yan, Y. 2005. "Of Hamburger and Social Space: Consuming McDonald's in Beijing." pp.70–9, in *The Cultural Politics of Food and Eating: A Reader*, edited by J. Watson and M. Caldwell. Malden, MA: Blackwell Publishing, LTD.
Yanklowitz, S. 2011. "A Yom Kippur of Mercy or Cruelty? Bringing an End to Kaporos!" *The Jewish Week*, September 26. Retrieved from: http://www.thejewishweek.com/features/street_torah/yom_kippur_mercy_or_cruelty
Yarborough, R. 1986. "Strategies of Black Characterization in *Uncle Tom's Cabin* and the Early Afro-American Novel." pp.45–84, in *New Essays on* Uncle Tom's Cabin*: The American Novel*, edited by E. Sundquist. New York, NY: Cambridge University Press.
Yarbrough, A. 2013. "How Whiteness and Patriarchy Hurt Animals." *Sistah Vegan Conference.* Web. September 14.

Yoder, K. and J. Decety. 2014. "The Good, the Bad, and the Just. Justice Sensitivity Predicts Neural Response during Moral Evaluation of Actions Performed by Others." *The Journal of Neuroscience* 34 (12): 4161–6.
York, R. and P. Mancus. 2013. "The Invisible Animal: Anthrozoology and Macrosociology." *Sociological Theory* 31 (1): 75–91.
Young, A. 2010. "Supreme Mystery." *VegNews* September/October: 45–9.
Yousif, Y. and C. Korte. 1995. "Urbanization, Culture, and Helpfulness." *Journal of Cross-Cultural Psychology* 26: 474–89.
Zacchino, M. 2013. "Vegan Strip Club Owner Johnny Diablo: We're All about Love and Compassion (Video)." *The Oregonian*, September 26. Retrieved from: http://www.oregonlive.com/multimedia/index.ssf/2013/09/vegan_strip_club_johnny_diablo.html
Zald, M. and R. Ash. 1966. "Social Movement Organizations: Growth, Decay and Change." *Social Forces* 44 (3): 327–41.
Zuberi, T. and E. Bonilla-Silva. 2008. *White Logic, White Methods: Racism and Methodology*. Lanham: MD: Rowman & Littlefield Publishers, Inc.

Index

269 Life, 99–100, 120, 201

ableism, 6, 106, 111, 131, 172, 187, 190, 199
abolitionism
  shortcomings, 9, 13, 16, 60, 123–5, 126–7, 158, 176, 196
  suppression of, xiv, 4, 5–6, 54, 198
  theory and tactics, 4–6, 16–17, 26–7, 42, 44–5, 60–1, 124–5, 126, 180–1, 184–5, 188, 190, 192–3, 195
Abolitionist Vegan Society, The, 125, 189, 197, 200
accountability, 141, 188–91, 194
ACE (Animal Charity Evaluators), 9, 34, 196
advocacy
  hindrances to, 31, 94–7, 115–19, 141, 146, 156–7, 161–2, 179, 182, 197, *see also* non-profits; racism; sexism; speciesism
  importance of, 26–7
AETA (Animal Enterprise Terrorism Act), 157
Africa, 130, 185, 200
age, 50, 77, 80, 85, 86, 88, 127, 186–7, 196
ag-gag laws, 92
alienation, 41–4, 60, 102, 140
alliance-building, *see* coalition-building
analogy, 21, 66–9, 72–8
  appropriateness of, 67–8, 77–8
anarchism, 26
Animal Liberation Front, ix
Animal Liberation Victoria, 99
animal rights movement
  history of, 8, 106, 121, 124, 134–6, 148–9, 201
  industrial complex, 32–3, 169
  negative reputation, 13, 156–7, 167, 169
  structure, 5, 94, 97, 173, 195

Animals Asia, 129, 202
anti-natalism, 131–2, *see also* population
appearance, 85–6, 102, 198
appropriation, 66–7, 107–8, 123–4, 126–7, 192, 193
Asia, 128–9, 133–4, 136, 149–50, 166–7, 202
atheism
  in animal rights, 7, 18, 23, 161–71, 190
  plus, 170–1, 203
  privilege, 163–6, 171, 203
  stigmatization, 23, 161–2, 167, 190

Best, Steve, ix, 12–13
body-shaming, *see* sizeism
bureaucratization, *see* rationalization
bystander effect, 89–90

capitalism
  role in advocacy, 24, 33, 76, 129, 147, 174, 175, 182–8, 193, 197
  typology, 30, 35, 73–5, 109, 128, 131–2, 143, 145, 147, 198
  see also Disneyization; fundraising; McDonaldization; non-profits
class
  discrimination, 39, 51, 70, 88, 96–7, 115–16, 122–3, 126, 127–33, 138–9, 142–3, 166–7, 184, 186–7, 190, 201, 202
  privilege, 39, 117, 121, 183, 184, 186, 188, 198–9
coalition-building, 22, 41, 140, 170, 172
cognition, *see* rationality
cognitive dissonance, 68–70, 77, 152–3, 164
Collins, Patricia Hill, 107, 126, 128, 130, 198, 199
colonialism, 121, 128, 130–3, 135, 145, 200

235

community, 88–9, 117, see also networks
companion animals, 38, 129, 180
compassion, xi, 15, 23–4, 55–6, 153–4, 168
compassion fatigue, 191–2, see also emotion
consumption, 96, 131–2, 133, 176, 183–5, 194, 197, 202, 203
critical thinking, see cognition; evaluation

death as a harm, 2, 157–8
decision paralysis, 76, 179
denial, 68, see also cognitive dissonance
direct action, 12–13, 90–3, 195, 196, 199
  see also violence
Disneyization, 55–9
diversity, 111–12, 126, 158
Durkheim, Émile, 142

EAA (Effective Animal Activism), see ACE (Animal Charity Evaluators)
education
  access to, 77, 87, 127–8, 138, 201
  importance of, 63–4, 76, 142, 188
egalitarianism, 115–16, 118–19, 166, see also diversity
Elise, Travis, 182, 189, 196
emotion
  labor, 57–9, 191–2
  motivation, 21, 37, 43, 55–6, 64–6, 67, 78–9, 81, 198
  see also compassion fatigue
environment, 131–2, 138–9, 180, 181, 197, 202
euthanasia, 53, see also shelters
evaluation
  examples of, 79–80, 87, 198
  failure, xii–xiii, 7, 9–15, 45–6, 47, 65, 173–4, 196
  need for, 8–9, 14–17, 64, 158, 172
  process of, 18–21
  experience, 11–12, 158, 200

factionalism, xiv, 4, 13, 16, 28, 36, 40, 45–6, 53–4, 116, 173

faith, see religion
FARM (Farm Animal Rights Movement), 79, 80, 155
Farm Sanctuary, 37–8, 39, 56, 57, 195, 197
fat-shaming, see sizeism
Faunalytics, see Humane Research Council
feminism
  in advocacy, 67, 105, 106–7, 114–15, 119, 164–5, 189
  choice, 95–8
  post-, 95–8, 111–12, 133
  in science, 22, 112, 118–19, 201
  third wave, 94–8, 114
films, 78–82, 188, 198, see also media
flexitarianism, see vegetarianism
food
  accessibility, 23, 81, 83–4, 88, 126, 127, 129–30, 139, 146, 199, 201
  as motivation, 80, 81–4, 188, 196
  production ethics, 51, 121–3, 185
  see also speciesism
Food Empowerment Project, 185
foundations, 34, 35, 117, 169, 183–4, see also fundraising; non-profits
Francione, Gary, 4, 23, 27, 28, 30, 45, 59, 75, 124, 127, 152, 168, 182, 184, 195, 196
Free from Harm, 133–4, 202
fundraising
  biasing evaluation, 10–11, 62, 174
  defining tactics, 8, 10, 13, 34–61, 76, 77, 122–3, 169, 179, 187–8, 196, 197

gender, 58, 65, 114–15, 159–61, 172, 195, 196, see also feminism; sexism
global inequality, 127, 128–33, 139, 180, 201
grassroots mobilization, 52, 88, 118, 137, 174, 188–90, 193, see also radical advocacy

Hai, Supreme Master Ching, see Loving Hut
Hall, Lee, 93, 101, 123, 196, 200

Harper, Breeze, 22, 120, 125, 127, 130–1, 139, 176, 200, 203
Harris, Sam, 157, 168, 170–1
Hawthorne effect, 79
health, x, 51, 83–4, 109, 138–9, 163–4, 175–6, 180, 181, 183–4
hero worship, *see* leadership
HSUS (Humane Society of the United States), 4, 5, 33, 56, 197
Humane League, The, 80
Humane Research Council, 80, 127
Humane use, 2, 145, 166
  see also welfare reform
humane washing, 3, *see also* speciesism, post-; welfare reform

identity, 86, 89, 114–15, 159–61, 165–6, 183
incarceration, 92–3, 121–2, 123, 138, 151–2, 192
inclusivity, 16, 111–19, 126, 170–1
individualism, 96–8, 102, 114, 131, 165, 176, 193, 200
inequality
  in movement structures, 39, 44, 60, 117, 186
  in society, 51, 63, 70–1, 96, 113–18, 141–4, 156, 160–2, 187, 202–3
  see also atheism, stigmatization; class; global inequality; oppression; racism; sexism
internet, 42–3, 60, 88, 191, 203
intersectionality, 95–6, 101, 106, 124, 197, 198
  resistance to, 120, 124–33, 136, 163–6, 190–1, 203
  as strategy, 23, 24, 66–7, 87, 117–18, 136, 170–1, 172, 178–82, 185–6, 190–1, 193, 203

James, William, 144, 198
just world phenomenon, 70–2, 77, 144

Kheel, Marti, 93, 103, 189, 195
kindness, *see* compassion
knowledge, *see* science

law, *see* policy
leadership

problems with, xii, 8–12, 38–9, 58, 126, 158, 163, 173, 189, 195, 196
  role of, 60, 196, 198
leafleting, 80, 82, 84–7, 127–8, 188, 196
legal reform, *see* policy
literacy, *see* education
lobbying, *see* policy
Loving Hut, 177–8, 185, 202
Lush Cosmetics, 98–9, 200

McDonaldization, 29–30, 49–55
Marx, Karl, 116, 142–3
masculinity, 12, 58, 90–1, 93, 146, 161, 170, 172, 181–2, *see also* patriarchy; sexism
media, 66, 78–89, 103, 156–7, *see also* pornography
merchandizing, 56–7, 188
Midgley, Mary, 108–9
moral relativism, 128, 136
moral shocks, 66, 78–82, 198
movies, *see* films

neoliberalism, 95–8, 114, 129–31, 183, 186–8
networks, 42–4, 48, 52, 55, 57, 60, 65, 78, 84, 89, 188–9
Nibert, David, 26, 45, 124, 182
no kill, 46, 70, 73–4
non-profits
  bias, 9–11, 14, 21, 25–61, 62, 174, *see also* fundraising
  industrial complex, 32–40, 62, 116–18, 169, 174, 186–9, 193
  structure, 4, 21, 25–61, 175, 178, 179–80, 189, 197
nonviolence, 12, 151, 175, 195, 203
Noske, Barbara, 33, 200

open rescue, 91–2
oppression, 24, 71, 73–5, 76, 93, 116, 137–8, 140, 142–5, 146–7, 151, 153, 162, 166, 170, 176, 180, 182, 184, 187, 191, 192–3, 197, 198, *see also* inequality
overpopulation, *see* population

Parkinson's law, 48–9
path dependency, 8, 11, 13

patriarchy, 19, 83, 93, 94, 102–5, 106–15, 140, 146–7, 160, 161, 170, 172, 175, 189, 195, 200, 201, *see also* Sexism
PETA (People for the Ethical Treatment of Animals), ix, x–xi, 13, 45–6, 52–3, 56, 57, 68, 98, 100–1, 104–5, 128, 131, 152–4, 196, 197, 200
persuasion, 21, 64–93, 176–7, 188, 198, 199
pets, *see* companion animals
philosophy, 1–2, 17, 144
policy, 11, 27, 63, 192, 195, 196
population, 131–3
pornography, x, 13, 66, 96, 100, 101–5, 114, 160, 174–5, 194, 196, 200
prayer, xi, *see also* religion; spirituality
prison abolition, *see* incarceration
privacy, 47–8, 60, 191–2, 197
professionalization
  benefits to, 31, 188, 189
  definition of, 28
  problems with, 32–61, 123, 174, 186–8
  see also rationalization

racism
  ideology, 23, 87, 111, 120, 133, 165–6
  in movement structures, 39, 120–1, 125, 134, 158, 165, 174, 176, 182, 190–1, 202, 203
  in society, 51, 111, 121–3, 126–7, 130–3, 134–9, 146–7, 151–2, 159–61, 185, 192, 199, 200, 201
  in tactics, x, 22–3, 67–8, 87–8, 121, 123, 126–7, 128–35, 139–40, 147
  see also anti-natalism; white-centrism; white privilege
  radical advocacy, 5, 17, 28, 39–40, 43, 44–5, 60–1, 118, 188, 190
  threats to, 35–6, 38, 41, 45–6, 49, 54, 60, 116–17, 140, 174, 186–7, 189–90
rape culture, 68, 70, 91, 99–100
rationality
  cognition, 21, 64–78
  definition, 6, 7, 17–18
  shortcomings, 22, 64, 105–15, 118, 141, 163–6, 172, 197
  theory, 15–16
  see also atheism
rationalization, 18, 20, 29–31, 41–61, 172
reciprocity norm, 82–3
Regan, Tom, 29, 63, 91, 195
religion
  in advocacy, 7, 23, 141, 155–6, 158, 161, 168, 176–7
  and animal rights, 129, 145–71, 177–8, 195, 202
  Buddhism, 129, 150, 155
  Christianity, 143, 146, 148, 150, 153, 156, 158, 202
  Hinduism, 145, 146, 150, 152, 166–7
  institution of, 18, 23, 141–5
  Islam, 145, 150, 202
  Jainism, 151, 195
  Judaism, 145, 150, 153–4, 202
  Rastafarian, 150
  see also spirituality
Ritzer, George, *see* McDonaldization

Salt, Henry, 149, 166
sanctuaries, 37
science, 22, 105–15, 116, 118, 134, 135, 164, 201, 202
scientific method, 6, 18–20, 79, 110, 112–13, 118
secularism
  in advocacy, 7–8, 13, 23–4, 149, 157, 170
  in society, 157, 162, 178
  see also atheism
self-care, 192
self-serving bias, 72
sexism
  in movement structures, 39, 58–9, 106–9, 118, 169, 170, 173–5, 185, 186–7, 189, 190–1, 191–2, 195, 201
  in science, 22, 105–15, 116–17, 135
  in society, 67, 68, 70, 94–7, 101, 122, 132–3, 134–6, 158–61, 164–5, 181–2, 199, 200, 203

sexism – *continued*
  in tactics, x–xi, 13, 22, 39–40, 45, 66, 83, 84, 86, 91, 93, 94–104, 118, 133, 140, 147, 174–5, 196, 200
  see also rape culture
shelters, 38, 45, 46
Singer, Peter, 9, 157–8
single-issue campaigning
  problems with, 18–19, 21–2, 24, 45, 52, 73–7, 136–40, 163–4, 178–82, 201
  purpose, 14, 47, 56–7, 195
sizeism, 102, 176, 202
Skepchick, 163–5, 171
skepticism, 7, 158, 163–71
slaughterhouses, 122–3
slavery, 66–7, 68, 92, 123–4, 127, 134, 138, 139, 151, 155–6, 159, 176, 181, 192, 193, 199, 202, 203
Socha, Kim, 67, 100, 184
social desirability bias, 79
social movements, 26–8, 30–1, 33–61, 141, 155–6
social psychology, 22, 64–93, 118, 144, 178–9, 191, 198
socialism, 26, 131, 182
sociology, 25–8, 110–11, 142–4, 157, 198, 202
speciesism
  causes, 68–72, 74, 81, 134, 145, 155–6, 169, 201
  economic benefits, ix, 51, 124, 145
  post-, 29, 77
  in society, 25, 67, 111, 124, 133, 163–8, 181, 183–4, 192, 202, 203
  in tactics, 10, 123, 129, 135–6, 140, 152, 192–3
  see also welfare reform
spirituality, xi, 18, 176–8
Stallwood, Kim, 11–12, 189, 196
state, 35–7, 63, 73, 92, 116, 142–3, 182, 184, 187, 193
Stowe, Harriet Beecher, 151–2, 156, 202, 203

tactics
  decision-making, xii, 14, 50–1, 168–70
  see individual tactics
third-world, *see* global inequality
Torres, Bob, 8–9, 26, 32–3, 41–2, 45, 158, 182, 187

UPC (United Poultry Concerns), 145, 153, 200
urban unhelpfulness effect, 191

Vegan Outreach, 5–6, 34, 45–6, 50, 58, 84, 86, 197
Vegan Society, The, 8, 125, 200, 201
veganism
  barriers to, 29, 34, 42, 45–7, 52, 57, 69, 76, 81, 89–90, 102, 126, 149, 163–4, 175–6, 179, 196
  conduciveness to, 63, 80, 84, 90, 129, 167–8, 176
  importance of, 26–7, 42, 45, 63, 65, 76, 118, 164, 176, 179–80, 186, 192, 197
  shortcomings, 27, 60, 120, 128, 183–5, 190, 197, 201
vegetarianism, 10, 34, 52, 83, 148, 149–50, 153, 166–7, 179, 192
VegNews, x, 178, 185, 200
violence, ix, 12–13, 90–3, 157, 175, 181, 190–1, 195, 199

Watson, Donald, 8, 121, 149
Weber, Max, 29–30, 41–50, 59, 143
welfare reform
  problems with, 3–4, 18–19, 29–30, 33, 45, 77, 140, 173–4, 192–3, 195–6
  theory and tactics, ix, 2–3, 27, 53–4, 122–3, 145, 157–8, 166, 196, 197
whiteness
  white privilege, 39, 93, 121, 123, 136, 161, 165, 190
  white-centrism, 22–3, 52, 87–8, 96–7, 111, 121, 126–8, 130–1, 133, 165–6, 175–6, 177, 203

The manufacturer's authorised representative in the EU is Springer Nature Customer Service Centre GmbH, Europaplatz 3, 69115 Heidelberg, Germany. If you have any concerns regarding our products, please contact ProductSafety@springernature.com

Printed and bound by CPI Group (UK) Ltd, Croydon, CR0 4YY

23/03/2026

02076682-0016